C000124801

Foundation Myths
in Ancient Societies

Foundation Myths in Ancient Societies

Dialogues and Discourses

Edited by

Naoíse Mac Sweeney

PENN

UNIVERSITY OF PENNSYLVANIA PRESS

PHILADELPHIA

Copyright © 2015 University of Pennsylvania Press

All rights reserved. Except for brief quotations used for
purposes of review or scholarly citation, none of this book
may be reproduced in any form by any means without
written permission from the publisher.

Published by
University of Pennsylvania Press
Philadelphia, Pennsylvania 19104-4112
www.upenn.edu/pennpress

Printed in the United States of America on acid-free paper

1 3 5 7 9 10 8 6 4 2

Library of Congress Cataloging-in-Publication Data
Foundation myths in ancient societies : dialogues and
discourses / edited by Naoíse Mac Sweeney. — 1st ed.
    p. cm.
Includes bibliographical references and index.
ISBN 978-0-8122-4642-1 (hardcover : alk. paper)
    1. Myth.   2. Mythology.   3. Mediterranean Region—
Civilization.   4. Civilization, Ancient.   5. Group
identity.   I. Mac Sweeney, Naoíse, 1982–
BL312.F68 2014
292.1'3—dc23

2014012639

CONTENTS

ABBREVIATIONS

Abbreviations for classical texts, corpora, and journals are those used in *L'Année philologique* or *The Oxford Classical Dictionary*, ed. S. Hornblower and A. Spawforth, 3rd ed. (Oxford: Oxford University Press, 1996). Abbreviations for Near Eastern reference works and corpora are those used in B. Mathieu, *Abréviations des periodiques et collections en usage à l'Institut français d'archéologie orientale* (Cairo: Institut français d'archéologie orientale, 2010), or the *Cuneiform Digital Library Initiative*. In addition to the more commonly used abbreviations, the following are also used in this book:

AE	*L'Année epigraphique*
ACO	E. Schwartz (ed.). 1922–74. *Acta consiliorum oecunenicorum.* Berlin-Leipzig: de Gruyter.
ANET	J. B. Pritchard (ed.). 1969. *Ancient Near Eastern Texts Relating to the Old Testament.* 3rd ed. Princeton, NJ: Princeton University Press.
ARV	J. D. Beazley. 1963. *Attic Red-Figure Vase-Painters.* 2nd ed. Oxford: Clarendon Press.
BMC	G. F. Hill. 1910. *Catalogue of the Greek Coins of Phoenicia.* A Catalogue of Greek Coins in the British Museum 23. London: Trustees of the British Museum.
CIL	*Corpus Inscriptionum Latinarum*
CJ	*Codex Justiniani*
CTA	A. Herdner. 1963. *Corpus de tablettes cunéiformes alphabétiques.* Mission de Ras Shamra 10. Paris: Imprimerie Nationale.
ETCS	J. A. Black et al. 1998–2006. *The Electronic Text Corpus of Sumerian Literature.* Oxford: Faculty of Oriental Studies, University of Oxford (http://etcsl.orinst.ox.ac.uk).
FGrH	F. Jacoby et al. (eds.). 1923–. *Die Fragmente der griechischen Historiker.* Berlin: Wiedmann.

FHG	C. F. W. Müller (ed.). 1841–70. *Fragmenta historicorum graecorum*. Paris: Editore Ambrosio Firmin Didot.
ID	1926–50. *Inscriptions de Délos*. 6 vols). Académie des Inscriptions et Belles Lettres. Paris: Champion.
IG	1873–. *Inscriptiones Graecae*
IGLSyr	1929–. *Inscriptions grecques et latines de la Syrie*. Beirut: Institut français d'archéologie du Proche-Orient.
IGLTyr	J.-P. Rey-Coquais. 2006. *Inscriptions grecques et latines de Tyr*. Bulletin d'Archéologie et d'Architecture Libanaises, special issue 3. Beirut: Ministère de la Culture Direction Générale des Antiquités.
IGRR	R. Cagnat et al. 1906–27. *Inscriptiones Graecae ad res Romanas pertinentes*. Paris: Librarie Ernest Leroux.
IGUR	*Inscriptiones Graecae Urbis Romae*
I.Didyma	A. Rehm. 1958. *Didyma II: Die Inschriften*. Berlin: Mann.
I.Ephesos	1979–. *Die Inschriften von Ephesos*. Bonn: Habelt.
I.Magnesia	O. Kern. 1900. *Die Inschriften von Magnesia am Maeander*. Berlin: Spermann.
I.Pergamon	1890–. *Die Inschriften von Pergamon*. Berlin: Spermann.
IRT	J. M. Reynolds and J. B. Ward-Perkins (eds.). 1952. *The Inscriptions of Roman Tripolitania*. Rome: British School at Rome.
KTU	M. Dietrich, O. Loretz, and J. Sanmartín. 1995. *The Cuneiform Alphabetic Texts from Ugarit, Ras Ibn Hani and Other Places*. 2nd ed. Münster: Ugarit-Verlag (abbreviation derives from title of 1st ed.: *Die keilalphabetische Texte aus Ugarit* 1. Neukirchen, 1976).
LIMC	1981–. *Lexicon Iconographicum Mythologiae Classicae*. Düsseldorf: Artemis Verlag.
OGI	W. Dittenberger. 1903–5. *Orientis Graeci inscriptiones selectae*. Leipzig: S. Hirzel.
PIR	*Prosopographia Imperii Romani Saeculi I, II, III*. 1st ed., E. Klebs and H. Dessau (1897–98); 2nd ed., E. Groag et al. (1933–). Berlin: de Gruyter.
PPM	*Pompei: Pitture e Mosaici*
RPC	1992–. *Roman Provincial Coinage*. London: British Museum.
SEG	1923–. *Supplementum Epigraphicum Graecum*

Foundation Myths
in Ancient Societies

Introduction

NAOÍSE MAC SWEENEY

Beginnings are important. The beginning sets the agenda, the tone, and the standard. Throughout antiquity, there was considerable interest in stories about beginnings, especially in those about the origins of cities, states, and peoples. Foundation myths were told across the ancient world in many different forms and through many different media. They can be found in poetry and prose, represented visually in monumental and decorative art, and played out in civic and religious rituals. Stories of origin were sometimes recounted in their entirety, forming the central narrative in a text. But even more frequently, foundation myths were alluded to obliquely or used as reference points for narratives on other subjects. Stories of beginnings and myths of foundation were ubiquitous in classical antiquity.

One notable characteristic of ancient foundation myths is their plurality. In many instances, several stories existed simultaneously to explain the origin of a single city or group of people. One foundation could have a range of myths attached to it, with several different accounts or alternative versions of a given story. In the classical period, for example, the Athenians were simultaneously said to be autochthonous and also to be descended from the Ionian branch of the Hellenic genealogy.[1] The existence of such alternative stories can present an interpretive challenge as from a modern perspective, these two accounts of Athenian beginnings may seem to be mutually exclusive. In antiquity, however, such apparent inconsistencies seem not to have been as problematic. Alternative versions of foundation myths were common, often circulating simultaneously among similar audiences, in similar social contexts, and sometimes even showcased alongside one another in direct recognition of their divergence. In one particularly well-known example, Herodotus recounts two conflicting stories about the foundation of Cyrene: one told by the Therans, who claimed to have founded Cyrene; and one by the Cyrenaicans themselves (Hdt 4.145–69).[2] Herodotus does not seek to integrate or rationalize the stories into a single narrative—indeed, he is happy to present the alternative versions, side by side (Hdt 4.154). In general, contrary stories and differing variants rarely seem to have been a cause for concern in antiquity; indeed, they seem to have been the rule rather than the exception.

This book addresses the variation in ancient foundation myths and proposes a new approach to interpreting this variation. Previous approaches have focused on individual myths or variants, considering how they fit together, support one another, or contradict one another. In contrast, this book argues for a shift of focus. Instead of concentrating on individual foundation myths, we suggest that much may be learned from considering complete foundation discourses. By this, we mean the sum total of several different myths together and the various relationships between the stories and variants. Individual myths, particular variants, and specific stories may all have their own social significance when considered separately. The myth of Athenian autochthony, for example, constructs a relationship between the Athenians and the land that they inhabited. The myth of Athenian descent from the Ionian branch of the Hellenes, in contrast, constructs a relationship between the Athenians and other Greek groups. Both these stories, therefore, have their own particular significance when approached individually as foundation myths. However, as both stories were in circulation simultaneously, something may also be learned from considering them together as elements in a wider foundation discourse.

The choice to tell one of these stories rather than the other is significant—it is a choice that entails not only selection of the story told but also rejection of the story not told. In recounting the myth of Athenian autochthony, not only is a certain type of relationship constructed with the land of Attica, but also a certain type of relationship with other Greeks is explicitly denied. The story serves to isolate the Athenians, not so much by the positive claim that it makes to the land, but more by the negative claims that it makes about wider bonds of Hellenic kinship. The myth of autochthony is therefore significant not only in itself, but also because it is emphatically not a myth of Hellenic origins. The simultaneous existence of an alternative myth that celebrates precisely these Hellenic origins highlights the significance of this point. Taken together, the different foundation myths of Athens suggest a fundamental plurality in the way Athenians conceived of their civic identity: a schizophrenic desire for splendid isolation and Athenian particularism on the one hand; and simultaneously for engagement with a wider Hellenic community on the other. The variety of the Athenian foundation myths implies a variety of perspectives about Athenian identity in the classical period, an uncertainty about what Athens was and what it should be. This uncertainty, and the existence of alternative views and identities, tells us something about classical Athens that we would not learn by looking at any one of the myths in isolation. Athens was neither simply autochthonous nor simply Hellenic. It was both simultaneously—not just despite, but also because of, the ambiguity that this allowed. By considering the Athenian foundation discourse as a whole, important insights may therefore be gained.

Foundation discourses include all the foundation myths relating to a particular city, state, or group of people in circulation at a given time. However, a foundation discourse consists not only of the full range of different stories and versions of stories, but also of the various ways in which they were told and the diverse social contexts of their telling. Crucial to this is the interaction between different foundation myths. Alternative versions of myths did not exist in isolation from or parallel with one another, but rather coexisted in the same social and cultural space. Alternative stories must therefore have interacted: feeding off one another, borrowing ideas and motifs from one another, contradicting or adding nuance to one another. This interaction or dialogue between individual myths means that any given foundation discourse is more than simply the sum of its individual mythic parts. Rather, it is a discourse in the fullest sense, comprising not only a range of mythic components but also the dialogue, interactions, and relationships between them. Before expanding on the theme of foundation discourses and the dialogues between individual myths further, it is necessary to consider existing approaches to classical foundation myths and current interpretations of mythic variation in antiquity.

Interpreting Foundation Myths

Foundation myths have long been a focus for research, and in recent decades the subject has attracted substantial scholarly attention. While myths in general are often discussed in the context of ritual and cult,[3] foundation myths are frequently considered separately, outside a ritual context. Instead, foundation myths are often considered as a form of historiography. By claiming to describe the origins of cities, states, and groups of people, foundation myths are fundamentally concerned with the past and necessarily engage at some level with historical explanation. Traditional approaches to foundation myths, therefore, have tended to consider them as a form of historiography, locating them at the intersection between myth and history. The distinction between myth and history in antiquity is itself the subject of much study, and will not be considered here.[4] However, for the purposes of this book it is significant that foundation myths have often been studied from a historical perspective. It is suggested that these myths contain kernels of historical truth, preserved and handed down over the generations through social memory and the oral tradition.[5] Over time, stories may be elaborated on and revised as part of this process, with imaginative additions, the changing of names, and poetic exaggeration. However, it is argued that at its core, a foundation myth is likely to preserve some historical facts concerning the foundation in question. Many traditional approaches to foundation myths therefore focus on attempting to strip away the layers of later invention to establish the historical kernel and uncover useful information about origins. For example, this approach has dominated the study of the "Ionian Migration." The idea of the Ionian Migration emerges from several of the best-known foundation myths of the Ionian cities of Asia Minor. These stories recount that the cities were established following a migration from Athens, name a range of founding heroes, and recount different stories about conflict and conquest upon arrival. It has often been assumed that these myths are, at their core, historically accurate and that a migration from Attica to Asia Minor did occur in the early Iron Age, resulting in the expulsion or suppression of indigenous groups and the establishment of the Ionian cities.[6]

In the last few decades, this approach to foundation myths has been criticized for being overly positivist. Instead, it was argued that foundation myths should be seen as social and literary constructs and should be situated in the time in which they were written and circulated.[7] This approach argued that foundation myths were shaped much more by the needs and agendas of those telling them in the historical present than by the objective facts of the historical past. It was argued that myths were altered, manipulated, and even created, for use in a strategic and political way. To return to the example of the Ionian Migration, instrumental interpretations of these myths have also been proposed. It is suggested that the idea that the colonists of the cities were originally migrants from Athens was promoted by Athens itself, as a means of justifying its expansionist ambitions in the eastern Aegean. If Athens could claim to be the mother city of the Ionians, this would give it a greater claim to influence over them.[8]

The contrast between these two approaches is perhaps not as great as might be suggested by some of the more polemical literature on the subject.[9] Most proponents of positivist approaches are careful to factor strategic and political concerns in when they consider the distorting influences on foundation myths. Similarly, most proponents of constructivist approaches would deny any possibility of some historical elements in the myths. Indeed, several scholars have now argued in favor of a compromise between the two extremes. A more pragmatic approach would recognize that strategic invention and instrumental manipulation must certainly have been crucial factors in shaping both the content and the expression of foundation myths, but these were necessarily constrained by popular expectation, generic conventions, and plausibility.[10] Investigating the audiences of myth, as well as the popular reception of foundation stories, is important to contextualize the literary or artistic expressions of these myths.

The two main schools of thought concerning ancient foundation myths—the positivist and the constructivist—may no longer determine all approaches to foundation myths, given the increasing interest in this more pragmatic third way. However, our understanding of variation in foundation myths is still dominated by these two schools. The existence of alternative myths and variants on individual stories is still usually explained in one of two ways. From a positivist perspective, different stories are interpreted as different fragments of collective memory from the distant past. The various stories can be seen as representing particular episodes within history, which can be stitched together to form one overarching historical narrative. For example, a wide range of foundation stories was told for the city of Miletus in Asia Minor.[11] The city was variously said to have been founded by Cretans under Sarpedon;[12] Ionians from Athens under the Codrid prince Neileus;[13] and an eponymous hero called Miletus, who, in some accounts, is a Cretan and in others is an autochthon.[14] In addition, some stories mention a settlement of Carians or Leleges predating the Greek foundation, while others do not. From a positivist perspective, each of these stories is considered to contain kernels of historical truth, and each is assumed to represent a different episode in the city's history.[15] Corroboration can therefore be sought for various elements within these individual stories, using archaeological evidence from the early Iron Age as well as by retrojecting aspects of ritual and civic practice known from later periods.[16] The different tales can then be combined into one coherent whole, to give a historically accurate overview of the Milesian past. It could be argued, for example, that an original Carian settlement was first conquered by Cretans, and later by migrants from Athens. The diverse foundation myths can be understood, using this framework, not as simultaneous stories but rather as sequential episodes. Any variants that do not fit into the sequential framework can be dismissed as the results of poetic invention or mythological hyperbole. This approach to mythic variation, therefore, sees alternative stories as the remnants of distinct historical memories, and aims to organize and combine them into one overarching narrative.

The second main approach to variation in foundation myths derives from the constructivist school. This approach casts individual myths as representative of different political or strategic positions. Alternative stories, it is argued, are the result of alternative visions of identity and different political stances. The different myths are seen as mutually exclusive traditions, each in direct rivalry or competition with the others. To return to the example of Miletus: under this framework, the different stories would be interpreted as standing for different factions either within the city or interest groups without. Stories of the Ionian migrants from Athens under Neileus can be explained as part of Athenian attempts to justify its influence over Miletus, while accounts of an eponymous autochthon founding the city may relate to a movement for Milesian autonomy rooted in localism. Similarly, myths of the Cretan migrants and Sarpedon may be the result of Milesian attempts to create kinship links with other groups in Asia Minor such as those in Lycia, while tying themselves in to heroic genealogies and the myths of the Trojan War. This approach to mythic variation sees the different stories as operating not sequentially but simultaneously. Each is a rival to the other, emphasizing a different aspect of identity and representing a different strategic viewpoint. The variation among the myths can be used not to reconstruct a historical narrative of the past but rather to understand the political and social dynamics of the period in which they were written and circulated.

Both these approaches to variation in foundation myth aim toward the singular. In the first approach, the many stories and variants must be merged into a single "true" account. In the second approach, each myth is treated singly, as a rival to and mutually exclusive with other accounts. However, there is potential for approaching mythic variation from yet another perspective—one that is neither positivist nor instrumental, that neither flattens variety nor sees it as oppositional. By adopting an approach based on foundation discourses, rather than on individual foundation myths, there is new scope for interpreting the plurality and diversity of classical foundation myths.

Approaching Foundation Discourses

The basic idea of a foundation discourse is not new. The individual elements of this concept have long been acknowledged. It has often been recognized that for each foundation in classical antiquity, there was usually a range of stories and variants in circulation. It has also been acknowledged that these alternative accounts would have been told, revised, and retold alongside one another, resulting in the interaction of different myths and the creation of relationships between them. The key elements of foundation discourses—mythic variations and the dialogue between them—are familiar features of existing scholarship on ancient foundation myths. This book does not, therefore, seek to establish a firm definition of a hitherto unrecognized phenomenon. Rather, it argues for a shift in emphasis to bring this phenomenon into sharper focus. It aims to demonstrate that adopting an approach based on foundation discourses allows us to view variation in foundation myths from a new perspective. Instead of privileging the singular, such an approach encourages the acknowledgment of the plural and the acceptance of complexity. Instead of identifying a single "correct" history or a set of discrete strategic stances, the key field of interest is the discourse itself—the ongoing process of mythopoesis and the continual dialogue between stories, storytellers, and their audiences.

There are many potential aspects to this dialogue. These include the way that different stories become more or less popular in relation to one another at different times, and among different audiences. It may be informative to consider which of the alternative stories are expressed in which media—in literature, in visual art, in civic iconography, in local cult, in onomastic practices—and also the changing patterns of this over time. Also relevant is how new versions or new stories incorporate elements of older myths, as well as how they rework, reimagine, and reject them. This intertextuality is a crucial element in the dialogue between myths—individual stories may corroborate, nuance, or contradict one another, but they would not have been told in a vacuum. The audiences of these myths would usually have been aware of a diverse range of alternatives and would have constructed the social meaning of any given story in relation to their understanding of these others.

To return to the many myths of Miletus, the different surviving stories can be seen to relate to one another in several complex ways. For example, Ephorus of Cyme in the fourth century BC claimed that Miletus had first been occupied by Leleges, before being officially founded by Cretans under Sarpedon, and later fortified by Neileus and his Attic Ionian followers (*FGrH* 70 F127). In his story, Ephorus seems to have picked up on several previous versions of the myth. The reference to military action and the fortification of the city by Neileus resonates with Herodotus' tale of the Ionians' violent arrival to the city (Hdt 1.146), while the story of Sarpedon's flight from Crete echoes the account found in Herodorus (*FGrH* 31 F45). Ephorus, then, brings together two separate stories that could be told independently of each other. This rationalization of variant myths perhaps involves a similar process to that undertaken by modern scholars adopting positivist approaches to mythic variation and may indeed be unsurprising, given Ephorus' wider aim of writing Universal History.[17] However, it also illustrates the dynamism of foundation myths and the interaction of different stories. The same narratives could be told separately, or they could be combined. They could be placed in a relationship of opposition to each other (Miletus *either* as a Cretan foundation *or* as an Ionian one), or they could be placed in a relationship of complementarity (Miletus first founded by Cretans but first fortified by Ionians). While different scholarly approaches may favor one of these interpretations over the other in a static form, the example of Ephorus indicates that both were possible in antiquity. The changing relationship between the stories—oppositional in some contexts, complementary in others—is an important part of the dialogue between them. It is also significant that in Ephorus' tale, the original inhabitants of the land prior to the Cretan arrival are Leleges. This directly contradicts a long-established tradition that held the original inhabitants of Miletus to be Carians, including not only Herodotus and Herodorus but also Homer (*Iliad* 2.867).[18] The substitution of Leleges for Carians was not an innovation of Ephorus himself (see Pherecydes *FGrH* 3 F155), but Ephorus' choice to follow this variant of the myth would not have gone unnoticed by his ancient audience. The rejection of a well-known and long-established part of the story is another aspect of the relationship between the myths. The decision to deviate and possibly to innovate is another element in the mythic dialogue.

The example of Ephorus demonstrates that over time, the variety and nature of Miletus' foundation myths changed, as did the relationships between them. While some of these developments can be glimpsed through the literary sources such as those considered here, a far more nuanced picture can be gained by also considering contemporary archaeological, epigraphic, and iconographic evidence. For example, Ephorus' rejection of the Carian origins of Miletus gains additional significance when we consider epigraphic evidence for the use of the Carian language and script, along with the continuing practice of choosing Carian names, in classical Miletus.[19] At the time that Ephorus was writing, not only was there a long-held tradition of Miletus' Carian prehistory (going back to Homer; see above), but Carian language and culture were an established part of Milesian life. In this context, Ephorus' mythic variation can be seen as going even more notably against the accepted grain. Even through dedicated interdisciplinary research, however, a complete understanding of these complex and changing relationships is unlikely to ever be possible. Nonetheless, it is these shifting mythic relationships and interactions, only partially discernible in the surviving sources, that constitute the central dynamic heart of Miletus' foundation discourse. The individual accounts of Herodotus, Herodorus, and Ephorus do not, by themselves or collectively, constitute a foundation discourse. Rather, the foundation discourse also embraces the relationships between these accounts and between these literary accounts and other forms of mythic representation, such as in the visual arts, social practices, and cult.

The case of Miletus cannot be taken as a pattern for other foundation discourses elsewhere in classical antiquity. In different circumstances, this dialogue between myths will necessarily take different forms, and the overall shape of each foundation discourse must necessarily be unique. It is not an aim of this book, therefore, to establish a fixed methodology for the investigation of variation in foundation myths, or for identifying the parameters or development of a foundation discourse. Instead, the chapters in this volume offer a selection of examples, exploring a variety of foundation discourses in action. By examining a broad range of different cases, we hope to demonstrate the potential for adopting an approach based on foundation discourses. We also hope to illustrate both some of the many forms that foundation discourses can take, and the many ways in which foundation discourses can function. In this book, as with foundation myths in classical antiquity themselves, variety and plurality are key.

Foundation Discourses Across Classical Antiquity

The contributors to this volume consider examples from across classical antiquity to explore how various foundation discourses operated and what might be learned from them. We make no claim to comprehensive coverage of the ancient world, chronologically or geographically. Neither do we claim to include all the best-known or most widely discussed cases of mythic variation from antiquity. Rather, the contributions highlight the diversity of foundation discourses and mythic variation that may be found in the classical world.

Two chapters take examples from what is often considered the "core" of classical antiquity: fifth-century Athens (Turner) and early imperial Rome (Squire). Other chapters focus on geographical areas that may be considered peripheral to the Greco-Roman world: Bactria (Mairs) and Phoenicia (Hirt). Others consider areas that were incontrovertibly part of the Greco-Roman world but that have often been treated as peripheral in modern classical scholarship: Sicily (Donnellan) and Alexandria (Ogden). One chapter is explicitly comparative in its approach, contrasting a classical and a nonclassical tradition in the form of Greek and Hebrew foundation myths (Malkin). A broad geographical and cultural range is therefore covered in this volume, allowing for a rich variety of foundation discourses to be discussed. The wide geographical and cultural range of the chapters is matched by their chronological range, which spans from the archaic period to the third century AD. The volume is arranged in roughly chronological order, making it easier for the reader to navigate the wide temporal span encompassed in this book. Just as the subject of each chapter is a foundation discourse, encompassing both mythic diversity and the relationship between mythic variants, we aim to achieve something similar with this volume as a whole. We hope that the diversity of the chapters, as well as the comparisons and relationships between the various insights offered, will form a loose discourse on the nature, variety, and functions of foundation myths and discourses in classical antiquity. The final contribution to this volume, the Epilogue (Osborne), revisits some of the themes highlighted in this Introduction, and returns to methodological questions of truth, falsity, and means of approaching foundation discourses.

The central issue of mythic variation is addressed directly in Chapter 1 by Irad Malkin, who compares Greek and Hebrew foundation myths, identifying plurality and variation as a key feature of Greek, as opposed to Hebrew, traditions. The chapter focuses on the motif of the foreign founder, the outsider who arrives from elsewhere and establishes his city on unfamiliar ground. In Hebrew traditions, Malkin notes, the arrival of the foreign founder is incorporated into a single linear foundation narrative, signifying a break with the past and heralding the establishment of a new order. In contrast, it seems that the foreign founders of Greek myth are embedded in plural foundation discourses, where multiple parallel narratives operated on different levels. These levels, Malkin argues, include the natural foundation of place, the origins of the *ethnos* (ethnic group or regional collective), and the political formation of the polis (city-state). The parallel stories of Greek myth, when compared with the more linear narratives of Hebrew foundation accounts, highlight the fundamental importance of plurality and variation in the Greek tradition. The contrast with Hebrew myths suggests, therefore, that foundation discourses were a central structuring principle of Greek mythic traditions.

In Chapter 2, Lieve Donnellan illustrates such a foundation discourse, played out in literary texts, local cult practices, and civic iconography. The chapter deals with the city of Naxos on Sicily and is the only chapter of this volume to address a Greek colonial foundation. Early textual accounts celebrated Theocles and Apollo Archegetes together as the human and divine founders of the city. Later traditions, however, tended to represent either one or the other of the founding figures, building on previous accounts while simultaneously incorporating new elements into the story. This acceptance, rejection, and elaboration of different elements with each new rendering depends on an appreciation of other versions of the story. Crucially, Donnellan explores not only the interaction between different stories told in the literary sources but also the relationships between literary representations of myths and the celebration of foundation stories in civic cult and on coin imagery. The different emphasis evident in the different mythic media allowed for a wider discourse to be developed, one where the full significance of any individual version of the foundation myth can be understood only in relation to the broader foundation discourse.

As demonstrated by the case of Naxos, foundation myths represented in different media often communicate different stories, or different "takes" on the same story. However, in Chapter 3, Susanne Turner shows that the portrayals of a foundation myth in two different media can also offer a similar overall vision of civic foundation. In this case, the shared vision of civic foundation focuses on duality and ambiguity as the central theme of the foundation discourse. Turner's chapter considers the figure of Theseus in classical Athens, specifically concentrating on the competing traditions that claimed that Theseus was simultaneously both the son of Aigeus and of Poseidon. Turner discusses how Theseus' relationship with his two fathers was portrayed in poetry and vase painting, highlighting the fact that scenes relating to both fathers can be found in both types of media. In both types of media and for both potential fathers, the scenes typically focus on the moment of paternal recognition. Crucially, Turner argues, in these scenes Theseus never achieves the official recognition of either father, and is instead eternally caught in the process of being acknowledged. In this way, Theseus is never committed to being the son of either Aigeus or Poseidon, and his ambiguous status is maintained. Contrary to what might initially be assumed, the subject of these scenes is not the recognition by one or the other of Theseus' mythic fathers. Rather, it is the uncertainty of Theseus' dual generation that is itself being emphasized. The indeterminate nature of Theseus' origins, Turner argues, was an essential part of the hero's appeal as a founder. Ambiguous, transformational, and continually on the cusp of achieving a new status, Theseus would have been an ideal civic hero for Athens around the time of its expansion in the Aegean. In the case of Theseus' indeterminate paternity, the very fact of mythic variation has itself become central in the representation of both variants. The dialogue between foundation myths has become a central theme of the discourse.

The reflexivity of foundation discourses, along with their potential to reflect on their own plurality, is also illustrated in the next two chapters, both of which consider Hellenistic examples. In the case described by Rachel Mairs in Chapter 4, it seems that greater variety among the mythic variants and greater complexity in the foundation discourse were desirable ends. The chapter discusses the foundation discourse at Ai Khanoum in Bactria (in modern Afghanistan). In addition to long-standing local and Achaemenid traditions and the conventional ideal of a foundation by Alexander, Mairs suggests that a fourth element was introduced to the foundation discourse in the mid-third century BC. Allusions to a Delphic foundation in the tradition of early Greek colonies were made, framed within the context of existing foundation narratives and civic cult. However, these allusions remained implicit, subtly changing the nature of a ritual space and a discourse previously concerned with civic foundation. Rather than foundation itself, the focus of the ritual space and discourse shifted to include the broader issue of civic origins. The shape and remit of the discourse at Ai Khanoum appear to have been expanded—perhaps deliberately—to go beyond the strict issue of foundations.

If the discourse at Ai Khanoum was even more expansive than those considered in previous chapters, the example discussed in Chapter 5 by Daniel Ogden lies at the other end of the scale. While Mairs considered a foundation discourse that spiraled out to include ever more stories and an increasingly vague sense of origins, Ogden explores a foundation discourse that spirals inward, pulling diverse traditions and stories into a single composite myth. Ogden argues that the story of Alexander slaying the serpent, the Agathos Daimon, in Alexandria brings together elements of a wide range of foundation traditions. Motifs are borrowed from early Greek foundation stories, Alexander's own personal mythology, Egyptian traditional tales, Jewish sacred imagery, and the conventional stories associated with Alexander's other foundations in the East. In the one story of the Agathos Daimon, Ogden argues that a variety of myths, traditions, and images are brought together. Within this tale, a vast pool of source material has been concentrated into a single coherent narrative, narrowing the foundation discourse into a tight space. Whereas the foundation discourse of Ai Khanoum was expansive and dispersed, that of the Agathos Daimon was focused, the stories and ideas converging into coherence.

Mairs's and Ogden's chapters deal with cases where the parameters of a new foundation discourse are being defined; in Chapter 6, Michael Squire is concerned with the potential flexibility of a foundation discourse when the shape and limits of this discourse have already been imposed. In early imperial Rome, an official foundation discourse was firmly established, which included not only the establishment of the city but also the origins of the ruling Julio-Claudian dynasty. But while the framework of this discourse and its basic components were already laid out, Squire's chapter demonstrates that there was still scope for flexibility and dialogue. Squire concentrates on the *Tabulae Iliacae*, a collection of handheld stone tablets from the first centuries BC and AD, conveying mythical subjects through inscriptions and scenes in relief. Many of the tablets depict stories of Rome's foundation, often focusing on the figure of Aeneas, in line with the official foundation discourse of the time. However, argues Squire, the way that Aeneas is presented on the tablets does not strictly conform to the typical official narrative. Instead, there is considerable space for narrative innovation—there is no clear way to read them from "start" to "finish" and no linear trajectory to the story. By their layout and their use of text and image, the tablets encourage viewers to take alternative routes and come to alternative endings. The tablets, then, actively introduce an element of discourse into the rigid official framework. They appear to have been deliberately designed to stimulate discourse, creating ambiguity where there was previously certainty, and introducing complexity where there was previously clarity. Squire's chapter suggests that foundation discourses were not the necessary means by which complex sets of foundation myths functioned, but rather an intrinsic part of the way ancient audiences engaged with myths. In a situation where mythic variation had been minimized as part of an official state-sponsored process, the example of the *Tabulae Iliacae* illustrates how ancient audiences could still shape a foundation discourse, finding flexibility and variation within a set framework.

Chapter 7, by Alfred Hirt, also considers the ancient audiences of foundation discourses. But where Squire illustrated the active potential of groups and individuals within an established structure, Hirt explicitly explores the range of potential audiences and their engagement with the foundation discourse of Tyre in the third century AD. Hirt focuses on the bronze coinage of Tyre, considering the contemporary articulation of a variety of foundation stories for the city through this widely used and easily accessible form of civic iconography. According to some versions, Tyre was a new city, founded as a Roman *colonia* in AD 198. According to others, it was the *metropolis* of Greco-Roman myth, whose role was to found rather than be founded, and to produce founding figures such as Dido, Europa, and Kadmos. Other stories again presented Tyre as an ancient Phoenician city, founded by the local heroes Ousoos and Samemroumos. Hirt identifies coin imagery related to all three of these visions of Tyre, and points out that the civic authorities saw no contradiction in representing their city in all ways at once. He suggests that these alternative versions appealed to different sections of Tyrian society, coexisting as a coherent composite discourse just as different social and cultural elements within the civic population coexisted in a composite and hybrid society.

Robin Osborne's Epilogue encourages us to reflect on our approaches and methodologies, bringing us back to the question of a third way between positivist and constructivist perspectives. Osborne addresses the charged terminology of "truth" and "lies" in foundation stories, deconstructing the dichotomy between the two. All our variant stories are, to some extent, "lies"—as none can be said to be wholly or exactly factually correct. Yet all variants are also simultaneously "true"—in that they reflect social realities and, when taken together as a collective discourse, hint at a broader and more abstract sense of historical truth. The Epilogue reminds us of what is at stake in our studies of ancient foundation discourses—not only our understanding of the origins, development, and dynamics of particular ancient societies but also our ideas about ancient historiography and the perception of historical time.

Despite the broad chronological, geographical, and cultural spread of this volume, the central theme remains the same: the variation of myths and traditions of foundation, the interaction and relationships between these variants, and the discourses of foundation that emerged in classical antiquity from this mythic variety and interaction. The chapters illustrate the vital importance of this sense of discourse within Greco-Roman traditions—Malkin by comparing Greek and Hebrew foundation myths, and Squire by considering the potentially subversive means of initiating discourse in the face of Rome's official narrative. The significance of discourse is also highlighted by Turner, in whose Athenian case study the ambiguity of a dual tradition was explicitly celebrated. Donnellan and Hirt provide detailed studies of specific foundation discourses, both drawing from a range of different types of evidence in an interdisciplinary way. These examples illustrate the potential range of audiences engaging with a foundation discourse and the complex internal functioning of these discourses. If Malkin, Squire, and Turner establish the importance of foundation discourses, and Donnellan and Hirt explore some of their key features and workings, Mairs's and Ogden's chapters consider their remit and extent. While it is evident that diverse myths and traditions were incorporated into foundation discourses, it seems that this could serve to broaden the discourse, as in the case discussed by Mairs, or to focus it, as in that discussed by Ogden. Taken as a whole, the chapters in this volume explore the concept of foundation discourses from several different perspectives. They offer examples drawn from across the ancient world to highlight the significance, the functioning, and the scope of these discourses, and they illustrate the wide range of insights that might be gained from adopting such an approach. It is the prospect of these new insights that leads us to argue for the significance of foundation discourses, rather than of individual foundation myths, in classical antiquity.

NOTES

1. For the various alternative accounts of Athenian origins, see Harding 2008; Loreaux 2000; Parker 1987; Rosivach 1987; and also Turner in this volume.

2. For discussions of the foundation myths associated with Cyrene, see Calame 1990, 2003; Giangiulio 2001; Malkin 2003.

3. For introductory discussions of the various approaches to Greek myths, see Bremmer 1987; Dowden and Livingstone 2011; Woodward 2007. For treatments of myth in the Roman world, see Braund and Gill 2003; Bremmer and Horsfall 1987; Wiseman 1995.

4. See Finley 1975 for a classic work on the subject. Other interesting discussions can be found in Calame 2003; Clarke 2008; Brilliante 1991; Fornara 1983; Fox 1996; Grethlein 2010; Griffiths 2011; Hartog 2000.

5. Examples of this approach include Boardman 1980; Carandini 2011; Desborough 1972.

6. E.g., Cook 1975; Herda 1998; Huxley 1966; Niemeier 2007; Sakellariou 1958; Van-schoonwinkel 2006.

7. Examples of this approach include Foxhall et al. 2010; Grandazzi 1997; Gehrke 2001; Hall 1997; Malkin 1998; Osborne 1998; Ungern-Sternberg 1988; Wiseman 1995.

8. E.g., Crielaard 2009; Hall 2002: 32, 67–71; Kowlazig 2005: 49–51; Mac Sweeney 2013; Nilsson 1951.

9. E.g., Zurbach 2012.

10. For critical overviews of the changing trends in the interpretation of foundation myths and for arguments in favor of this third way, see Hall 2008; Kerschner 2006. See Patterson 2010: 22–44; and Clarke 2008: 245–303, for discussions of fiction, belief, and plausibility in the context of ancient foundation myths. See also Osborne's Epilogue in this volume for a more abstract discussion of truth and foundation myths.

11. For a fuller discussion of Milesian foundation myths, see Mac Sweeney 2013.

12. E.g., Ephorus *FGrH* 70 F127; Aristokritos *FGrH* 493 F3; Apollod. *Bibl.Epit.* 3.1–2; Ant. Lib. *Met.* 30.1–2.

13. E.g., Hdt 9.97; Pherecydes *FGrH* 3 F155; Hellanicus *FGrH* 4 F125; Callim. *Hymn to Artemis* 225–27; Polyb. 16.12; Paus. 7.1.4; Ael. *VH* 8.5; Amm. Marc. 22.8.12; Nicolaus of Damascus *FGrH* 90 F53. A variant of this story has Neileus as hailing from Pylos: Str. 14.1.3 (Neileus, founder of Miletus, is not to be confused with Nēleus, king of Pylos and father of Nestor. As son of Codrus, Neileus was supposedly a descendant of Nēleus but is a distinct figure.) Yet another variant claims that Neileus was a Phoenician, who founded Miletus after being exiled from the Levant: Douris of Samos *FGrH* 70 F74; Diog. Laert. *Life of Thales* 1.1.

14. E.g., Herodorus *FGrH* 31 F45; Konon *FGrH* 16 F1.2; Apollod. *Bibl.Epit.* 1.9.16; Ap. Rhod. *Argon.* 1.185.

15. See Sourvinou-Inwood 2005: 268–309 for a detailed example of this interpretive approach to Miletus' foundation myths.

16. E.g., Herda 1998 surveys the evidence for the figure of Neileus, while Roebuck 1962 argues that the organization of tribes in later periods at Miletus and in its colonies provides evidence for the city's original foundation.

17. For Ephorus, see Barber 1935.

18. Indeed, the idea of Miletus' specifically Carian origins persisted long after Ephorus wrote, e.g., Paus. 7.2.5; Strabo 7.7.2.

19. Herda 2009; Herda and Sauter 2009.

REFERENCES

Barber, E. 1935. *The Historian Ephorus.* Cambridge: Cambridge University Press.

Boardman, J. 1980. *The Greeks Overseas.* London: Thames and Hudson.

Braund, D., and D. Gill (eds.). 2003. *Myth, History and Culture in Republican Rome: Studies in Honour of T. P. Wiseman.* Exeter: Exeter University Press.

Bremmer, J. N. (ed.). 1987. *Interpretations of Greek Mythology.* London: Croom Helm.

Bremmer, J. N., and N. M. Horsfall. 1987. *Roman Myth and Mythography.* London: Institute of Classical Studies.

Brilliante, C. 1991. "Myth and History: History and the Historical Interpretation of Myth." In *Approaches to Greek Myth,* ed. L. Edmunds, 93–138. Baltimore: Johns Hopkins University Press.

Calame, C. 1990. "Narrating the Foundation of a City: The Symbolic Birth of Cyrene." In *Approaches to Greek Myth,* ed. L. Edmunds, 277–341. Baltimore: Johns Hopkins University Press.

Calame, C. 2003. *Myth and History in Ancient Greece,* tr. D. W. Berman. Princeton, NJ: Princeton University Press.

Carandini, A. 2011. *Rome: Day One.* Princeton, NJ: Princeton University Press.

Clarke, K. 2008. *Making Time for the Past: Local History and the Polis.* Oxford: Oxford University Press.

Cook, J. M. 1975. "Greek Settlement in the Eastern Aegean and Asia Minor." In *The Cambridge Ancient History,* vol. 2, part 2: *History of the Middle East and the Aegean Region, c. 1380–1000 BC,* ed. I. E. S. Edwards, N. G. L. Hammond, and E. Sollberger, 773–804. Cambridge: Cambridge University Press.

Crielaard, J. P. 2009. "The Ionians in the Archaic Period: Shifting Identities in the Changing World." In *Ethnic Constructs in Antiquity: The Role of Power and Tradition,* ed. T. Derks and N. Roymans, 37–84. Amsterdam: Amsterdam University Press.

Desborough, V. R. d'A. 1972. *The Greek Dark Ages.* London: Benn.

Dowden, K., and N. Livingstone (eds.). 2011. *A Companion to Greek Mythology.* Oxford: Wiley-Blackwell.

Finley, M. I. 1975. "Myth, Memory and History." In *The Use and Abuse of History,* ed. M. I. Finley, 11–33. London: Chatto & Windus.

Fornara, C. W. 1983. *The Nature of History in Greece and Rome.* Berkeley: University of California Press.

Fox, M. 1996. *Roman Historical Myths: The Regal Period in Augustan Literature.* Oxford: Clarendon.

Foxhall, L., H.-J. Gehrke, and N. Luraghi (eds.). 2010. *Intentional History: Spinning Time in Ancient Greece*. Stuttgart: Franz Steiner.

Gehrke, H.-J. 2001. "Myth, History, and Collective Identity: Uses of the Past in Ancient Greece and Beyond." In *The Historian's Craft in the Age of Herodotus*, ed. N. Luraghi, 286–313. Oxford: Oxford University Press.

Giangiulio, M. 2001. "Constructing the Past: Colonial Traditions and the Writing of History. The Case of Cyrene." In *The Historian's Craft in the Age of Herodotus*, ed. N. Luraghi, 116–37. Oxford: Oxford University Press.

Grandazzi, A. 1997. *The Foundation of Rome: Myth and History*. Ithaca, NY: Cornell University Press.

Grethlein, J. 2010. *The Greeks and Their Past: Poetry, Oratory and History in the Fifth Century BCE*. Cambridge: Cambridge University Press.

Griffiths, A. 2011. "Myth in History." In *A Companion to Greek Mythology*, ed. K. Dowden and N. Livingstone, 195–207. Oxford: Wiley-Blackwell.

Hall, J. M. 1997. *Ethnic Identity in Greek Antiquity*. Cambridge: Cambridge University Press.

Hall, J. M. 2002. *Hellenicity: Between Ethnicity and Culture*. Chicago: University of Chicago Press.

Hall, J. M. 2008. "Foundation Stories." In *Greek Colonisation: An Account of Greek Colonies and Other Settlements Overseas*, vol. 2, ed. G. R. Tsetskhladze, 385–425. Leiden: Brill.

Harding, P. 2008. *The Story of Athens: The Fragments of the Local Chronicles of Attika*. London: Routledge.

Hartog, F. 2000. "The Invention of History: The Pre-History of a Concept from Homer to Herodotus." *History and Theory* 39: 384–95.

Herda, A. 1998. "Der Kult des Grunderheroen Neileos und die Artemis Kithone in Milet." *Jahreshefte des Österreichischen Archäologischen Institutes* 88: 1–48.

Herda, A. 2009. "Karkiša-Karien und die sogenannte Ionische Migration." In *Die Karer und die Anderen*, ed. F. Rumscheid, 27–108. Bonn: Habelt.

Herda, A., and E. Sauter. 2009. "Karerinnen und Karer in Milet: Zu einem späklassischen Schlüsselchen mit karischem Graffito aus Milet." *Archäologische Anzeiger*: 51–112.

Huxley, G. L. 1966. *The Early Ionians*. London: Faber and Faber.

Kerschner, M. 2006. "Die Ionische Wanderung im Lichter neuer archaologischer Forschungen in Ephesos." In *"Troianer sind wir gewesen": Migrationen in der antiken Welt. Stuttgart Kolloquium zu Historischen Geographie des Altertums 8, 2002*, ed E. Olhausen and H. Sonnabend, 364–82. Stuttgart: Franz Steiner Verlag.

Loraux, N. 2000. *Born of the Earth: Myth and Politics in Athens*. Tr. S. Stewart. Ithaca, NY: Cornell University Press.

Kowalzig, B. 2005. "Mapping Out *Communitas*: Performances of *Theoria* in Their Sacred and Political Context." In *Pilgrimage in Graeco-Roman and Early Christian Antiquity: Seeing the Gods*, ed. J. Elsner and I. Rutherford, 41–72. Oxford: Oxford University Press.

Mac Sweeney, N. 2013. *Foundation Myths and Politics in Ancient Ionia*. Cambridge: Cambridge University Press.

Malkin, I. 1998. *The Returns of Odysseus: Colonization and Ethnicity.* Berkeley: University of California Press.

Malkin, I. 2003. "'Tradition' in Herodotus: The Foundation of Cyrene." In *Herodotus and His World: Essays from a Conference in Memory of George Forrest,* ed. P. Derow and R. Parker, 153–70. Oxford: Oxford University Press.

Niemeier, W.-D. 2007. "Westkleinasien und Ägais von den Anfängen bis zur ionischen Wanderung: Topographie, Geschichte und Beziehungen nach dem archäologischen Befund und den hethitischen Quellen." In *Frühes Ionien: Eine Bestandsaufnahme. Akten des Symposions: 100 Jahre Milet, 1999,* ed. J. Cobet et al., 37–96. Mainz: Philip von Zabern.

Nilsson. M. P. 1951. *Cults, Myths, Oracles and Politics in Ancient Greece, with Two Appendices: The Ionian Phylae, the Phratries.* Lund: C. W. K. Gleerup.

Osborne, R. 1998. "Early Greek Colonisation? The Nature of Greek Settlement in the West." In *Archaic Greece: New Approaches and New Evidence,* ed. N. Fisher and H. van Wees, 251–70. London: Duckworth.

Parker, R. 1987. "Myths of Early Athens." In *Interpretations of Greek Mythology,* ed. J. Bremmer, 187–214. London: Croom Helm.

Patterson, L. E. 2010. *Kinship Diplomacy in Ancient Greece.* Austin: University of Texas Press.

Roebuck, C. 1962. "Tribal Organization in Ionia." *Transactions of the American Philological Association* 92: 495–507.

Rosivach, V. J. 1987. "Autochthony and the Athenians." *Classical Quarterly* 37: 294–306.

Sakellariou, M. B. 1958. *La migration grecque en Ionie.* Athens: Institut Français d'Athènes.

Sourvinou-Inwood, C. 2005. *Hylas, the Nymphs, Dionysios and Others: Myth, Ritual, Ethnicity.* Stockholm: Svenka Institutet i Athen.

Ungern-Sternberg, J. von. 1988. "Überlegungen zur frühen römischen Überlieferung in Licht der Oral-Tradition-Forschung." In *Vergangenheit in mündlicher Überlieferung,* ed. J. von Ungern-Sternberg and H. Reinau, 237–65. Stuttgart: Teubner.

Vanschoonwinkel, J. 2006. "Greek Migrations to Aegean Anatolia in the Early Dark Age." In *Greek Colonisation: An Account of Greek Colonies and Other Settlements Overseas,* vol. 1, ed. G. R. Tsetskhladze, 115–41. Leiden: Brill.

Wiseman, T. P. 1995. *Remus: A Roman Myth.* Cambridge: Cambridge University Press.

Woodward, R. D. (ed.). 2007. *The Cambridge Companion to Greek Mythology.* Cambridge: Cambridge University Press.

Zurbach, J. 2012. "Mobilités, réseaux, ethnicité: Bilan et perspectives." In *Mobilités grecques: Mouvements, réseaux, contacts en Méditerranée de l'époque archaïque à l'époque hellénistique,* ed. L. Capdetrey and J. Zurbach, 261–79. Bordeaux: Ausonius.

CHAPTER I

Foreign Founders: Greeks and Hebrews

IRAD MALKIN

Nous sommes tous des étrangers sur la terre!
—A rallying cry in French demonstrations
against immigration laws

Greeks mostly saw themselves as newly arrived, foreigners in the lands that they were occupying. This is true of most mainland Greeks, those who considered themselves migrants to the Aegean and Asia Minor (in what we call the "Dark Ages"), and of the settlers in the new foundations in the Mediterranean and the Black Sea, following the second half of the eighth century BC. Such self-images are quite different from those we meet in the ancient Near East. The city of Eridu, for example, seems to have existed since the creation of the world.[1]

In the extremely rich corpus of ancient Near Eastern writings, aside from those of the ancient Israelites, there are hardly any stories about collective migration and foundation.[2] In contrast, the notion of autochthonous origins is rarely found among Greeks, and, when it is found, it is often problematic: Was the idea that Athenians were autochthonous truly universal? Most think that it was one among other, rival strategies.[3] On the one hand, Herodotus, for example, has his fun with the Athenians, pointing out that if they keep insisting on their autochthonous origins, this would imply that originally they were not Greeks but Pelasgians.[4] On the other hand, we may find statements to the effect that "We [Athenians] are pure Hellenes, who have not mixed with barbarians [*amigeis barbarôn*]. For we are not like descendants of Pelops or Kadmos, Aegyptus or Danaus, nor any others who, being barbarians by nature [*phusei*] and Hellenes by convention [*nomos*], dwell among us—we reside here as genuine Hellenes, not as half-barbarians [*meixobarbaroi*]."[5]

An autochthonous model suggests evolution and growth, not foundation. In contrast, every new foundation usually consists of a story about someone coming "here" from elsewhere and hence, almost by definition, as a "foreigner." The title of this chapter, "Foreign Founders," may appear redundant: most founders are foreigners. Sometimes founders were deliberately portrayed as having foreign ethnic origins: according to some versions, Cadmus, a "founder" of Thebes, was supposedly a Phoenician. Pelops, the eponymous hero of the Peloponnese, whose tomb was venerated at panhellenic Olympia, was a Phrygian. Danaus came from Egypt. This notion of foreign ancestors applies also to Greek notions of non-Greeks: in terms of *origines gentium*, Greeks could project the "foreign" Medea as the ancestress of the Medes, Perseus of the Persians, or Odysseus as cofounder of Rome and the leader of the migration of the Etruscans.[6]

In fact, the most popular framework for collective foundation stories in Greece was that of the newcomer, the immigrant, the conqueror. It is true of Ionian migration lore, as it is for foundation stories about historical colonies. The founder is new in relation to a place that is already in existence. The Boiotians came to Boiotia some sixty years after the Trojan War, and the Herakleidai, descendants of Hercules of Thebes, led their Dorian army into the Peloponnese twenty years later. Yet both Boiotia and Lacedaemon—more specifically, both Thebes and Sparta—were not founded by the new arrivals. They were there earlier, some from primordial times.[7] Thus it is at the point of dissonance with the past that the origins of a new collective identity, in relation to the place that also partly defines it, can begin. Like other chapters in this book, this one examines alternative foundation stories. However, instead of analyzing individual settlements, I shall be looking at entire categories of foundation myths, the constant dialogue among them, and, especially, the common tension between foreignness and belonging.

Foundation and "Place"

We may need to clarify three categories of stories that connect the notions of foundation to that of place, especially in view of the misguided tendency to see all such myths as a priori "political," in the sense of justification and legitimation of conquest, settlement, and possession.[8] Yet not all myths relating to territory serve that purpose.

First, we can observe the myths about "founders of the land"—primordial and not political founders such as Apollo and the nymph Cyrene, Helios and the nymph Rhodes, or Hercules' vanquishing of Antaeus and opening of Libya for general human habitation. To this category belong also "genealogies of the land," such as Lacedaemon, Sparte, Taÿgetus, and Eurotas. Pausanias relates the conventional genealogy, according to which the autochthonous ruler Lelex had a grandson named Eurotas who channeled the marshy waters to the sea, thus creating the river Eurotas. His daughter Sparte married Lacedaemon, son of the eponymous nymph Taygete.[9] "Once in power he first of all renamed the *country and the people* [Lacedaemonians] after himself and then founded a city and named it after his wife; the city is called Sparta to this day."[10] Lelex may be indeed autochthonous, but it is precisely the rupture with his line that would be at the heart of the (Dorian) Sparta's foundation. The hero "of the land" is sharply contrasted with the invading Dorians who in "this day" (Pausanias') inhabit Argos, Sparta, and Corinth. Both the genealogies of the land and the "civilizing or culture myths," such as that of Hercules and Antaeus, explain not specific political foundations and the formation of territories but rather the emergence of places as such, and how they became free for human habitation. Needless to say, the founders of the land usually disappear by the time political founders arrive.

The second category of story also involves mythic characters who were not directly connected with the historical present: somehow, after the primordial first people, Greek collective memory could celebrate a second-tier genealogy of heroes. For example, the kings of those glorious cities of heroic epochs, especially in the Peloponnese, were epic heroes. The House of Tyndareus, which was tenuously linked with the primordial Peloponnesian genealogies, was replaced through marriage with the Atreidai, among whose proud descendants we find kings of Argos, Mycenae, and Sparta: Agamemnon, Menelaus, Orestes, and Teisamenos.[11]

Finally, we have explicit *ktiseis*, myths of immigration and foundation that directly link historical societies with their own past, now building on a rupture with the primordial heroes of the land and the epic heroes who replaced them. This is a third category of foundation that we find in the historical period as the constitutive framework for most discrete Greek collective identities: a new polity and its territory, defined with perceived notions of territorial boundaries, in contrast to the open-ended, undemarcated land myths with their springs, mountains, and monsters. The whole point of the Herakleidai charter myth, partly first articulated by Tyrtaeus, was the obliteration of the Atreid line and the refoundation of Corinth, Argos, and Sparta as new, Dorian cities. They had all been in existence before; what were new were the Dorians and their Herakleid kings and aristocrats, such as the Spartan royal houses or the Corinthian Bakchiads.

Yet we note some uneasiness with the idea of the absolute foreignness: unlike the invading Dorians, the Herakleidai were supposedly only "returning," since their ancestor Hercules (himself a Theban and certainly not a Dorian) had acquired the right of possession when he restored Tyndareus to the throne. The notion of the "right of return" through heroic figures and ancestors provides some legitimacy in stories about immigration and foundation and allows holding the stick at both ends: the Dorians were newcomers, but their leaders were returning. By analogy, the Books of Joshua and Judges in the Hebrew Bible proudly tell stories of conquest, settlement, and displacement; however, in the background is the ancestor Abraham, who spent his life in the Land of Canaan. This provides the story in Joshua with a color of the "return" of his descendants.

With the Dorian myths, we see rupture emphasized over continuity, yet with attempts to connect to the past of the land and bridge the link to its ancient heroes: the Herakleidai were "returning," and rituals were consecrated to Helen, Menelaus, Orestes, and Teisamenos, all belonging to the dynastic genealogy that was deposed and replaced by the Herakleidai.[12] We also find rhetorical tropes: when Gelon demanded to become the supreme commander of the joint Greek force, the Spartans retorted that Agamemnon would be turning in his grave; and Agamemnon had not even been a king of Sparta.[13]

In general, however, being new immigrants, conquerors, and newly arrived seems to have been a point of pride and a common reference for collective identity. Similarly to Tyrtaeus, when Mimnermus sings about the foundation of Colophon, he says, "We came," thus emphasizing a common collective action of migration that also constitutes a positive focus of common memory and collective identity. By "positive," I mean the reverse of a negative self-definition, a self-definition that depends on contrast. It is an identity defined in its own terms precisely because it rests on the notion of common historical action and not negatively, Greeks as "not barbarians."[14]

The Herakleidai illustrate the overlap between "founder" in the sense of a founder of a colony, such as Sparta, and in the sense of a founder of a new genealogical line, such as the Spartan royal houses. This is a general characteristic:

there is something inherent in the logic of foundation stories that makes it necessary for the new ancestor to have come from elsewhere. A community can see itself as new in relation to a new place, simply by immigrating there. In contrast, blood has no beginning. Had the ancestor not wandered away but stayed home, he would never have become an ancestor but another link in some other genealogical matrix. For what would have distinguished him from his father, grandfather, uncles, and so on? As Plato said, "Every single man has countless hosts of ancestors, near and remote, among whom are to be found, in every instance, rich men and beggars, kings and slaves, Greeks and barbarians, by the thousand. When men pride themselves on a pedigree of twenty-five ancestors, and trace their descent back to Hercules the son of Amphitryon, they seem to him to be taking a curious interest in trifles. As for the twenty-fifth ancestor of Amphitryon, what *he* may have been is merely a matter of luck, and similarly with the fiftieth before him again" (Plato, *Theaetetus* 174E–175B).

According to the account in the Hebrew Bible (mostly in Genesis but mentioned in other books; see below), Abraham must leave the house of Terah and Nahor in the land of the Chaldeans (Ur Kasdim) "across the river" to go to Canaan, the land later promised to his descendants. A new beginning is possible only there. He gets a new land to live in and even a new personal name: it is changed from Avram to Avraham (Abraham). Only in Canaan can he become an "ancestor": the father and grandfather of Isaac and Jacob, whose numerous sons would become eponymous ancestors of the Hebrew tribes. By analogy, it is no wonder that the two royal houses in Sparta, while considered Herakleidai, were not named after the specific Herakleidai who belonged to the first generation of conquest. That would have kept them too closely linked to a non-Spartan Hercules and to too many other genealogies. As Ephorus says, although Eurysthenes and Procles were both *oikistai* (founders) of the Spartan state and of its two royal dynasties, neither was recognized as *archêgetês*, and their descendants were not named after them.[15]

Distancing allows for a new beginning, acquiring the foreigner's trait. Initially, the sons of Hercules mistook the oracle regarding their return and understood it to instruct them to wait three years. They were defeated. Success had to wait for three generations to pass. Had it been only three years after the death of Hercules, they would be truly returning—but without the distancing effect of some hundred years. The four hundred years that the Israelites spent in Egypt (and the extra forty years in the desert prescribed to forge them into a people that would forget Egypt) are thematically parallel to the time of "three generations" of the Herakleidai. Thus we see an interesting dialectic in the mentality of foundation stories: while expressing the connection with the country in terms of "return," there is a much richer body of historicizing myths that puts the emphasis on the novelty and foreignness of the settlers, providing them with a sense of new beginnings—a primordial, constitutive moment of foundation.

Any place, or any land, must, by definition, be old, predating human arrival. What is important is the founder coming from elsewhere. It could be simply another place within the orbit of familiar geography (such as the Herakleidai coming from just north of the Peloponnese) or an "elsewhere" that could acquire an ethnic emphasis when ethnic differences came to matter more. Concerns about Kadmos as Phoenician, Danaus as Egyptian, or Pelops as Phrygian seem to belong more to fifth-century emphases and projections and indicate Greek ambivalence about foreign ancestry: those foreign origins rooted in ancient, rich civilizations that were highly respected also provided validation and connectedness with the venerable past of the "other." Yet they could also articulate difference when difference rather than affinity might become a rallying cry. The past is a "scarce resource," claims Arjun Appadurai, and Romans identifying and validating their "Trojan" origins in a Greek myth were doing just what Greeks had been doing with respect to the foreign civilizations that they were acquainted with and respected.[16]

As noted, some myths relate the emergence of places as such, but these relate more to the gods and to primordial eras and belong to the category of land myths. For example, the island of Rhodes emerged from the sea to provide Helios with a land to worship him (Pindar, *Olympian* 7). Divine itineraries sometimes provide names and thus differentiate places. In the *Homeric Hymn to Apollo*, for example, that is how the itinerary of the god on his way to Delphi seems to function, creating primordial paths and puncturing space with place names. Or the nymph Cyrene, an eponymous "founder of the land" kidnapped and taken to Libya by Apollo, is the *aition* for the spring named after her. Yet she is primordial and disconnected from the actual colonization by the Therans.[17]

Places might have their own force field or identity, perceived in metahuman terms. Generally speaking, Greeks also saw gods and heroes as "holding the land" (*echein tên gên*), hence the importance they would attach to such heroes as embodying the place. Think, for example, of the sacrifice made before the Battle of Plataea to the seven anonymous heroes of the field of battle.[18] No wonder, perhaps, that Helen and Menelaus, heroes of the land, received cultic honors in Dorian Sparta already in the seventh century.[19]

The polytheistic and poly-heroic matrix of Greek religion was helpful in that respect, allowing for the newly arrived to ritually recognize the local divinities, such as Arethousa (Syracuse) or Orthia (Sparta), and heroes, such as Rhesus at Amphipolis, whose bones were "returned" to his fatherland (now an Athenian colony) by the Athenian founder Hagnon. Rhesus, son of the local river Strymon (hence truly of the land), was also an ally of Priam and needed appeasement when the Athenians settled in his land, an area that had known disastrous colonial failures at the hands of the Thracians (enemies, analogous to the Trojans, on whose side Rhesus had fought).[20] To oversimplify, polytheistic systems recognize that names for gods may be foreign but not so the gods themselves, as if one were speaking of the same thing yet in a different language (religion is *langue*; divine names are *parole*). So Hercules might be his name in Greek; but in Phoenician, he is Melqart. Thus, for newly arrived Greek settlers, bridging the gap from primordial to historical times can be easier, since collective identity need not be defined in adverse contrast to the heroes and gods of the land, necessarily replacing them with one's own, "true" god.

Let us observe an ideology of conquest and forceful settlement that does precisely that, backed by a religion that would not allow this polytheistic mechanism to integrate with the *epichorioi theoi*. An explicit, somewhat proud, claim for rupture and discontinuity comes at the end of the Book of Joshua (chapter 24), which recounts the conquest of the Land of Canaan by the Israelites. At first glance, the Hebrew conquest and the return of the Herakleidai appear similar: both conquering peoples divided their new land by a lottery (see below); and for both, the land had been promised by a god. The Hebrew God "gave" Canaan to Abraham, and Zeus, says Tyrtaeus, "gave this country [*polis*] to the Herakleidai, with whom we came from windy Erineos." But whereas the Spartans bridged the gap by establishing the Menelaion and told stories about the nymph Taygete, the ancient Hebrews would have none of that.

First, let us look at what is glaringly absent. It is curious how little attention is paid in the colonization narrative in the Hebrew Bible to the land myths of Canaan—to how its springs burst from the ground, how a particular river was formed, why certain mountains look the way they do. The exceptions might be precedents set by the patriarchs (parallel to such precedents by Hercules in the Peloponnesos): Abraham buys property in Hebron (Genesis 12); Jacob buys land by Shechem and sets up an altar to El (Genesis 33) or at Bet El (Genesis 35). This is very different, for example, from the water springs associated with the Danaids in the Argolis or the springs of Cyrene or Arethousa in Syracuse. There is no mention of the original founders of the cities that the Israelites were conquering. It is all happily foreign: a new people invading a land promised by their exclusive God. Despite the archeological evidence, which points to very little destruction and shows no evidence of wholesale conquests (the Book of Joshua is apparently full of wishful thinking),[21] this is the image that the biblical author of Joshua wanted to convey.

Discontinuity is a matter to be proud of, as is well articulated at the end of the Book of Joshua, chapter 24. In this chapter, God summarizes the history of the relation of the people to the land, starting with the first genealogical founder, Abraham, whose foreign origins "over there" and his previous foreign gods are emphasized:

ב וַיֹּאמֶר יְהוֹשֻׁעַ אֶל-כָּל-הָעָם, כֹּה-אָמַר יְהוָה אֱלֹהֵי יִשְׂרָאֵל, בְּעֵבֶר הַנָּהָר יָשְׁבוּ אֲבוֹתֵיכֶם מֵעוֹלָם, תֶּרַח אֲבִי אַבְרָהָם וַאֲבִי נָחוֹר; וַיַּעַבְדוּ, אֱלֹהִים אֲחֵרִים.

[2]And Joshua said unto all the people: Thus says the LORD, the God of Israel: Your fathers dwelt of old time *beyond the River*, even Terah, the father of Abraham, and the father of Nahor; *and they served other gods.*

God proceeds with the historical summary, recounts the Exodus from Egypt, and ends by making an explicit declaration about the new land:

יג וָאֶתֵּן לָכֶם אֶרֶץ אֲשֶׁר לֹא-יָגַעְתָּ בָּהּ, וְעָרִים אֲשֶׁר לֹא-בְנִיתֶם, וַתֵּשְׁבוּ, בָּהֶם; כְּרָמִים וְזֵיתִים אֲשֶׁר לֹא-נְטַעְתֶּם, אַתֶּם אֹכְלִים. יד וְעַתָּה יְראוּ אֶת-יְהוָה, וְעִבְדוּ אֹתוֹ—בְּתָמִים וּבֶאֱמֶת; וְהָסִירוּ אֶת-אֱלֹהִים, אֲשֶׁר עָבְדוּ אֲבוֹתֵיכֶם בְּעֵבֶר הַנָּהָר וּבְמִצְרַיִם, וְעִבְדוּ, אֶת-יְהוָה.

[13]And I gave you a land whereon thou hadst not labored, and cities which ye built not, and ye dwell therein; of vineyards and olive-yards which ye planted not do ye eat. [14]Now therefore fear the LORD, and serve Him in sincerity and in truth; and put away the gods which your fathers served beyond the River, and in Egypt; and serve ye the LORD.

This is repeated in Deuteronomy 6:

י וְהָיָה כִּי יְבִיאֲךָ יְהוָה אֱלֹהֶיךָ, אֶל-הָאָרֶץ אֲשֶׁר נִשְׁבַּע לַאֲבֹתֶיךָ לְאַבְרָהָם לְיִצְחָק וּלְיַעֲקֹב—לָתֶת לָךְ: עָרִים גְּדֹלֹת וְטֹבֹת, אֲשֶׁר לֹא-בָנִיתָ. יא וּבָתִּים מְלֵאִים

כָּל-טוּב, אֲשֶׁר לֹא-מִלֵּאתָ, וּבֹרֹת חֲצוּבִים אֲשֶׁר לֹא-חָצַבְתָּ, כְּרָמִים וְזֵיתִים אֲשֶׁר
לֹא-נָטָעְתָּ, וְאָכַלְתָּ, וְשָׂבָעְתָּ.

[10]And it shall be, when the LORD thy God shall bring thee into the land which He swore unto thy fathers, to Abraham, to Isaac, and to Jacob, to give thee—great and goodly cities, *which thou didst not build*, [11]and houses full of all good things, *which thou didst not fill*, and cisterns hewn out, *which thou didst not hew*, vineyards and olive-trees, *which thou didst not plant*.

Here the Israelites are not founders of new cities, nor are they the first to appropriate the land by tilling it. It is theirs, again, by a covenant of keeping faith with God, who gave them all that, while rejecting the local. The "over there" (beyond the river) is linked with "other gods"; Abraham moved "over here," and now Yahweh is to be worshiped alone. Other gods (*elohim acherim*) are clearly associated with those citied built by the others, not by the Hebrews. The link is explicit, and this is how the text of Joshua 24 concludes:

יד וְעַתָּה יְראוּ אֶת-יְהוָה, וְעִבְדוּ אֹתוֹ—בְּתָמִים וּבֶאֱמֶת; וְהָסִירוּ אֶת-אֱלֹהִים, אֲשֶׁר
עָבְדוּ אֲבוֹתֵיכֶם בְּעֵבֶר הַנָּהָר וּבְמִצְרַיִם, וְעִבְדוּ, אֶת-יְהוָה. טו וְאִם רַע בְּעֵינֵיכֶם
לַעֲבֹד אֶת-יְהוָה, בַּחֲרוּ לָכֶם הַיּוֹם אֶת-מִי תַעֲבֹדוּן—אִם אֶת-אֱלֹהִים אֲשֶׁר-עָבְדוּ
אֲבוֹתֵיכֶם אֲשֶׁר בעבר (מֵעֵבֶר) הַנָּהָר, וְאִם אֶת-אֱלֹהֵי הָאֱמֹרִי אֲשֶׁר אַתֶּם יֹשְׁבִים
בְּאַרְצָם; וְאָנֹכִי וּבֵיתִי, נַעֲבֹד אֶת-יְהוָה.

[14]Now therefore fear the LORD, and serve Him in sincerity and in truth; and put away the gods which your fathers served beyond the River, and in Egypt; and serve ye the LORD. [15]And if it seem evil unto you to serve the LORD, choose you this day whom ye will serve; whether the gods which your fathers served that were beyond the River, or the gods of the Amorites, in whose land ye dwell; but as for me and my house, we will serve the LORD.

Not bound by any monotheistic exclusiveness, the Dorians found no difficulty in being at once proud of their conquests, claiming the divine right to do so (because, like the Hebrews, Zeus "gave" it to the Herakleidai) yet accepting a measure of continuity and worshiping the gods and heroes of the land. Ideas associated with alternative foundations could coexist. Through mythological and cultic modalities, continuity was established, somehow subsuming earlier, local identities in the process. That this was not always successful is evident from the case of Sikyon, where the tyrant Cleisthenes forbade the performance of the Homeric poems because they celebrated (heroic) Argos, as Argos, in his day, was considered an enemy. For similar reasons, Cleisthenes had asked Delphi's permission to expel the hero Adrastos but was refused; finally, he also renamed the three Dorian tribes of Sikyon, giving them derogatory names, while naming his own tribe "masters of the People" (Archelaoi). The example of Sikyon demonstrates that the difference between Dorians and non-Dorians was still an important issue in the sixth century. Yet Cleisthenes' actions also show that he recognized the framework of validation and mediation based on cult and precedence. Moreover, contemporary (Dorian) Argos, Cleisthenes' enemy, was acknowledged by him as the direct extension of Homeric Argos (in his canceling of Homeric recitations). The case for continuity could not have had a better advocate.[22]

We may perceive more aspects of the mentality of settlements by the newly arrived, or the foreigner, though practices of foundation. In contrast to the monotheistic emphasis on difference, which sees integration as a threat to the cult to Yahweh, other Hebrew practices of foundation seem similar to Greek ones. In and of itself, this similarity implies the similar perspective of foreigners arriving into the land. I am claiming here thematic similarity, leaving the complex yet separate question of possible mutual influences aside.[23]

Land Allotment

In both Greek and Hebrew foundation stories, the "land" (or "country") is objectified and perceived as an entity to be divided by lottery among the settlers. This signifies "being new" on a concrete level: a parceling and division of plots of land. The Hebrew notion of *nachala*[24] is comparable with the Greek *klêros*, although, unlike *klêros*, it does not imply sortition. Zeus, Hades, and Poseidon had famously divided the cosmos through lottery; the Herakleidai similarly split up the Peloponnese among themselves; and historically, individual settlers would receive their *klêroi* by lottery. Archilochus (mid-seventh century), for example, tells of the miserable Aethiops, who, while still en route to the colony, had gambled away his future plot in the new settlement.[25] The Spartan quasi-founder Lycurgus supposedly split up the Lacedaemonian domains into 30,000 inalienable lots (not to be sold or split up).²⁶ Allotment (mostly egalitarian) and sortition seem to have been integral to Greek practices of foundation, as we can also see on the ground—for example, at Megara Hyblaia in the last third of the eighth century.²⁷

The interdiction on sale of the individual *klêros* at Sparta is very similar to Lev. 25:23, where God provides two reasons for the inalienability of the *nachala*. First, because the land is "His" to give. It seems to indicate God's status as "giver," which is not all that different from the notion that Zeus "gave" (Tyrtaeus' *dedôke*) the polis to the Herakleidai, thus also legitimating fighting those who possess it. Second, because of the foreignness of the founders as well as their status as settlers (ibid.):

כג וְהָאָרֶץ, לֹא תִמָּכֵר לִצְמִתֻת—כִּי-לִי, הָאָרֶץ: כִּי-גֵרִים וְתוֹשָׁבִים אַתֶּם, עִמָּדִי.

²³And the land shall not be sold in perpetuity; for the land is Mine; *for ye are strangers and settlers with Me.*

Allocation of land through lottery is also a common theme. In Joshua 18, we hear of seven tribes that still await allocation of lands. Joshua sends three men from each tribe to spy the land in order "to write [or 'describe'] it":

ח וַיָּקֻמוּ הָאֲנָשִׁים, וַיֵּלֵכוּ; וַיְצַו יְהוֹשֻׁעַ אֶת-הַהֹלְכִים לִכְתֹּב אֶת-הָאָרֶץ לֵאמֹר, לְכוּ וְהִתְהַלְּכוּ בָאָרֶץ וְכִתְבוּ אוֹתָהּ וְשׁוּבוּ אֵלַי, וּפֹה אַשְׁלִיךְ לָכֶם גּוֹרָל לִפְנֵי יְהוָה, בְּשִׁלֹה. ט וַיֵּלְכוּ הָאֲנָשִׁים וַיַּעַבְרוּ בָאָרֶץ, וַיִּכְתְּבוּהָ לֶעָרִים לְשִׁבְעָה חֲלָקִים עַל-סֵפֶר; וַיָּבֹאוּ אֶל-יְהוֹשֻׁעַ אֶל-הַמַּחֲנֶה, שִׁלֹה. י וַיַּשְׁלֵךְ לָהֶם יְהוֹשֻׁעַ גּוֹרָל בְּשִׁלֹה, לִפְנֵי יְהוָה; וַיְחַלֶּק-שָׁם יְהוֹשֻׁעַ אֶת-הָאָרֶץ לִבְנֵי יִשְׂרָאֵל, כְּמַחְלְקֹתָם.

⁸And the men arose, and went; and Joshua charged them to describe the land, saying: "Go and walk through the land, and describe it, and come back to me, and I will cast lots for you here before the LORD in Shiloh." . . . ¹⁰And Joshua cast lots for them in Shiloh before the LORD; and there Joshua divided the land unto the children of Israel according to their divisions.

The lottery is conducted by the *archêgetês*-like figure Joshua, as well as by the counterpart of the Greek seer, such as the Iamidai who joined Archias, founder of Syracuse, or Onymastus the Delphian, who may have accompanied the Battos to Cyrene.²⁸ At Josh. 19:51, that role is played by Eleazar the Priest:

נא אֵלֶּה הַנְּחָלֹת אֲשֶׁר נִחֲלוּ אֶלְעָזָר הַכֹּהֵן וִיהוֹשֻׁעַ בִּן-נוּן וְרָאשֵׁי הָאָבוֹת לְמַטּוֹת בְּנֵי-יִשְׂרָאֵל בְּגוֹרָל בְּשִׁלֹה, לִפְנֵי יְהוָה—פֶּתַח, אֹהֶל מוֹעֵד; וַיְכַלּוּ, מֵחַלֵּק אֶת-הָאָרֶץ.

These are the inheritances, which Eleazar the priest, and Joshua the son of Nun, and the heads of the fathers' houses of the tribes of the children of Israel, distributed for inheritance by lot in Shiloh before the LORD, at the door of the tent of meeting. So they made an end of dividing the land.

Was there a Greek equivalent to "the heads of the fathers' houses of the tribes"? The Israelite settlement is described in terms of mass migration, and therefore the households (and their "heads") are on the move. Similarly, the return of the Herakleidai is also told in terms of mass migration of Dorians. In contrast, in historical Greek colonization (understood in historical terms as relating to the phenomenon of foundations following the second half of the eighth century), the points of origin remain in existence and keep an affinity with the settlers. The *metropolis* is not abandoned, and the newly founded *apoikia* seems to have been an affair of young *apoikioi*, potential heads of new *oikoi* (households), and sometimes forming, by virtue of being first, a kind of aristocracy of first settlers.[29] Primary land allocation (*temenê* to the gods; *klêroi* to settlers) was the responsibility of the *oikistês*, the founder, who seems to have had plenipotentiary powers during the generation of foundation.[30] New *oikoi* would be established based on the new *klêroi*. Unlike migration, colonization implied a notion of "new" and "foreign" in yet another sense: the young settlers were less constrained by tradition and the authority of their elders. They were less prone to simply replicate previous social patterns and, both by necessity and choice, were freer to abstract and implement their own social and political order.

Foundation Oracles

Shiloh was the Israelites' oracle, which, like Delphi, provided settlement prophecies that connected specific groups with specific allotments, thus providing a charter that mediated between the foreigner and the land.[31] The content of the question addressed to the oracle is quite similar to Greek formulas, "To which land should I go?"[32] In Judges 1, the entire tribe of Judah is given a specific area for conquest, although its inquiry is phrased in terms of leadership:

א וַיְהִי, אַחֲרֵי מוֹת יְהוֹשֻׁעַ, וַיִּשְׁאֲלוּ בְּנֵי יִשְׂרָאֵל, בַּיהוָה לֵאמֹר: מִי יַעֲלֶה-לָּנוּ
אֶל-הַכְּנַעֲנִי בַּתְּחִלָּה, לְהִלָּחֶם בּוֹ. **ב** וַיֹּאמֶר יְהוָה, יְהוּדָה יַעֲלֶה: הִנֵּה נָתַתִּי
אֶת-הָאָרֶץ, בְּיָדוֹ.

[1]And it came to pass after the death of Joshua, that the children of
Israel asked the LORD, saying: "Who shall go up for us first against
the Canaanites, to fight against them?" [2]And LORD said: "Judah
shall go up; behold, I have delivered the land into his hand."

Similarly, "apportionment is the property of Zeus," as Walter Burkert says,[33]
which is probably implied in the "gift" to the Herakleidai and in the triple division by lottery of the entire Peloponnese among them.[34] The same proportion-
ate relation holds in both civilizations: the god gives the land, followed by
mechanisms of lottery (for entire groups and individual settlers) for divisions of
countries or household plots. There is, however, a subtle difference with regard
to historical Greek colonization (as contrasted with the Dorian migration): the
oracle of Delphi, the most prominent to hand out foundation oracles, points
the way, orders to go, but hardly "gives," explicitly, any particular land. One
could argue that since Apollo was a mediator, an *exêgêtês* (expounder) of the
gods' will (especially that of his father Zeus), such a gift was implied; this is
certainly a possibility, but we need to be careful not to press the matter too far.
I have argued elsewhere that the degree of explicit justification of conquest and
taking possession stands in direct proportion to the threat posed against the
realization of such conquest and possession. No wonder that only in the Spartan Mediterranean do we find this: Tyrtaeus sang of the gift of Zeus probably
in the context of the Second Messenian War; the foundation oracle to Taras,
Sparta's colony just following the First Messenian War, is the only one in the
entire corpus of fictitious and real foundation oracles to command the settlers
to be a "plague to the Iapygians," a command perhaps comparable to the terri-
ble injunctions against the Amalekites in the Hebrew Bible.[35]

In a more trivial sense, both the oracle of Delphi and the Hebrew oracle
confer leadership status on the conqueror and founder: it was Delphi that
would speak directly to the *oikistês*, and the oracle in Shiloh is also consulted,
via the mediation of the seer, to confirm the nomination of Joshua as the military leader and, by implication, as the successor of Moses. Num. 27:21:

כא וְלִפְנֵי אֶלְעָזָר הַכֹּהֵן יַעֲמֹד, וְשָׁאַל לוֹ בְּמִשְׁפַּט הָאוּרִים לִפְנֵי יְהוָה: עַל-פִּיו יֵצְאוּ
וְעַל-פִּיו יָבֹאוּ, הוּא וְכָל-בְּנֵי-יִשְׂרָאֵל אִתּוֹ—וְכָל-הָעֵדָה.

[21]And he shall stand before Eleazar the priest, who shall inquire for him by the judgment of the Urim [= the oracular device] before the LORD; at his word shall they go out, and at his word they shall come in, both he, and all the children of Israel with him, even all the congregation.

Women and Colonization

Finally, through the Hebrew accounts concerning allotment, we get a glimpse of the role of women as foreign participants in foundation, a problem that must have existed among Greek settlers with regard to their new *klêroi*. It also indicates how colonization may have enhanced the status of women in society.[36] Among Greeks, lots inherited through women guaranteed the preservation of the individual *oikos*; hence, for example, the celebrated status of the Spartan *patriouchos* or *epiklêros* (the terms are significant), the woman who inherits the *klêros*, and thus keeps it intact instead of joining it to her husband's family.[37] In the Hebrew Bible, this is precisely the status claimed by the daughters of Zelophehad. It was apparently important, since the case and the arguments are repeated twice. Their case was recognized by the leaders of Israel: in Numbers 36, the elders from the "families" of Joseph (not quite a discrete "tribe") come to Moses with the following complaint and demand:

ב וַיֹּאמְרוּ, אֶת-אֲדֹנִי צִוָּה יְהוָה, לָתֵת אֶת-הָאָרֶץ בְּנַחֲלָה בְּגוֹרָל, לִבְנֵי יִשְׂרָאֵל; וַאדֹנִי, צֻוָּה בַיהוָה, לָתֵת אֶת-נַחֲלַת צְלָפְחָד אָחִינוּ, לִבְנֹתָיו. ג וְהָיוּ לְאֶחָד מִבְּנֵי שִׁבְטֵי בְנֵי-יִשְׂרָאֵל, לְנָשִׁים, וְנִגְרְעָה נַחֲלָתָן מִנַּחֲלַת אֲבֹתֵינוּ, וְנוֹסַף עַל נַחֲלַת הַמַּטֶּה אֲשֶׁר תִּהְיֶינָה לָהֶם; וּמִגֹּרַל נַחֲלָתֵנוּ, יִגָּרֵעַ.

[2]and they said: "The LORD commanded my lord [Moses] to give the land for distribution by lot as *nachala* to the children of Israel; and my lord was commanded by the LORD to give the inheritance of Zelophehad our brother unto his daughters. [3]And if they be married to any of the sons of the other tribes of the children of Israel, then will their inheritance be taken away from the inheritance of our fathers, and will be added to the inheritance of the tribe whereunto they shall belong; so will it be taken away from the lot of our inheritance [*nachala*].

Their claim is recognized, and the daughters become legitimate inheritors but are forced to marry within the family. This is cast in more general terms elsewhere in the Book of Numbers, as an answer to the direct demand of the women, spoken in their own voice. In Num. 27:4, the women ask:

ד לָמָּה יִגָּרַע שֵׁם-אָבִינוּ מִתּוֹךְ מִשְׁפַּחְתּוֹ, כִּי אֵין לוֹ בֵּן; תְּנָה-לָּנוּ אֲחֻזָּה, בְּתוֹךְ אֲחֵי אָבִינוּ. ה וַיַּקְרֵב מֹשֶׁה אֶת-מִשְׁפָּטָן, לִפְנֵי יְהוָה.

[4]Why should the name of our father be done away from among his family, because he had no son? Give us an *achuza* [equivalent to *nachala*] among our father's brothers.

God's answer in Num. 27:8 is at once explicit and goes beyond the ad hoc:

ח וְאֶל-בְּנֵי יִשְׂרָאֵל, תְּדַבֵּר לֵאמֹר: אִישׁ כִּי-יָמוּת, וּבֵן אֵין לוֹ—וְהַעֲבַרְתֶּם אֶת-נַחֲלָתוֹ, לְבִתּוֹ.

[8]And thou shalt speak unto the children of Israel, saying: If a man die, and have no son, then ye shall cause his inheritance [*nachala*] to pass unto his daughter.

Conclusion

The idea of foundation expresses a perception of an event, punctuating time. Greek colonists in the historical period perceived it in terms of actions done during the lifetime of the founder, solemnly sealed with heroic ritual at the time of his death, followed by burial in the agora and an annual hero cult. The founder, whether mythical or historical, represents beginnings and the focus of collective identity. He is always a foreigner, with more emphasis on arrival from elsewhere, another place (rather than another ethnic group). It would be useful to develop this issue also with regard to ancient Rome, where Aeneas was such a foreign founder but Romulus was indigenous.[38]

Autochthony is a rare self-image. Notions of immigration and new settlement form the more common idea of one's beginnings and collective identity. This implies at once an inherent foreignness and, on the other hand, some expression of mediation and integration with the place.

Sometimes preexisting places would have their own identity in the form of alternative land myths. Among Greeks, the foundation of new polities rather belongs to the third stratum of foundation and origin myths, preceded by myths of the land as well as those of epic heroes. Both are expressly disconnected from the later, political foundations that are foreign in their aspect of migration, conquest, and settlement. I have pointed out three strata of myth and land, but we may note that these are not so neatly discrete. Sometimes the disconnection with the heroic past is deliberately compensated through rituals (cult accorded to local heroes) or mythic notions, portraying the connection with the land as one of return. Polytheism made it easier to connect to local gods and heroes; in comparison, because of explicit religious reasons that forbid such integration, the foreignness of the Israelite settlers emphasizes abruptness and difference rather than sameness and continuity.

Aside from this major difference, the thematic parallels of practices of settlement and appropriation are noteworthy and perhaps merit further study encompassing Near Eastern practices. Both Hebrews and Dorians took over existing cities that they had not built and rich lands for which they had not labored; both received similar foundation oracles; both used seers and priests; both distributed entire countries and individual plots of lands by means of lottery; and both needed to consider the legal status of women.

There is more overlap between Greek and Hebrew foundation myths when relating to mass migration (the Israelites, the Dorians, and perhaps the Ionians) rather than to practices of historical Greek colonization (involving the *metropolis*, *apoikia*, and Delphi); but some practices and circumstances seem to bear comparison nonetheless, even for historical Greek colonization.

The question of what is comparable as such and what is owed to actual contacts and influence is often debated. I would leave these important issues for further study and cooperation with scholars specializing in biblical history and archaeology. Much would also depend on the conflicting dating of biblical passages (including claims that some might have been influenced by Greeks) and the tortured relations of text and archaeology. Former approaches tended to regard the issue of influence literally—"in-fluence," "flowing into"—as if cultural contacts are necessarily unidirectional; their "source," therefore, needed to be identified and located in a hierarchy that is either temporal ("who was first?") or spatial ("first from where?"). Such approaches may indeed be valid at times. Conversely, one might argue that situations of conquest, appropriation, and colonization evoke similar responses as they address the perennial conflict between our essential attribute as traveling beings who settle down, strike roots, and possess lands that we claim to own.

Foundation and foreignness appear as major components of collective identity: the self-awareness of being collectively young in an old land and—just as with ancestors who start a new genealogical line, being foreign allows for a notion of beginning—the focus of a new collective identity and the answer to a perennially posed question: "What am I doing here?"[39]

NOTES

1. Green 1975; Leick 2001. See articles in Azara 2000.

2. Weinfeld 1993.

3. Rosivach 1987; Loraux 1993. The few cases of autochthonous origins include the Theban Spartoi (Pherecydes *FGrH* 3 F22 and F88; Hellanicus *FGrH* 4 F1 and F96; Eur. *Phoen.* 638–89), on which see Vian 1963. However, the Boiotians, says Thuc. 1.12, arrived there only in consequence of the Trojan War, similarly to the Dorians. The autochthonous Arcadians (Strabo 5.2.4) are famous, yet are often seen as exceptional.

4. Hdt. 1.57–58.

5. Plato *Menex.* 245D. Quoted in Finkelberg 2005: 37.

6. For a comprehensive and nuanced discussion, see Gruen 2011.

7. Discussed in detail in Malkin 1994: ch. 1.

8. See, e.g., Dougherty 1993.

9. Calame 1987.

10. Paus. 3.2.2.

11. On the "Homeric Lords of the Land," see Malkin 1994: 26–33.

12. Malkin 1994: 46–47.

13. Hdt. 7.159

14. Mimnermus: F9 in West 1993, and F3 in Gentili and Prato 1988; Tyrtaeus: F1a in Prato 1968 and F2 in Gerber 1999.

15. Ephorus *FGrH* 70 F118.

16. Appadurai 1981. Cf. Malkin 1998: 178–209; Gruen 2011.

17. Clay 1989.

18. Plut. *Aristides* 11.3.

19. For the archaeology and inscriptional epigraphy, see Catling 1976–77; Catling and Cavanagh 1976.

20. Homer *Iliad* 10.435; Polyaenus *Strat.* 6.53 with other references in Malkin 1987: 81–84.

21. Finkelstein and Silberman 2001.

22. Hdt. 5.67.

23. For the most up-to-date treatment and bibliography for the issues of contacts between the ancient Near East and Greece, see López-Ruiz 2010. See, specifically, Weinfeld 1988a, 1988b, 1993.

24. A terrestrial possession of a plot of land; an inheritance; allocated land; *nachalat avot*: an ancestral plot. In Modern Hebrew, the words for a "colonist" or "colony" (*mitnachel, hitnachalut*) are derivatives.

25. Archilochus F293 West.

26. Plut. *Lycurgus* 8.

27. Megara: Gras et al. 2004.

28. Malkin 1987: ch. 2.

29. Aristotle *Pol.* 1290b 12; *Rh. Al.* 1423a 37. The Gamoroi (sharers in land plots) of Syracuse may serve as example. Dunbabin 1948: 57–58; cf. Asheri 1966: 31–32.

30. Graham 1983: ch. 3; Malkin 2009.

31. On Delphi's role in Greek colonization, see Malkin 1987: 17–91; cf. Morgan 1990.

32. That is the conventional question that the Spartan Dorieus had failed to ask. Hdt. 5.43; Malkin 1987: 79.

33. Burkert 1985: 129–30.

34. Isocrates *Archidamos* 18, with more references and a full discussion in Malkin 1994: 33–43.

35. Taras: Malkin 1987: 47–52; Malkin 1994: ch. 4. Sparta: Malkin 1994: passim. For a more nuanced picture of the relations with indigenous Iapygians (notable at L'Amastuola, some fifteen kilometers from Taras) and Taras, concerning also this oracle, see Burgers and Crielaard 2007.

36. For women in Greek colonization, see Graham 1984; Coldstream 1992; Hodos 1999.

37. On the Greek *epiklêros* (and the Spartan *patroiouchos*), see Cartledge 1981; Finkelberg 1991, esp. on royal succession through women; Hodkinson 1986; Patterson 1998; Schaps 1979; Cantarella 2005.

38. Cf. Wiseman 1995; Dench 2005; Malkin 1998: 178–211 (I wish to thank Jeanne Pansard-Besson for discussing this matter with me).

39. This is the title of a book by Bruce Chatwin, the travel writer who spoke for nomadism: Chatwin 1988.

REFERENCES

Appadurai, A. 1981. "The Past as a Scarce Resource." *Man* 16: 201–19.
Asheri, D. 1966. *Distribuzioni di terre nell' antica Grecia: Memoria.* Turin: Accademia delle Scienze.
Azara, P. (ed.). 2000. *La Fundació de la ciutat: Mesopotàmia, Grècia i Roma.* Barcelona: CCCB.

Burgers, G.-J., and J. P. Crielaard. 2007. "Greek Colonists and Indigenous Populations at L'Amastuola, Southern Italy." *BABesch* 82: 77–114.

Burkert, W. 1985. *Greek Religion*. Cambridge MA: Harvard University Press.

Calame, C. 1987. "Le récit généalogique spartiate: La représentation mythologique d'une organisation spatiale." *Quaderni di Storia* 26: 43–91.

Cantarella, E. 2005. "Gender, Sexuality, and Law." In *The Cambridge Companion to Ancient Greek Law*, ed. M. Gagarin and D. Cohen, 236–53. Cambridge: Cambridge University Press.

Cartledge, P. 1981. "Spartan Wives: Liberation or Licence?." *Classical Quarterly* 31: 84–105.

Catling, H. W. 1976. "New Excavations at the Menelaion." In *Neue Forschungen in griechischen Heiligtümern*, ed. U. Jantzen, 77–90. Tübingen: Wasmuth.

Catling, H. W. 1976–77. "Excavations at the Menelaion, Sparta, 1974–1976." *Archaeological Reports* 23: 24–42.

Catling, H. W., and H. Cavanagh. 1976. "Two Inscribed Bronzes from the Menelaion, Sparta." *Kadmos* 15: 145–57.

Chatwin, B. 1988. *What Am I Doing Here?*. London: Vintage (1998 publication).

Clay, J. S. 1989. *The Politics of Olympus: Form and Meaning in the Major Homeric Hymns*. Princeton, NJ: Princeton University Press.

Coldstream, J. N. 1992. "Mixed Marriages at the Frontiers of the Early Greek World." *Oxford Journal of Archaeology* 12: 89–107.

Dench, E. 2005. *Romulus's Asylum: Roman Identities from the Age of Alexander to the Age of Adrian*. Oxford: Oxford University Press.

Dougherty, C. 1993. *The Poetics of Colonization: From City to Text in Ancient Greece*. New York: Oxford University Press.

Dunbabin, T. J. 1948. *The Western Greeks: The History of Sicily and South Italy from the Foundation of the Greek Colonies to 480 B.C.* Oxford: Clarendon.

Finkelberg, M. 1991. "Royal Succession in Heroic Greece." *Classical Quarterly* 41 (2): 303–16.

Finkelberg, M. 1995. "Odysseus and the Genus 'Hero.'" *Greece and Rome* 42: 1–14.

Finkelstein, I., and N. A. Silberman. 2001. *The Bible Unearthed: Archaeology's New Vision of Ancient Israel and the Origin of Its Sacred Texts*. New York: Free Press.

Gentili, B. and C. Prato. 1968. *Poetarum elegiacorum testimonia et fragmenta*. Rev. 2nd ed. Bibliotheca scriptorium Graecorum et Romanorum Teubneriana. Leipzig: Teubner.

Gerber, D. E. 1999. *Greek Elegiac Poetry: From the Seventh to the Fifth Centuries BC*. Loeb Classical Library. Cambridge, MA: Harvard University Press.

Graham, A. J. 1983. *Colony and Mother City in Ancient Greece*. 2nd ed. Chicago: Aris.

Graham, A. J. 1984. "Religion, Women and Greek Colonization." In *Religione e città nel mondo antico (Atti, Centro ricerche e documentazione sull' antichità classica)*, 293–314 (reprinted in Graham, A. J. 2001. *Collected Papers on Greek Colonization*, 327–48. Leiden: Brill).

Gras, M., H. Tréziny, and H. Broise. 2004. *Mégara Hyblaea*, vol. 5: *La ville archaïque*. Paris: École française de Rome.

Green, M. W. 1975. *Eridu in Sumerian Literature*. Chicago: University of Chicago Press.

Gruen, E. S. 2011. *Rethinking the Other in Antiquity*. Princeton, NJ: Princeton University Press.

Hodkinson, S. 1986. "Land Tenure and Inheritance in Classical Sparta." *Classical Quarterly* 36: 378–406.

Hodos, T. 1999. "Intermarriage in the Western Greek Colonies." *Oxford Journal of Archaeology* 18: 61–78.

Leick, G. 2001. *Mesopotamia: The Invention of the City*. London: Allen Lane.

López-Ruiz, C. 2010. *When the Gods Were Born: Greek Cosmogonies and the Near East*. Cambridge, MA: Harvard University Press.

Loraux, N. 1993. *The Children of Athena: Athenian Ideas About Citizenship and the Division Between Sexes*, tr. Caroline Levine. Princeton, NJ: Princeton University Press.

Malkin, I. 1987. *Religion and Colonization in Ancient Greece*. Leiden: Brill.

Malkin, I. 1994. *Myth and Territory in the Spartan Mediterranean*. Cambridge: Cambridge University Press.

Malkin, I. 1996. "The Polis Between Myths of Land and Territory." In *The Role of Religion in the Early Greek Polis: Third International Seminar on Ancient Greek Cult*, ed. R. Hägg, 9–19. Stockholm: Swedish Institute at Athens.

Malkin, I. 1998. *The Returns of Odysseus: Colonization and Ethnicity*. Berkeley: University of California Press.

Malkin, I. 2009. "Foundations." In *A Companion to Archaic Greece*, ed. K. Raaflaub and H. van Wees, 373–94. Malden, MA: Wiley-Blackwell.

Morgan, C. 1990. *Athletes and Oracles: The Transformation of Olympia and Delphi in the 8th Century BC*. Cambridge: Cambridge University Press.

Patterson, C. B. 1998. *The Family in Greek History*. Cambridge, MA: Harvard University Press.

Prato, C. 1968. *Trytaeus: Fragmenta*. Lyricorum Graecorum quae extant 3. Rome: Athenaeum.

Rosivach, V. J. 1987. "Autochthony and the Athenians." *Classical Quarterly* 37: 294–306.

Schaps, D. M. 1975. "Women in Greek Inheritance Law." *Classical Quarterly* 25: 53–57.

Schaps, D. M. 1979. *Economic Rights of Women in Ancient Greece*. Edinburgh: Edinburgh University Press.

Schaps, D. M. 1998. "What Was Free About a Free Athenian Woman?." *Transactions of the American Philological Association* 128: 161–88.

Vian, F. 1963. *Les origines de Thèbes: Cadmos et les Spartes*. Paris: C. Klincksieck.

Weinfeld, M. 1988a."The Promise to the Patriarchs and Its Realization: An Analysis of Foundation Stories." In *Society and Economy in the Eastern Mediterranean (c. 1500–1000 BC)*, ed. M. Heltzer and E. Lipiński, 353–69. Orientalia Lovaniensia Analecta 23. Louvain: Peeters.

Weinfeld, M. 1988b. "The Pattern of the Israelite Settlement in Canaan." Supplement to *Vetus Testamentum* 40: 270–83. Leiden: Brill.

Weinfeld, M. 1993. *The Promise of the Land: The Inheritance of the Land of Canaan by the Israelites*. Berkeley: University of California Press.

West, M. L. 1993. *Lyric Greek Poetry*. Oxford: Oxford University Press.

Wiseman, T. P. 1995. *Remus: A Roman Myth*. Cambridge: Cambridge University Press.

CHAPTER 2

Oikist and Archegetes in Context: Representing the Foundation of Sicilian Naxos

LIEVE DONNELLAN

Introduction: Foundations and Representations

La fondation des cités italiotes et sicéliotes . . . était rattachée par une tradition que nous ont transmise les auteurs anciens, au grand mouvement de la colonisation hellénique des VIII–VIIe siècles. Mais, à côté de cette tradition "historique," une tradition "fabuleuse" faisait remonter leur origine à une époque beaucoup plus reculée, à l'âge héroïque de la Guerre de Troie.

—Jean Bérard[1]

In his 1941 book, Jean Bérard, the great French historian of Greek colonization, developed a revolutionary approach: in the written sources referring to the western Greek colonial foundations, he sought to distinguish history from myth. By drawing a chronological boundary between heroic narratives and historical events in the eighth century BC, he tried to reconstruct the truth of a city's foundation.[2] Foundation myths, especially those of the Greek colonial settlements, are an exceptional source. The relatively recent beginnings of these new settlements offered an opportunity for reshaping existing myths and genealogies and especially for developing new ones.

We may with difficulty get at the truth behind such stories, but what is of equal or even greater interest is how the Greeks understood these beginnings. It is around the past and ideas of origins that human societies construct their collective identity. Greek *apoikiai* are not different in this respect, and it is significant that a standard pattern developed for these colonial foundation stories. These cities typically traced their origins back to a leader-founder, the *oikist*, responsible for the initiation of their settlement.[3] In most cases, the *oikist* was honored with a monumental funerary tomb on the agora and a yearly festival.[4] The sanctuary of Apollo in Delphi also frequently appears in colonial foundation stories.[5] Foundation stories, however, did not constitute an independent genre until the Hellenistic period. Earlier foundation narratives usually functioned as topos or themes that added geographical detail and etiological focus to catalog poetry, or they were integrated into choral contexts such as *epinikion*, *paian*, or drama.[6] Carol Dougherty has pointed out that the narrative patterns, metaphors, and language of Greek foundation myths are informed by aspects of contemporary culture. These include purification practices, the Delphic oracle, marriage ideology, and Panhellenic competition. She stressed an analogy of colonial foundations in particular with purification rituals after murder.[7]

Despite these commonalities between Greek foundation myths, there is generally much more variety than similarity. The structure of Greek foundation myths was actually quite flexible, the main common factor being the beginning of the new settlement portrayed as a single act, carried out by a single (or a few) founder(s), and a single (or a few) named mother city(ies). Therefore, while murder and marriage analogies are found in several foundation myths, they are absent in many others, as, for example, in Sicilian Naxos.

There is variation not only between the foundation myths of different cities but also within the foundation traditions belonging to individual cities. This diversity of myth is to be found in written texts and also in the other contexts in which foundation myths were depicted, such as cult space, public architecture, or coinage. Every foundation discourse, therefore, whether sung, written, or sculpted, had its own focus, and was creative in stressing or elaborating different details. Usually, the foundation discourses represented in the spatial, architectural, or numismatic contexts are studied as illustrations of the narratives known from the written sources. But instead of considering them as elements of a unified discourse, we should see these representations as fundamentally different from one another and as equally creative contexts, or perhaps even competitive contexts, where the representation of foundation narratives could be questioned, improved on, or elaborated. As will be demonstrated, the representations used in one context can differ quite significantly from those used in another. This indicates not only that adaptations occurred in the spoken or written discourse but that the foundation narratives were altered, modified, and elaborated in other media, too.

In this chapter, I focus on the evidence relating to the foundation narratives of the city of Naxos on Sicily. Naxos is located on the east coast of Sicily (Fig. 2.1), about five kilometers south of modern-day Taormina. Although the remains of the ancient city had already been identified in the nineteenth century, it was not until the 1950s that systemic excavations began.[8] These revealed the existence of a typically Greek-style settlement from the eighth century BC onward, and an adjacent necropolis. Remains of "indigenous" habitation were found very recently underneath the "Greek colonial settlement," but the evidence is too scanty to draw firm conclusions about interethnic relations. The nature of the earliest objects found at Naxos testifies to links with

2.1. Map of eastern Sicily with the location of the most important sites mentioned in the text. Author's own.

Euboea, Samos, and, especially, Corinth. Because of the name of the city, scholars have attempted to identify Cycladic traits in the material record, which would prove the origins of the colonists. However, apart from one inscription dated to the seventh century BC, a link with Cycladic Naxos has not yet been identified.[9]

The written sources of the classical and Hellenistic periods, discussed below, offer us an external and non-Naxian view of Naxos' foundation. These authors' representations of the Naxian foundation should be seen as part of wider strategies to project a positive image of the Hellenes in general, and the Athenians in particular. These external textual representations of Naxian origins are markedly different from local views, which can be seen in Naxian self-representation through coinage and spatial organization of cult. First, these local views focus much more on the cult of Apollo Archegetes, whereas the texts fail to recognize the importance of this cult. However, this cult was used by the Naxians not only as a symbol for their foundation but also as a tool to negotiate political and military alliances with neighboring cities. These cities could claim kinship through a common discourse of collective foundation represented by Apollo Archegetes. This was an effective and strategic choice in the face of threatening enemies such as Syracuse, which attached itself to another competing Greek *ethnê* (Dorian).

Second, while the relationship with overseas metropoleis is an important element in the texts, it seems to have been a less important factor in Naxian self-representation and politics. Naxos sought close relationships with nearby Leontini and Catane, rather than its supposed mother city(ies) overseas. Both Leontini and Catane are located to the south of Naxos (Fig. 2.1); Leontini lies inland, and Catane (modern Catania) is on the coast. Archaeological research at Catane has been very limited because of the intensive nature of modern occupation and repeated eruptions of Mount Etna, but the information available reveals occupation, especially Corinthian links in pottery, found in a sanctuary deposit, from the late eighth century BC onward.[10] Significant Corinthian links have equally been found at Leontini.[11] Leontini is noted for the intensive "indigenous" presence before and during the first centuries of the "Greek colonial settlement." There are also indications of a Phocaean connection, which, however, does not figure in the foundation myths.[12]

Contextualizing the various representations of Naxos' foundation provides an interesting insight into the dynamics of mythic discourse. Greek colonial foundation narratives were used to negotiate citizenship, relationships with neighboring and overseas poleis, and historical and cultural discourses of Athenian intellectuals.

Thucydides

Three texts refer to the foundation of the city of Naxos on Sicily. They date from the fifth to the second century BC. The earliest of these is Thucydides:

Ἑλλήνων δὲ πρῶτοι Χαλκιδῆς ἐξ Εὐβοίας πλεύσαντες μετὰ Θουκλέους οἰκιστοῦ Νάξον ᾤκισαν καὶ Ἀπόλλωνος Ἀρχηγέτου βωμόν, ὅστις νῦν ἔξω τῆς πόλεώς ἐστιν, ἱδρύσαντο, ἐφ' ᾧ, ὅταν ἐκ Σικελίας θεωροὶ πλέωσι, πρῶτον θύουσιν . . . Θουκλῆς δὲ καὶ οἱ Χαλκιδῆς ἐκ Νάξου ὁρμηθέντες ἔτει πέμπτῳ μετὰ Συρακούσας οἰκισθείσας Λεοντίνους τε, πολέμῳ τοὺς Σικελοὺς ἐξελάσαντες, οἰκίζουσι καὶ μετ' αὐτοὺς Κατάνην· οἰκιστὴν δὲ αὐτοὶ Καταναῖοι ἐποιήσαντο Εὔαρξον.

Of the Hellenes, on the other hand, the first to sail over were some Chalcidians from Euboea who settled Naxos with Thucles as founder, and built an altar in honor of Apollo Archegetes. This is now outside the city, and on it sacred deputies, when they sail from Sicily, first offer sacrifice. . . . In the fifth year after the settlement of Syracuse, Thucles and the Chalcidians, setting forth from Naxos, drove out the Sicels in war and settled Leontini, and after it Catane. The Cataneans, however, chose for themselves Evarchos as founder.

Thucydides 6.3.1–3[13]

The reference to Naxos' foundation forms part of an ethnological description of Sicily, known as the "Sicilian Archaeology." The Sicilian Archaeology is considered by scholars to be Thucydides' explanation for the Athenians' failure in the Sicilian expedition. Athens underestimated the Sicilian cities' capacities and resources, which led to a humiliating defeat instead of a brilliant victory. This disastrous invasion proved to be a pivotal turn for Athenian prosperity during the Peloponnesian Wars.[14]

Thucydides begins the Sicilian Archaeology by listing all the inhabitants of Sicily chronologically. He starts with a nod to Homer, claiming that the Cyclopes and Laestrygones were the first inhabitants of the island.[15] After the list of inhabitants, Thucydides' narrative focuses on the arrival of the Greeks. He discusses the foundation of the different Greek poleis in chronological order. In each case, Thucydides indicates the name of the *oikist*, the mother city, and an important event that had influenced the act of foundation, such as the erection of the altar for Apollo Archegetes, or a war with the indigenous population over Leontini. Thucydides seeks to divide the Greek cities of Sicily according to their origins, through a connection with the mother city: Naxos was Chalcidian, as were Leontini and Catane; Syracuse was a Corinthian foundation; and so on. The loyalty of the Sicilian colonies to their mother cities was claimed as an important factor in the course of the Athenian invasion, and the connections between colonies and metropoleis therefore features strongly in Thucydides' story.[16] Despite an appeal by the Syracusan ambassador, Hermocrates, to close ranks and support a common Siceliot case, civic and ethnic (Dorian versus Ionian) oppositions prevailed.[17] Naxos and the other Euboean foundations chose the Athenian side during the Athenian invasion, whereas the Dorian cities supported Syracuse.

These Euboean origins connected Naxos with the earliest Greek colonial movements and with the oldest colonies, such as Pithekoussai and Cumae.[18] This gave Naxos a sense of antiquity and primacy among the Sicilian foundations, a claim that proved to be very successful. This primacy seems to have brought great prestige, as several other Sicilian cities tried to link themselves to Naxos by claiming Naxian descent. Apart from Leontini and Catane, Thucydides mentions that Zancle also claimed to have been refounded by Naxos, after having been occupied by Cumean pirates.[19] The Megarian colony Hyblaea has also been connected with Theocles' expedition, and the story of the founder Lamis is closely linked with the early years of Leontini's occupation.[20] The idea of primacy among the Sicilian cities was important enough that, after the destruction of Naxos in 403 BC, it continued to be a powerful political claim. This concern for primacy and antiquity among the Sicilian cities in Thucydides seems to be due to actual Sicilian concerns. Thucydides' source for the primacy of Naxos and the chronology of the other Sicilian foundations was probably Antiochos of Syracuse, and it is suggested that the chronology is linked to dedications in the sanctuary of Apollo Archegetes at Naxos.[21]

Through the connection with Apollo Archegetes, the foundation of Naxos and the *oikist* Theocles are shrouded in a mythic aura. As Archegetes— literally, "the founder"—Apollo protected the foundation of Naxos and was a point of reference for Naxian self-identification and civic cult. The regional significance of the cult of Apollo Archegetes has been much discussed. It is thought that the sanctuary at Naxos was the focus for regional cult practice and local Siceliot identity.[22] Some scholars argue for a connection between Apollo Archegetes of Naxos and the sanctuary of Apollo in Delos because of the supposed Cycladic Naxian involvement in the foundation of Naxos in Sicily.[23] However, as there is no clear evidence for Naxian domination or influence over the sanctuary at Delos in the eighth century BC, or for the subsequent "export" of the cult to Sicilian Naxos, this hypothesis is unlikely. Alternatively, Apollo of Naxos has sometimes been connected with the oracle of Apollo at Delphi. But the link with Delphi is problematic, as there is relatively little known about it in the second half of the eighth century BC and the installation of the oracle.[24]

By linking the human founder Theocles with Apollo Archegetes, Naxos is cast as a divinely inspired foundation and given a divine mandate. Thus, Thucydides presents his version of the foundation of Naxos as the classic foundation—inspired by Apollo, led by an *oikist* from a single city, Chalcis.

Ephorus

Only slightly later than Thucydides is Ephorus' account of the foundation of Naxos, preserved as a fragment in Strabo's *Geography*.[25]

φησὶ δὲ ταύτας Ἔφορος πρώτας κτισθῆναι πόλεις Ἑλληνίδας ἐν Σικελίᾳ δεκάτῃ γενεᾷ μετὰ τὰ Τρωικά· τοὺς γὰρ πρότερον δεδιέναι τὰ ληστήρια τῶν Τυρρηνῶν καὶ τὴν ὠμότητα τῶν ταύτῃ βαρβάρων, ὥστε μηδὲ κατ᾽ ἐμπορίαν πλεῖν. Θεοκλέα δ᾽ Ἀθηναῖον παρενεχθέντα ἀνέμοις εἰς τὴν Σικελίαν κατανοῆσαι τήν τε οὐδένειαν τῶν ἀνθρώπων καὶ τὴν ἀρετὴν τῆς γῆς, ἐπανελθόντα δὲ Ἀθηναίους μὲν μὴ πεῖσαι, Χαλκιδέας δὲ τοὺς ἐν Εὐβοίᾳ συχνοὺς παραλαβόντα καὶ τῶν Ἰώνων τινάς, ἔτι δὲ Δωριέων, ὧν οἱ πλείους ἦσαν Μεγαρεῖς, πλεῦσαι τοὺς μὲν οὖν Χαλκιδέας κτίσαι Νάξον, τοὺς δὲ Δωριέας Μέγαρα, τὴν Ὕβλαν πρότερον καλουμένην.

According to Ephorus, these were the earliest Greek cities to be founded in Sicily, that is, in the tenth generation after the Trojan war;

for before that time men were so afraid of the bands of Tyrrhenian
pirates and the savagery of the barbarians in this region that they
would not so much as sail thither for trafficking; but though Theocles, the Athenian, borne out of his course by the winds to Sicily,
clearly perceived both the weakness of the peoples and the excellence of the soil, yet, when he went back, he could not persuade the
Athenians, and hence he took as partners a considerable number of
Euboean Chalcidians and some Ionians and also some Dorians, most
of whom were Megarians, and made the voyage; so the Chalcidians
founded Naxos, whereas the Dorians founded Megara, which in earlier times had been called Hybla.

Strabo 6.2.2[26]

The references to the Greek foundations of Sicily were part of a total of thirty
books forming a "universal history," a new genre of which Ephorus, according
to Polybius, was the first practitioner.[27] The original work is largely lost, but
parts remain known through references in the work of the historian Diodorus,
especially books 11–16, and others. It is not clear which sources Ephorus may
have used for his foundation story of Sicilian Naxos; he probably drew upon
several works, including Thucydides and Hellanicus.[28]

Ephorus' treatment of the foundation of Naxos is not radically different
from that of Thucydides, but does vary in a number of key details. There is
no reference to the god Apollo overseeing the colonial expedition. Nor does
Ephorus mention the cult of Apollo Archegetes, which Thucydides claimed
was founded upon arrival by the colonists and which we know was of great
local significance.[29] In general, it has been noted that Ephorus displays some
hostility toward myth; rationalism and historical interpretation of mythology (euhemerism) are detectable throughout his work and are clearly evident
in his treatment of the foundation of Naxos.[30] Instead of Apollo, Ephorus
places the human founder, Theocles, in the foreground. Theocles takes the
initiative, and it is he, not Apollo, who is the "archegetes," leading the colonists
to Sicily. Theocles is, moreover, not an "intentional founder": while seafaring,
he landed by accident in Sicily.[31] Having landed fortuitously, he observed the
suitability of the land for settlement. Apollo's imperative of the traditional
colonial enterprise is replaced by *tychê* and human initiative.[32] This is a more
down-to-earth idea of foundation, with the motive of material advantage.
Ephorus' Theocles fits the profile of the early Greek seafarer-adventurer.

Theocles follows in the footsteps of Odysseus or Heracles, embodying ideas about early Greek seafaring and elite contacts. He has strategic interests in the discovery of rich uninhabited lands, suitable for settlement, or perhaps hopes to return home as a wealthy man.[33]

Although both Catane and Leontini are said by Ephorus to be Naxian foundations, he does not link them with Theocles, as Thucydides does.[34] Another difference between Thucydides' and Ephorus' accounts can be found in the connection with Athens made by Ephorus. According to Ephorus, Theocles was an Athenian but guiding a motley group of Chalcidians and others. It seems clear that Theocles' alleged Athenian background is an indication of Athenian interest in the southern Italian region.[35] In this period, Naxos' mother city of Chalcis was under Athenian control, and thus Athens could claim a connection as the "mother city" of Naxos' mother city—Naxos' "grandmother city." If Ephorus was indeed a contemporary of Theopompus at Isocrates' school, as has been argued, that would explain his ideological pro-Athenian positioning. Echoes of Isocrates' pro-Athenian and pro-Hellenic thought can be found throughout Ephorus' account. The Ephorean Theocles resembles the Isocratean Theseus: he is a hero with an ideal virtuous character and acts as a successful leader in uniting Greeks to overcome barbarian resistance, initiating civilization and settlement.[36] Theocles serves as a mirror for the contemporary political realities at the time Ephorus was writing. He thus supports Ephorus' pro-Athenian opinions—Athenian domination of other Greek states but with the accompanying rhetoric of alliance, kinship, and agreement. Naxos chose the Athenian side during the Sicilian expedition, and Ephorus projects the alliance back into the past by giving the colony an Athenian founder. By linking Athens with the oldest of Sicilian cities, Ephorus is justifying the Sicilian expedition and supporting Athenian claims. By not linking the foundation of Naxos to any one place, but rather representing it as a collaborative effort by a number of Greek poleis that are persuaded through argument to act under the leadership of an Athenian in the past, Ephorus can minimize contemporary accusations of Athenian imperialism.[37]

The presence of the indigenous inhabitants is mentioned by Ephorus, but their position in comparison with the Greeks is clearly stated as inferior. Although Thucydides mentions conflict accompanying the foundation of Leontini and Catane, he does not stress barbarian weakness in the same way that Ephorus does, who alludes, a priori, to the victory of the Greeks. Reflecting

Isocratean ideas, panhellenism and anti-barbarian attitudes are also clearly evident in Ephorus' narrative.

Pseudo-Scymnus

Ephorus' account of the foundation of Naxos seems to have been closely followed by pseudo-Scymnus' *Periodos Gês:*[38]

... Σικελία νῆσος, εὐτυχεστάτη, ἣν τὸ πρότερον μὲν ἑτερόγλοσσα βάρβαρα λέγουσι πλήθη κατανέμεσθ' Ἰβιρικά. ... εἶθ' Ἑλληνικὰς ἔσχεν πόλεις, ὥς φασιν, ἀπὸ τῶν Τρωϊκῶν δεκάτη γενεᾷ μετὰ ταῦτα Θεοκλέους στόλον παρὰ Χαλκιδέων λαβόντος· ἦν δ' οὗτος γένει ἐκ τῶν Ἀθηνῶν· καὶ συνῆλθον, ὡς λόγος, Ἴωνες εἶτα Δωριεῖς οἰκήτορες. Στάσεως δ' ἐν αὐτοῖς γενομένης, οἱ Χαλκιδεῖς κτίζουσι Νάξον, οἱ Μεγαρεῖς δὲ τὴν Ὕβλαν, τὸ δ' ἐπὶ Ζεφύριον τῆς Ἰταλιας [οἱ] Δωριεῖς κατέσχον. ... Μετὰ ταῦτα δ' ἀπὸ Νάξου Λεοντίνη [πόλις], ἡ τὴν θέσιν τ' ἔχουσα Ῥηγίου πέραν, ἐπὶ τοῦ δὲ πορθμοῦ κειμένη τῆς Σικελίας, Ζάγκλη, Κατάνη, Καλλίπολις ἔσχ' ἀποικίαν.

The most fortunate island of Sicily was first inhabited by barbarians speaking different languages, who came from Iberia. ... Then she received Greek cities, in the tenth generation after the Trojan War, as they say, when Theocles instructed a fleet from Chalcis, although he came from Athens. With him, according to tradition, came Ionians, then Dorians, as settlers. Because of disagreement, the Chalcidians founded Naxos, the Megarians Hybla, whereas the Dorians took possession of Zephyrion in Italy. ... After these events, it is from Naxos that Leontini, the one located in front of Rhegion, on the border of the Street, on the Sicilian side, Zancle, as well as Catane and Callipolis, received their colonists.

Pseudo-Scymnus, vv. 264–97[39]

In his version of the story, tentatively dated to the later second century BC, pseudo-Scymnus, by adding "as they say," and "according to the tradition," is clearly more reluctant than Thucydides or Ephorus to provide a firm view of the beginnings of Naxos.[40] Although pseudo-Scymnus seems to have been less concerned about rationalization than Ephorus was—he addresses Apollo of Didyma and the Muses to guide him in the composition of his work—the involvement of Delphi or the erection of the altar for Apollo Archegetes in Naxos is not mentioned. Pseudo-Scymnus thus rejects the traditional format of a colonial foundation, with its Delphic consultation. His characterization of Theocles, moreover, differs from that of the typical *oikist* with his single foundation act from one mother city. The pseudo-Scymnian Theocles was the leader of one single Greek expedition of mixed origin, uniting Ionians and Dorians alike. Only in a second stage, we are told, was the decision taken to split up and found several separate cities. Pseudo-Scymnus writes that this decision was motivated by disagreement between the Ionians and Dorians, who were unable to act together. The importance of Naxos' primacy among the Sicilian foundations is therefore minimized, and Theocles now appears as the *oikist* of all the Greek foundations of Sicily, rather than just of Naxos.

Pseudo-Scymnus' Theocles did not land accidentally in Sicily, as did Ephorus' Theocles. Instead, he is described as having planned the expedition and instructed the fleet. Here, Theocles is modeled after successful army leaders. Neither Apollo nor *tychê* has anything to do with the colonial foundation; it is, rather, the result of successful and rational organization and cooperation between different Greek groups.

Pseudo-Scymnus identifies the *oikist* Theocles as Athenian; but unlike Ephorus, he conveys no sense of Athenian dominance over the colonizing project. The Chalcidian origins of the fleet are given just as much prominence as Theocles' Athenian origins. Like Ephorus, pseudo-Scymnus represents the expedition as a mixed Ionian-Dorian enterprise under Athenian leadership. But in pseudo-Scymnus the Ionian-Dorian opposition comes to the foreground, and the expedition is divided according to the groups with which the metropoleis identified: Chalcis with the Ionians, versus Megarians and other Dorians. The motif of strife between the Dorians and the Ionians during the act of foundation is new. Clearly, historical events have shaped the author's understanding of the remote past and account for a way particular representation that is not used by the earlier authors. In pseudo-Scymnus' account, no mention is made of Greek-barbarian conflict, in contrast to the accounts of Ephorus and Thucydides. Pseudo-Scymnus refers to the presence of other peoples, barbarians, speaking different languages, but they are placed in a remote past, predating Greek settlement on the island. In pseudo-Scymnus, the conflict is strictly inter-Greek.

Pseudo-Scymnus was writing in a period when several of the colonies whose foundation he discusses, such as Naxos or Megara, had been destroyed for many years. Their foundation stories, although no longer related to an active citizen body, had been picked up and integrated into the foundation stories of other cities in Sicily. Tauromenion was founded by the survivors of the Naxian destruction. Tauromenion was quick to claim descent from the Naxians and incorporated the figure of Apollo Archegetes into its civic identity. The prestige attached to Naxos, drawing from its antiquity and primacy, was a powerful tool to establish a new city and reinforce a newly composed citizen body. As a result, this Hellenistic foundation story had shifted away from the focus on the *oikist*, Delphi, and mother city that we saw in the classical accounts. Instead, emphasis is laid on the successful claims of descent by a second generation of foundations. This second generation of foundations did not seek the connections with the homeland which had been so important for the earliest foundations, but sought them instead with prominent local Sicilian cities. The involvement of the "big players" of early colonization, the colonial mother cities, became a topos in later representations such as pseudo-Scymnus' story. During this time, lines of Dorian and Ionian ethnicity within Sicily were far more important than connections between individual colonies and an original mother city.

Coinage and Shifting Naxian Identity

So far, I have discussed only literary accounts of Naxos' foundation myths. In the next two sections, I will look at coins and cults. These classes of evidence inform us about local Naxian views, whereas the textual evidence offers only external views. It will become clear that coinage presents a different picture of Naxos' foundation from that of the literary sources.[41] In the texts, the figure of the *oikist* Theocles is prominent: he is the key to the discovery of a site suitable for occupation, according to Ephorus; he was the founder of the cult of Apollo Archegetes, according to Thucydides; and he was the *oikist* of the whole colonial expedition of Sicily, according to pseudo-Scymnus. From Theocles' prominence in the literary sources, we might presume a starring role for the *oikist* in the local foundation myths and cult of Naxos, or perhaps even in the whole of eastern Sicily. This, however, is not the case. There is no evidence for a cult of Theocles, not even in Naxos, and the frequent occurrence of Apollo on the coins of Naxos, Leontini, and Catane suggests that Apollo, rather than Theocles, was the preferred figure for expressing kinship between the cities.[42]

2.2. Silver tetradrachm of Catane showing the head of Apollo and a quadriga, c. 450–440 BC. Reproduced with permission of Gemini Numismatic Auctions.

2.3. Silver didrachm of Naxos showing the head of Apollo and a Silen, c. 420–403 BC. Reproduced with permission of Fritz Rudolf Künker GmbH & Co. KG, Osnabrück; and Lübke & Wiedemann, Stuttgart.

Apollo appears first on a series of tetradrachms of Leontini, dated to the 460s BC.[43] Probably slightly later, or even contemporary, are the Catanian tetradrachms depicting the head of Apollo (Fig. 2.2).[44] Naxos depicts Apollo on its coins only from the 420s BC onward (Fig. 2.3). Prior to this, Naxian coins feature Dionysiac imagery.[45] Dionysus was the tutelary deity of Naxos. The shift to Apolline imagery in the fifth century BC was therefore a strategic break with tradition set within a specific historical context, rather than a passive reflection of ideas of communal descent. In 476 BC, the tyrant of Syracuse, Hieron, destroyed Catane and Naxos, and deported the inhabitants to Leontini. With the fall of the tyranny of the Deinomenids in 461 BC, the inhabitants of Naxos and Catane were able to return to their homes. During the time that the exiled Naxians were in residence in Leontini, it is significant that Leontini started issuing coins with the head of Apollo. The close link between Naxos and Leontini—and the use of Apollo as a figure to articulate that link—is clear here.

Thucydides tells us that the Catanians had chosen to honor a certain Euarchos as *oikist*, despite the initial foundation of Theocles.[46] This suggests that a distinct foundation tradition had initially developed in Catane, centered around Euarchos, in contrast to the Naxian Theocles narrative. In the second half of the fifth century BC, this distinction was downplayed in favor of the Naxian connection. Catanian coinage imagery was brought in closer harmony with the images on the Naxian and Leontinian coins. New motifs on the Catanian coins included the head of Apollo and the head of a Silen, both distinctive symbols of Naxos. This strongly suggests that Catane was increasingly interested in connections with Naxos and Leontini. The destruction of Catane in 476 BC by Hieron of Syracuse and the reassertion of Syracusan power shortly after the fall of the Deinomeid tyrants may well have motivated these choices.

After the return of the citizens from Leontini to Naxos in 461 BC, following the fall of the Syracusan tyrants, the coinage of Naxos continued to portray Dionysiac themes, which had been used in emissions before the destruction of the city in 476 BC. Some scholars argue that these references to Dionysos have a Cycladic origin, given Dionysus' significance on Cycladic Naxos, and Cycladic Naxos' supposed participation in the foundation of Sicilian Naxos. However, as evident from the previous discussion, this is not mentioned in the sources.[47] The choice of Dionysiac motifs at Sicilian Naxos can be seen as an attempt by the Naxians to set themselves apart from the other Sicilian cities, and the continuation of the symbols on the emissions after the destruction as a desire to confirm continuity with the older city. After 420 BC, the Dionysiac images are supplemented by bronze emissions depicting the head of Apollo. These motifs link to the strategic choices made by Leontini and Catane, and suggest that Naxos was also part of this movement. The emphasis on Apollo may perhaps be seen as stressing a more unified Euboean narrative across all three cities. This unified narrative would replace the earlier independent ones, perhaps related to Euarchos at Catane and Dionysos at Naxos. In the face of a continuing Syracusan threat, it was probably very important for the allies to underline their unity, not their diversity. For the forging of unified identities, Apollo, with a commonly respected cult in Naxos, seems to have been the perfect tool. Through the figure of Apollo Archegetes, Naxos could point to her primacy among the Sicilian colonies and demonstrate its authority. Through a connection with Naxos via foundation narratives and Apollo Archegetes, other Sicilian cities were able to sharpen boundaries against an enemy that claimed contrasting origins, such as Syracuse, which was said to be a Corinthian foundation.

As mentioned, this idea of primacy among the Sicilian cities was so important that even after the final destruction of Naxos—again, by Syracuse—in

2.4. Bronze *dilitron* of Tauromenion showing the head of Apollo Archegetes and a bull, c. 300 BC. Reproduced with permission of the Classical Numismatic Group, Inc. (http://www.cngcoins.com).

403 BC, the city remained an important source of symbolic capital. Its successor cities of Neopolitoi and Tauromenion made a clear statement about their
affiliation by choosing Apollo as the main symbol for their coinage (Fig. 2.4).
In a post-Naxian context, Apolline imagery would have almost certainly referred to Apollo Archegetes, the most famous Apollo cult of the area and one
closely linked to civic history. Significantly, Apollo Archegetes was again the
preferred symbol to express a Naxian connection. By housing the first cult of
Sicily, prestige was assured and kinship could be stressed.

Performance and Evocation of Naxian Origins

The images used on the coins of Naxos, Leontini, and Catane testify to the
powerful role of Apollo Archegetes as a symbol of unity and communal identity. But what of Apollo Archegetes in Naxos itself? Apollo Archegetes was
initially a Naxian cult, and aspects of this cult practiced by means of performance in a sacred space will be analyzed in this section.

The importance of space in the construction of identities has been stressed
in social sciences and ancient Greek scholarship alike.[48] Rather than being the
background against which events happen, it is now accepted that space is actively shaped and defined by its users. In the ancient Greek world, cults and
temple sites were actively used to define society, and a vast literature has been
built around this subject.[49] For the purposes of this chapter, it is important to
note that the agora of a Greek city was one of the most important spaces in a
Greek polis, where civic identity was represented and celebrated through the
erection of monuments. In many Greek colonies, these would include the
tomb of the founder, around which (part) of the civic celebrations focused.[50] It
was the tomb of the founder that, for a colonial city, represented its origins,
foundation, and mother city, as well as its distinct identity.

The location of the agora of Naxos has been established recently through
excavations, and this seems to suggest an intimate connection with the sea.
Rather than being inland, as was the case for most cities, the Naxian agora
was next to the harbor (Fig. 2.5). This was also the location of the ship sheds,
which had been in use from the late sixth to the end of the fifth century BC.[51]
This arrangement of urban space finds a parallel in Thasos, where the agora
was also near the harbor.[52] The agora was a very significant space for the polis,
and its location next to the harbor is important. It suggests that the sea occupied an important place in the mental landscape of the Naxians, and it seems

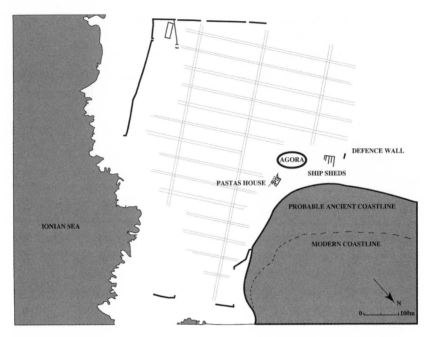

2.5. Plan of Naxos. Author's own, adapted from M. C. Lentini, *Naxos di Sicilia: L'Abitato Coloniale e l'Arsenale Navale, Scavi 2003–2006* (Messina: Sicania, 2009).

likely that the sea figured prominently in their ideas about their foundation. The textual references we have for Apollo Archegetes also connect this cult to a coastal location. Thucydides says that *theoroi* would offer sacrifices to the god directly before embarking on board ship, and Appian indicates that the sanctuary was located where ships were able to land.[53] While we cannot be absolutely sure of this yet, there are nonetheless several reasons to hypothesize a location of the sanctuary of Apollo Archegetes on or near the agora.[54] These arguments suggest that both worship and the civic cult on the agora centered topographically on the sea. The sea, travel, and overseas connections are therefore likely to have played an important role in the Naxian founder cult and Naxian ideas about foundation.

Conclusion: Naxos' Foundation Myths in Context

In this chapter, I have considered several representations of the foundation myths associated with Naxos on Sicily. Three literary representations have been discussed, each presenting a different view of the Naxian foundation. These literary sources offer us an external, non-Sicilian perspective on the issue, written as they were by external commentators who mention Naxos' foundation as part of their wider writings. I have also discussed the way different foundation stories were likely viewed within Naxos and the neighboring cities of Leontini and Catane. The sources for this internal view are not literary but rather include the strategic use of imagery linked to foundation stories in coins and the location and significance of cults linked to foundation. Interesting insights can be gained about how foundation myths worked in the Greek world: first, by comparing the changing representations of Naxian foundation found in the three literary accounts; and second, by comparing the external literary sources with the local Sicilian evidence from coinage and archaeology.

Traditionally, the study of Naxos' foundation myths has focused on the historicity of the texts, especially on establishing the identity of the mother city.[55] But instead of reading these texts in a quest for the "facts" of foundation, it is more helpful to consider what they tell us about the dynamics of political representation in their own times. The account of Thucydides casts the foundation of Naxos as a divinely inspired act under the guidance of Apollo Archegetes, carried out by a single founder, Theocles, from a single mother city, Chalcis in Euboea. This version falls most neatly into the standard pattern for colonial foundation stories of the classical period, linked as they usually are to the Delphic oracle and featuring a clear mother city and *oikist* figure. Thucydides, therefore, was following the common practice of his day in the way he represented Naxos' foundation. Ephorus' version of the story undermines the idea of a single mother city, making the colonists a mixed group from various *ethnê* and places. However, the position of the *oikist* retains its significance, as Theocles is credited with the initiative for the foundation, opportunistically taking advantage of his accidental discovery. The Athenian origin of Theocles is therefore significant, especially given the emphasis on Theocles as *oikist* and the increased importance of the *oikist* above the notion of the mother city. Ephorus' representation of Naxos' foundation is therefore also very much of his time. The idea of Athenian influence and leadership in the Naxian myth echoes a wider discourse of Athenian primacy among the Greeks, a discourse that Ephorus was most likely exposed to during his education. Finally, pseudo-Scymnus' account of Naxos' foundation is even less concerned with the concept of the mother city than that of Ephorus. However, the role of Theocles as *oikist* seems to be diminished. What replaces it is an emphasis on conflict between groups—between different Greek *ethnê* and between Greeks and the indigenous Sicilians.

The shifts in the Naxian foundation myth highlight how a single story can undergo many revisions within a relatively short time—in this case, over only three centuries. They also highlight interesting points about the plurality of the Naxian myth. The figure of Theocles is of particular interest. In contrast to the traditional *oikists*, Theocles founds more than one colony.[56] Thucydides cites him as the *oikist* of Naxos, Leontini, and Catane. Ephorus says that he is the founder of Naxos and at least involved partly in establishing Megara Hyblaea. According to pseudo-Scymnus, Theocles was directly responsible for Naxos and Megara Hyblaea, as well as for Zephyrion, Leontini, Catane, Zancle, and Callipolis, as these were all founded from Naxos. It might initially seem that this role as multiple should be problematic. Of course, not every city could claim to have Theocles' tomb in its agora. So where did Theocles have his tomb and cult—Naxos? Leontini? Nowhere? Such questions did not necessarily pose problems on a practical level. As seen throughout this volume, plurality in foundation myths was not necessarily as much of a problem in ancient society as we might expect. Theocles could belong to every city—or to none. In addition, it seems that each city could recognize a multiple founder. While Theocles may have been shared by several cities, he may have shared his position within some cities, too. For example, Theocles' *oikist* status did not seem to have prevented the Catanians from honoring Euarchos as an *oikist* as well.[57] In addition, it seems that Zancle held an annual festival for unnamed but plural founders.[58] Plurality in foundations does not seem to have been a problem for the colonial foundations of eastern Sicily.

There is also a striking difference between literary representations of Naxos' foundations and the way that foundation stories were deployed and used on the ground in Sicily. The general story of Theocles, though it seems to have been widely known elsewhere in the Greek world, was not necessarily the most significant origin myth for Naxians and their neighbors. The existence of alternative *oikists* has already been suggested; in addition, there seems to have been a preference among the eastern Sicilian cities for focusing on the divine figure of Apollo Archegetes rather than on the human Theocles. Thucydides' comment about Euarchos at Catane is significant: it implies that the different cities had their own independent foundation traditions in the early classical period. During the fifth century BC, however, this individuality was downplayed to forge stronger intercity bonds in the face of military threat, which is evident from the politics of coinage in Leontini, Catane, and

Naxos. Rather than seeking the protection of a mother city overseas, Naxos, Leontini, and Catane stressed links with one another. The cult of Apollo Archegetes seems to have been used as a unifying element, which was symbolized by his image on the coinage. Through this cult, some Sicilian poleis (re)-forged their identities and stressed a common Euboean foundation narrative. In addition to binding the three cities together, claiming a Euboean identity was a powerful way to distance themselves from opposing cities, which instead claimed a Dorian origin. The primary position of Naxos was a powerful tool in this self-conceptualization and the source of considerable prestige. After the destruction of Naxos in 403 BC, this claim was quickly recovered and recycled by the Naxian successor cities. The cult of Apollo Archegetes continued in a very prominent way in Tauromenion.

Many representations of Naxos' foundations have been discussed here. There are differences along chronological lines in the literary texts. There are differences, too, along perspective lines between the external textual views and the internal evidence of coins and cult. But these different versions were not necessarily in oppositional conflict with one another. Instead, they depend on their differences to make their point—it is only by being different from another version that they gain their full meaning. The representations of Greek foundations were numerously varied and sometimes deliberately in conflict with one another. Whether we get the story "crooked," the code cracked, or the message decoded, the history we presented should not be de-mythified, but rather simply contextualized.[59]

NOTES

I would like to thank Naoíse Mac Sweeney for her kind invitation to participate in this volume, and for her and the anonymous readers' very helpful suggestions. My research has been made possible by the generous financial support of the Fund for Scientific Research Flanders (project FWO-G.0162.06) and Foundation Utopa.

1. Bérard 1941: 11.

2. Ibid. *Contra*: Pais 1894: 10–17; 251–53 already casts doubt on the practice of reading foundation myths for their historical content.

3. Greek colonial foundation narratives: Malkin 1987, 1998, 2009; Dougherty 1993a, 1993b; Osborne 1998; Calame 2003; Giangiulio 2001; Hall 2006.

4. The *oikist* and cult: Leschhorn 1984; Malkin 1987: 199–202; Dougherty 1993a; Antonaccio 1999. Veneration of the *oikist* is attested in several places. This is often in the

form of a cenotaph because actual bodies have never been found. E.g., Cyrene (Stucchi 1965: 58–65, 111–14); Poseidonia (Greco and Theodorescu 1983: 25–33; Greco 1994). In both Selinunte (Mertens 2003: 407–8) and Megara Hyblaea (Gras and Tréziny 2001: 59–62), an *oikist* cult was identified on the agora. For the role of the agora in the polis, see Martin 1951; Kenzler 2000; Hansen 2004: 138–43. Traditionally, the "duties of the *oikist*" are read in the achievements of Nausithoos in Homer *Odyssey* 6.7–10.

5. Delphi and Greek colonization: Defradas 1954; Forrest 1957; Fontenrose 1978: 49–81; Leschhorn 1984: 86; Malkin 1987: 17–91; Morgan 1990: 172–78; Londey 1990; Dougherty 1993a, 1993b: 18; Rougemont 1995: 173–77; Giangiulio 2010.

6. Dougherty 1993b: 27 n. 1, 83–156; Dougherty 1994: 35–37; Bowie 1986. On performance: Kowalzig 2007.

7. The canon of foundation myths: Calame 2003: 31–34. Analogies: Dougherty 1993a, 1993b.

8. The first and also the most recent systematic survey of Naxos is Rizzo 1894. A summary of the excavations can be found in Pelagatti 1993. Recent research at Naxos: Lentini 1998, 2004, 2009.

9. For the inscription, see Guarducci 1985.

10. A summary of research in the Catanian area: Rizza 1987; Gentili 1996. Corinthian pottery: Grasso 1998.

11. A complete overview of the archaeological research at Leontini: Frasca 2009. Corinthian pottery of the sanctuary at Alaimo: Grasso 2008.

12. Thuc. 5.4.4 refers to a toponym "Phokaiai." For the consequences, see Frasca 2009: 60.

13. Tr. Smith 1952 (Loeb Classical Library).

14. The underestimation of the Sicilian resources: Alcibiades: Thuc. 6.17.2–3. On Thucydides' Sicilian Archaeology in general: Rawlings 1981: 58–125. Tsakmakis 1995: 157–75; Zahrnt 2006: 629–30; Hornblower 2008. For a taste of the vast literature on Thucydides, see Rood 1998b; Rutherford 2005: 111–14; Rengakos and Tsakmakis 2006; Hornblower 2011. On Sikelika in general: Fornara 1983: 36–38.

15. On Homer's influence on Thucydides in general: several examples in Hornblower 1994; Rood 1998a; Grethlein 2010: 257–61. Homer's influence on the Sicilian Archaeology in particular: Frangoulidis 1993; Mackie 1996; Rood 1998a, contra: Grethlein 2010: 260.

16. An exception is Camarina, a Dorian foundation, but on the Chalcidian side instead of joining the other Dorian cities on several occasions: Thuc. 3.86.2; 4.25.7; 6.52.1; 6.75.3.

17. On the speech of Hermocrates: Hammond 1973. Its significance for Siceliot identity: Antonaccio 2001: 121–22; Cardete del Olmo 2008; Donnellan 2012. Speeches in Thucydides in general: Stadter 1973.

18. On Euboean colonization: Ridgway 1992; contributions in Euboica 1998; d'Agostino 2006. Contra: Papadopoulos 1997.

19. Thuc. 6.5.4. Also in Ps. Scymn. *Per.* 283–86 and Strabo *Geog.* 6.268. Discussion by Consolo Langher 1985; Antonelli 1996. In general on Zancle: Vallet 1958; Scibona 1992; Gentili and Pinzone 2002.

20. Lamis and Leontini: Thuc. 6.4.1 and Polyaenus, *Strat.* 5.5.

21. The sources of Thucydides for the foundation of the Sicilian colonies: van Compernolle 1950–51; Gomme et al. 1970: 198–210. Chronology of Greek colonization in Sicily: van Compernolle 1956, 1959; Miller 1970; in general: Hall 2006. The dependence of Thucydidean chronology on dedications in the sanctuary of Apollo Archegetes: Murray 1993: 113.

22. On theoria: Rutherford and Elsner 2005; Rutherford 2007. Theoria in Naxos: Rutherford 1998. The regional importance of Apollo Archegetes: Brelich 1964: 45; Malkin 1986, 1987: 19, 2001: 8; Morgan 1990: 176; Antonaccio 2001: 134; Cordano 2004: 96; Donnellan 2012.

23. The Delphic connection of Apollo Archegetes of Naxos: Rizzo 1894: 11; Cahn 1944: 92; Lacroix 1965: 139–42; Malkin 1984–85: 55; Malkin 1986, 1987: 19, 2001: 8; Morgan 1990: 176. The Delian connection: van Compernolle 1950–51: 181–83; Brelich 1964: 45; Kontoleon 1967; Valenza Mele 1977: 508; Brugnone 1980; Guarducci, 1985: 20; Guarducci 1996; Lentini, 2001: 5; Cordano, 2004.

24. Morgan 1990: 127, 134 with bibliography.

25. Strabo *Geog.* 6.2.2 = *FGrH* 70 F 137. On the use of Ephorus by Strabo: Prandi 1988.

26. Tr. Jones 1954 (Loeb Classical Library).

27. Polybius 5.33.2. On Ephorus' life and work in general: Barber 1935; Schepens 1977. Universal history: Fornara 1983: 42–46.

28. The sources of Ephorus: Barber 1935: 113–37.

29. See n. 23 above.

30. Ephorus' euhemeristic treatment of myth: Avagianou 1998: 121–22; Graf 1993: 121–41.

31. On unintentional "surprised *oikists*": Dougherty 1993b: 18; Malkin 1987: 27–28.

32. On ἔτυχε in Thucydides: Grethlein 2010: 252–54.

33. Odysseus as proto-colonial hero: Malkin 1998. Heracles: Malkin 2005. The elite nature of early Greek seafaring and exchange: Osborne 1998; Crielaard 2000, 2006.

34. The Naxian foundation of Catane: Strabo *Geog.* 6.2.3. The Naxian foundation of Leontinoi: Strabo *Geog.* 6.2.7.

35. Bérard 1941: 89.

36. The influence of Isocrates on Ephorus: Barber 1935: 75–83; Avagianou 1998: 134–35; Isocrates in general: Saïd 2006.

37. On Ephorus as historical source: Parker 2001.

38. Ps. Scymn. *Per. Gês* vv. 264–97 (ed. Les Belles Lettres). On pseudo-Scymnus: Diller 1952: 165; Marcotte 2000: XIII–CLXIV. The sources of pseudo-Scymnus: Marcotte 2000: 18, 106.

39. Translation adapted from Marcotte 2000.

40. For comparison, see the following on authority and distance in Herodotus: Marincola 2001: 31–39; Rösler 2002: 79–94 esp. 90–91; van Wees 2002: 321–49, esp. 322–23; Cartledge and Greenwood 2002. In general: Marincola 1997.

41. Greek coinage and civic identity: Rutter 2000; Papadopoulos 2002.

42. For a detailed discussion on the politics of Naxian coinage: Donnellan 2012.

43. The coinage of Leontini: Boehringer 1998; Fisher-Hansen et al. 2004: 210; Frasca 2009: 115–17.

44. The coinage of Catane: Manganaro 1996 (with earlier bibliography); Fisher-Hansen et al. 2004: 207.

45. The coinage of Naxos: Cahn 1944; Fisher-Hansen et al. 2004: 220.

46. Thuc. 6.3.3.

47. It must be mentioned, however, that Cycladic Naxos did not issue coins for the largest part of the fifth century BC and that there was no adoption of the symbol of Cycladic Naxos (a kantharos: see Nicolet-Pierre 1999) by the colony, which could be clearly read in favor of an undisputed statement of recognized kinship, in contrast to what is claimed by some scholars. When Cycladic Naxos began issuing coins again in the fourth century BC, a visual language closer to that of the homonymous colony was adopted. By then, Sicilian Naxos had been destroyed, and the successor cities referred to Apollo, rather than Diony-sus; see Consolo Langher 1964: 179–81; Fisher-Hansen et al. 2004: 232. If there was any statement made in the Naxian cities' coinage, it was not by the colony, connecting to the mother city, but the other way around. On the possible link between Sicilian Naxos and Cycladic Naxos: Hell. *FGrH* 4 F82 and Guarducci 1985; Pelagatti 1993; Lentini 2001, 2004.

48. Theory of space and place in general: Tilley 1994; Low et al. 2003. Recently on Greek cultic space: Scott 2010. Sculpture and cultic experience: Marconi 2007; Osborne 2009.

49. Part of the study of the relationship between Greek cult and space has focused on rural sanctuaries as a demarcation of territory. The placing of sanctuaries in the landscape did not happen randomly but was an active and strategic choice to demarcate physically the *chora* of a polis and psychologically distinguish nature from culture and citizens from noncitizens. Participation in extra-urban cult was the defining and unifying tool for citizenship, according to these theories (de Polignac 1984; Veronese 2006).

50. See n. 4 above.

51. Blackman and Lentini 2003; Lentini et al. 2008; Lentini 2009; Lentini and Pakkanen 2012; Lentini, Blackman, and Pakkanen forthcoming.

52. Martin 1959; Kenzler 2000; Hansen 2004: 138–43.

53. Thuc. 6.3.1; Appian *B Civ.* 5.12.109. Thucydides does, however, mention that the altar was moved in the sixth century to a location outside the city.

54. This is argued in more detail in Donnellan 2012.

55. Bérard 1941: 87–91. Bérard's opinion on the possibility of Athenian propaganda to explain the Athenian origins of Theocles has been accepted by most scholars but has never been studied in detail: Leschhorn 1984: 9. Significantly, Bérard attached little importance to the cult of Apollo Archegetes, dismissing it as being of great antiquity and therefore irrelevant to civic foundation (Bérard 1941: 88–89). As has been argued here, as well as by many other scholars, this cult was crucial in identity constructions in several Sicilian Greek cities.

56. The career of Theocles: Malkin 2002; Donnellan 2012.
57. Thuc. 6.3.3.
58. Callimachus 43 F69–79 (Pfeiffer).
59. Getting the story "crooked": Kellner 1989.

REFERENCES

Antonaccio, C. M. 1999. "Colonization and the Origins of Hero Cult." In *Ancient Greek Hero Cult: Proceedings of the Fifth International Seminar on Ancient Greek Cult, Organised by the Department of Classical Archaeology and Ancient History*, Göteborg University, April 21–24, 1995, ed. R. Hägg, 109–21. Stockholm: Svenska Institutet i Athen.

Antonaccio, C. M. 2001. "Ethnicity and Colonization." In *Ancient Perceptions of Greek Ethnicity*, ed. I. Malin, 113–57. Washington, DC: Center for Hellenic Studies.

Antonelli, L. 1996. "Considerazioni sulla Prima Fondazione di Zancle." *Kokalos* 42: 315–25.

Avagianou, A. 1998. "Ephorus on the Founding of Delphi's Oracle." *Greek, Roman and Byzantine Studies* 39: 121–36.

Barber, G. L. 1935. *The Historian Ephorus*. Cambridge: Cambridge University Press.

Bats, M., and B. d'Agostino. 1998. *Euboica: L'Eubea e la Presenza Euboica in Calcidica e in Occidente*. Atti del Convegno Internazionale, Naples, November 13–16, 1996. Naples: Centre Jean Bérard.

Bérard, J. 1941. *La Colonisation grecque de l'Italie Méridionale et de la Sicile dans l'Antiquité: L'Histoire et la Légende*. Paris: De Boccard.

Blackman, D., and M. C. Lentini. 2003. "The Shipsheds of Sicilian Naxos, Researches 1998–2001. A Preliminary Report." *Annual of the British School at Athens* 98: 387–435.

Boehringer, C. 1998. "Zur Münzgeschichte von Leontinoi in klassischer Zeit." In *Studies in Greek Numismatics in Memory of Martin Jessop Price*, ed. R. Ashton and S. Hurter, 43–53. London: Spink & Son.

Bowie, E. 1986. "Early Greek Elegy, Symposium, and Public Festivals." *Journal of Hellenic Studies* 106: 13–35.

Brelich, A. 1964. "La Religione Greca in Sicilia." *Kokalos* 10–11: 35–54.

Brugnone, A. 1980. "Annotazioni sull'Apollo Archegete di Naxos." In *Filias Kharin: Miscellanea di Studi Classici in Onore di E. Manni*, 277–94. Rome: Bretschneider.

Cahn, H. A. 1944. *Die Münzen der griechischen Stadt Naxos: Ein Beitrag zur Kunstgeschichte des griechischen Westens*. Basel: Birkhäuser.

Calame, C. 2003. *Myth and History in Ancient Greece: The Symbolic Creation of a Colony*. Princeton, NJ: Princeton University Press.

Cardete del Olmo, C. 2008. "De Griegos a Siceliotas: La Dimensión Etnica del Congreso de Gela." *Annuario della Scuola archeologica di Atene e delle Missioni italiane in Oriente* 86: 153–67.

Cartledge, P. A., and E. Greenwood. 2002. "Herodotus as a Critic: Truth, Fiction, Polarity." In *Brill's Companion to Herodotus*, ed. E. J. Bakker, I. J. F. de Jong, and H. van Wees, 351–71. Leiden: Brill.

Consolo Langher, S. 1964. *Contributo alla Storia dell'Antica Monetazione Bronzea in Sicilia*. Milan: Giuffrè.

Consolo Langher, S. 1985. "Zancle: Dalle Questioni della Ktisis ai Problemi dell' Espansionismo Geloo." In *Xenia: Scritti in Onore di P. Treves*, ed. F. Broilo, 45–65. Rome: La Fenice.

Cordano, F. 2004. "Naxos di Sicilia e l'Egeo." In *Le Due Città di Naxos: Atti del Seminario di Studi*, October 29–31, 2000, ed. M. C. Lentini, 100–105. Giardini Naxos: Comune di Giardini Naxos.

Crielaard, J. P. 2000. "Honour and Value as Discourse for Early Greek Colonization (8th–7th Centuries BC)." In *Die Ägäis und das westliche Mittelmeer: Beziehungen und Wechselwirkungen 8. bis 5. Jh. v.Chr. Akten des Symposions*, Vienna, March 24–27, 1999, ed. F. Krinzinger, 499–506. Vienna: Österreichische Akademie der Wissenschaften.

Crielaard, J. P. 2006. "Basileis at Sea: Elites and External Contacts in the Euboian Gulf Regions from the End of the Bronze Age to the Beginning of the Iron Age." In *Ancient Greece: From the Mycenaean Palaces to the Age of Homer*, ed. S. Deger-Jalkotzy and I. Lemos, 271–97. Edinburgh: Edinburgh University Press.

d'Agostino, B. 2006. "The First Greeks in Italy." In *Greek Colonisation: An Account of Greek Colonies and Other Settlements Overseas*, ed. G. R. Tsetskhladze, 201–37. Leiden: Brill.

Defradas, J. 1954. *Les Thèmes de la Propagande Delphique*. Paris: Klincksieck.

de Polignac, F. 1984. *La Naissance de la Cité Grecque*. Paris: La Decouverte.

Diller, A. 1952. *The Tradition of the Minor Greek Geographers*. Oxford: Blackwell.

Donnellan, L. 2012. "Apollo Mediating Identities in Ancient Greek Sicily." *BaBesch* 87: 173–86.

Dougherty, C. 1993a. "It's Murder to Found a Colony." In *Cultural Poetics in Archaic Greece. Cult, Performance, Politics*, ed. C. Dougherty and L. Kurke, 178–98. Cambridge: Cambridge University Press.

Dougherty, C. 1993b. *The Poetics of Colonization: From City to Text in Archaic Greece*. Oxford: Oxford University Press.

Dougherty, C. 1994. "Archaic Greek Foundation Poetry: Questions of Genre and Occasion." *Journal of Hellenic Studies* 114: 35–46.

Eucken, C. 1983. *Isokrates: Seine Position mit den zeitgenössischen Philosophen*. Berlin: De Gruyter.

Fisher-Hansen, T., T. H. Nielsen, and C. Ampolo. 2004. "Sikelia." In *An Inventory of Archaic and Classical Poleis*, ed. M. H. Hansen and T. H. Nielsen, 172–248. Oxford: Oxford University Press.

Fontenrose, J. 1978. *The Delphic Oracle: Its Responses and Operations*. Berkeley: University of California Press.

Fornara, C. W. 1983. *The Nature of History in Ancient Greece and Rome*. Berkeley: University of California Press.

Forrest, W. G. 1957. "Colonisation and the Rise of Delphi." *Historia* 6: 160–75.

Frangoulidis, S. A. 1993. "A Pattern from Homer's Odyssey in the Sicilian Narrative of Thucydides." *Quaderni urbinati di cultura classica* 44: 95–102.

Frasca, M. 2009. *Leontinoi: Archeologia di una Colonia Greca.* Rome: Bretschneider.

Gentili, B. (ed.). 1996. *Catania Antica: Atti del Convegno della S.I.S.A.C.* Pisa and Rome.

Gentili, B., and A. Pinzone. 2002. *Messina e Reggio nell'Antichità: Storia, Società, Cultura. Atti del Convegno della S.I.S.A.C, Messina-Reggio Calabria,* May 24–26, 1999. Messina.

Giangiulio, M. 2001. "Constructing the Past: Colonial Traditions and the Writing of History. The Case of Cyrene." In *The Historian's Craft in the Age of Herodotus,* ed. N. Luraghi, 116–37. Oxford: Oxford University Press.

Giangiulio, M. 2010. "Collective Identities, Imagined Past, and Delphi." In *Intentional History: Spinning Time in Ancient Greece,* ed. L. Foxhall, H. J. Gehrke, and N. Luraghi, 121–35. Stuttgart: Franz Steiner.

Gomme, A. W., A. Andrewes, and K. J. Dover. 1970. *A Historical Commentary on Thucydides,* vol. 4, books V(25)–VII. Oxford: Oxford University Press.

Graf, F. 1993. *Greek Mythology: An Introduction.* Baltimore: Johns Hopkins University Press.

Gras, M., and H. Tréziny. 2001. "Mégara Hyblaea: Retours sur l'agora." In *Architettura, Urbanistica, Società nel Mondo Antico: Giornata di Studi in Ricordo di Roland Martin,* February 21, 1998, ed. E. Greco, 51–63. Paestum: Pandemos.

Grasso, L. 1998. *Stipe Votiva del Santuario di Demetra a Catania: Kotylai, Coppe Corinzie Figurate.* Catania: Consiglio Nazionale delle Ricerche.

Grasso, L. 2008. *La Stirpe des Santuario di Alaimo a Lentini.* Catania: IBAM.

Greco, E. 1994. "L'agora de Posidonia: Une mise au point." *Comptes rendus de l'Academie des Inscriptions et Belles-Lettres:* 227–37.

Greco, E., and D. Theodorescu. 1983. *Poseidonia—Paestum. 2. L'agora.* Rome: Collection de l'École française de Rome.

Grethlein, J. 2010. *The Greeks and Their Past: Poetry, Oratory and History in the Fifth Century BC.* Cambridge: Cambridge University Press.

Guarducci, M. 1985. "Una Nuova Dea a Naxos in Sicilia e gli Antichi Legami fra la Naxos Siceliota e l'Omonima Isola delle Cicladi." *Melanges d'archeologie et d'histoire de l'École Française de Rome* 97: 7–34.

Guarducci, M. 1996. "Apollo di Delfi o Apollo di Delo? Contributo alla Storia di Naxos Cicladica e Siceliota." In *Le Cicladi ed il Mondo Egeo: Seminario Internazionale di Studi,* Rome, November 19–21, 1992, ed. E. Lanzillotta and D. Schilaroli, 13–19. Rome: Università degli studi di Roma "Tor vergata," Dipartimento di storia.

Hall, J. 2006. "Foundation Stories." In *Greek Colonisation: An Account of Greek Colonies and Other Settlements Overseas,* ed. G. R. Tsetskhladze, 383–426. Leiden: Brill.

Hammond, N. G. L. 1973. "The Particular and the Universal in the Speeches in Thucydides: With Special Reference to That of Hermocrates at Gela." In *The Speeches in Thucydides: A Collection of Original Studies with a Bibliography,* ed. P. A. Stadter, 49–59. Chapel Hill: University of North Carolina Press.

Hansen, H. M. 2004. "Introduction." In *An Inventory of Archaic and Classical Poleis,* ed. H. M. Hansen and T. H. Nielsen, 3–153. Oxford: Oxford University Press.

Heilbrunn, G. 1977. "The Composition of Isocrates' Helen." *Transactions and Proceedings of the American Philological Association* 107: 147–59.

Hornblower, S. 1994. "Narratology and Narrative Techniques in Thucydides." In *Greek Historiography*, ed. S. Hornblower, 131–66, Oxford: Oxford University Press.

Hornblower, S. 2008. *A Commentary on Thucydides*, vol. 3, bks. 5.25–8.109. Oxford: Oxford University Press.

Hornblower, S. 2011. *Thucydidean Themes*. Oxford: Oxford University Press.

Jones, H. L. 1954. *The Geography of Strabo*, vol. 3. Cambridge, MA: Harvard University Press.

Kellner, H. 1989. *Language and Historical Representation: Getting the Story Crooked*. Madison: University of Wisconsin Press.

Kenzler, U. 2000. "Vom dörflichen Verzammlungsplatz zum urbanen Zentrum: Die Agora im Mutterland und in den Kolonien." In *Die Ägäis und das westliche Mittelmeer: Beziehungen und Wechselwirkungen 8. bis 5. Jh. v.Chr. Akten des Symposions*, Vienna, March 24–27, 1999, ed. F. Krinzinger, 23–28. Vienna: Österreichische Akademie der Wissenschaften.

Kontoleon, N. M. 1967. "Zur Gründung von Naxos und Megara auf Sizilien." In *Europa. Studien zur Geschichte und Epigraphik der frühen Aegaeis: Festschrift für Ernst Grumach*, ed. W. C. Brice, 181–90. Berlin: De Gruyter.

Kowalzig, B. 2007. *Singing for the Gods: Performances of Myth and Ritual in Archaic and Classical Greece*. Oxford: Oxford University Press.

Lacroix, L. 1965. *Monnaies et Colonisation dans l'Occident grec*. Brussels: Palais des Académies.

Lentini, M. C. 1998. "Le Ultime Esplorazioni a Naxos (1983–1995)." In *Naxos a Quarant'anni dall' Inizio degli Scavi: Atti della Tavola Rotonda*, Giardini Naxos, October 26–27, 1995, ed. M. C. Lentini, 71–100. Messina: Museo archaeologico di Naxos.

Lentini, M. C. (ed.). 2001. *The Two Naxos Cities: A Fine Link Between the Aegean Sea and Sicily*. Palermo: Kalós.

Lentini, M. C. 2004. *Le Due Città di Naxos: Atti del Seminario di Studi*, October 29–31, 2000. Giardini Naxos: Comune di Giardini Naxos.

Lentini, M. C. 2009. *Naxos di Sicilia: L'Abitato Coloniale e l'Arsenale Navale, Scavi 2003–2006*. Messina: Sicania.

Lentini, M. C., et al. 2008. "The Shipsheds of Sicilian Naxos: A Second Preliminary Report (2003–06)." *Annual of the British School at Athens* 103: 299–366.

Lentini, M. C., and J. Pakkanen. 2012. "Nouvelles découvertes sur l'agora de Naxos en Sicile." In *Tout vendre, tout acheter: Structures et équipements des marchés antiques*. Actes du colloque d'Athènes, June 16–19, 2009, ed. V. Chankowski and P. Karvonis. Paris: École Française d'Athènes.

Lentini, M. C., D. J. Blackman, and J. Pakkanen. Forthcoming. "The Port in the Urban System of Sicilian Naxos (5th c. BC)." In *Ancient Ports: The Geography of Connections*, conference at Dept. of Archaeology and Ancient History, Uppsala University, September 24–25, 2010. Uppsala: Uppsala University.

Leschhorn, W. 1984. *Gründer der Stadt: Studien zu einem politisch-religiösen Phänomen der griechischen Geschichte.* Stuttgart: Franz Steiner.

Londey, P. 1990. "Greek Colonists and Delphi." In *Greek Colonists and Native Populations: Proceedings of the First Australian Congress of Classical Archaeology,* Sydney, July 9–14 1985, ed. J.-P. Descoeudres, 117–27. Oxford: Clarendon.

Low, S. M., et al. 2003. *The Anthropology of Space and Place: Locating Culture.* Oxford: Wiley-Blackwell.

Mackie, C. J. 1996. "Homer and Thucydides: Corcyra and Sicily." *Classical Quarterly* n.s. 46: 103–13.

Malkin, I. 1984–85. "Dieux et Colons dans la Sicile Archaïque." *Kokalos* 30–31: 155–59.

Malkin, I. 1986. "Apollo Archegetes and Sicily." *Annali della Scuola Normale Superiore di Pisa, Serzione di Lettere* 16: 959–72.

Malkin, I. 1987. *Religion and Colonisation in Ancient Greece.* Leiden: Brill.

Malkin, I. 1998. *The Returns of Odysseus: Colonization and Ethnicity.* Berkeley: University of California Press.

Malkin, I. 2001. "Introduction." In *Ancient Perceptions of Greek Ethnicity,* ed. I. Malkin, 1–28. Cambridge, MA: Center for Hellenic Studies.

Malkin, I. 2002. "Exploring the Validity of the Concept of Foundation: A Visit to Megara Hyblaia." In *Oikistes: Studies in Constitutions, Colonies, and Military Power in the Ancient World, Offered in Honor of A. J. Graham,* ed. E. W. Robinson and V. B. Gorman, 195–225. Leiden: Brill.

Malkin, I. 2005. "Herakles and Melquart: Greeks and Phoenicians in the Middle Ground." In *Cultural Borrowings and Ethnic Appropriations in Antiquity,* ed. E. Gruen, 238–57. Stuttgart: Franz Steiner.

Malkin, I. 2009. "Foundations." In *A Companion to Archaic Greece,* ed. K. Raaflaub and H. van Wees, 373–94. Malden, MA: Wiley-Blackwell.

Manganaro, G. 1996. "La Monetazione di Katane dal V al I sec. a.C." In *Catania Antica: Atti del Convegno della S.I.S.A.C.,* Catania, May 23–24, 1992, ed. B. Gentile, 303–21. Pisa: Istituti editoriali e poligrafici internazionali.

Marconi, C. 2007. *Temple Decoration and Cultural Identity in the Archaic Greek World: The Metopes of Selinus.* Cambridge: Cambridge University Press.

Marcotte, D. 2000. *Les Géographes Grecs. I. Pseudo-Scymnos: Circuit de la terre.* Paris: Les Belles Lettres.

Marincola, J. 1997. *Authority and Tradition in Ancient Historiography.* Cambridge: Cambridge University Press.

Marincola, J. 2001. *Greek Historians.* Cambridge: Cambridge University Press.

Martin, R. 1951. *Recherches sur l'Agora Grecque: Études d'Histoire et d'Architecture Urbaines.* Paris: Boccard.

Martin, R. 1959. *L'Agora.* Paris: Boccard.

Mertens, D. 2003. "Die Agora von Selinunt: Neue Grabungsergebnisse zur Frühzeit der griechischen Kolonialstadt. Ein Vorbericht." *Mitteilungen des Deutschen Archäologischen Instituts* 110: 389–412.

Miller, M. 1970. *The Sicilian Colony Dates.* Studies in Chronography 1. Albany: State University of New York Press.

Morgan, C. 1990. *Athletes and Oracles: The Transformation of Olympia and Delphi in the Eighth Century B.C.* Cambridge: Cambridge University Press.

Murray, O. 1993. *Early Greece.* Cambridge, MA: Harvard University Press.

Nicolet-Pierre, H. 1999. "Les cratérophores de Naxos (Cyclades): Emissions monétaires d'argent à l'epoque hellénistique." *Revue Numismatique* 154: 95–119.

Osborne, R. 1998. "Early Greek Colonisation? The Nature of Greek Settlement in the West." In *Archaic Greece: New Approaches and New Evidence*, ed. N. Fischer and H. van Wees, 251–70. London: Duckworth.

Osborne, R. 2009. "The Narratology and Theology of Architectural Sculpture Or: What You Can Do with a Chariot but Can't Do with a Satyr on a Greek Temple." In *Structure, Image, Ornament: Architectural Sculpture in the Greek World.* Proceedings of a conference at the American School of Classical Studies, November 27–28, 2004, ed. P. Schulz and R. Von den Hoff, 2–12. Oxford: Oxbow.

Pais, E. 1894. *Storia della Sicilia e della Magna Grecia.* Turin: Causen Carlo.

Papadopoulos, J. 1997. "Phantom Euboians." *Journal of Mediterranean Archaeology* 10: 191–219.

Papadopoulos, J. 2002. "Minting Identity: Coinage, Ideology and the Economics of Colonization in Akhaian Magna Graecia." *Cambridge Archaeological Journal* 12: 21–55.

Parker, V. 2001. "Ephorus and Xenophon on Greece in the Years 375–372 B.C." *Klio* 83: 353–68.

Pelagatti, P. 1993. "Nasso." In *Bibliografia Topografica della Colonizzazione Greca in Italia e nelle Isole Tirreniche*, ed. G. Nenci and G. Vallet, 268–312. Pisa: Scuola normale superiore.

Prandi, L. 1988. "Strabone ed Eforo: Un'ipotesi sugli Historikà Hypomnémata." *Aevum* 62: 50–60.

Rawlings, H. R. 1981. *The Structure of Thucydides' History.* Princeton, NJ: Princeton University Press.

Rengakos, A., and A. Tsakmakis (eds.). 2006. *Brill's Companion to Thucydides.* Leiden: Brill.

Ridgway, D. 1992. *The First Western Greeks.* Cambridge: Cambridge University Press.

Rizza, G. 1987. "Catania." In *Bibliografia Topografica della Colonizzazione Greca in Italia e nelle Isole Tirreniche*, ed. G. Nenci and G. Vallet, 157–66. Pisa: Scuola normale superior.

Rizzo, P. 1894. *Naxos Siceliota: Storia, Topografia, Avanzi, Monete.* Catania: Monaco.

Rood, T. 1998a. "Thucydides and His Predecessors." *Histos* 2: 230–67.

Rood, T. 1998b. *Thucydides: Narrative and Explanation.* Oxford: Oxford University Press.

Rösler, W. 2002. "The Histories and Writing." In *Brill's Companion to Herodotus*, ed. E. J. Bakker, I. J. F. de Jong, and H. van Wees, 79–94. Leiden: Brill.

Rougemont, G. 1995. "Delphes et les cités grecques d'Italie du Sud et de Sicile." In *La Magna Grecia e i Grandi Santuari della Madrepatria: Atti del Trentunesimo Convegno di Studi sulla Magna Grecia*, October 4–8, 1991, 157–92. Taranto: Istituto per la storia e l'archeologia della Magna Grecia.

Rutherford, I. 1998. "The Amphikleidai of Sicilian Naxos: Pilgrimage and Genos in the Temple Inventories of Delos." *Zeitschrift fur Papyrologie und Epigraphik* 122: 81–89.

Rutherford, I. 2005. *Classical Literature: A Concise History.* Oxford: Wiley-Blackwell.

Rutherford, I. 2007. "Network Theory and Theoric Networks." *Mediterranean Historical Review* 22: 23–37.

Rutherford, I., and J. Elsner (eds.). 2005. *Pilgrimage in Graeco-Roman and Early Christian Antiquity.* Oxford: Oxford University Press.

Rutter, N. K. 2000. "Coin Types and Identity: Greek Cities in Sicily." In *Sicily from Aeneas to Augustus: New Approaches in Archaeology and History,* ed. C. Smith and J. Serrati, 73–83. Edinburgh: Edinburgh University Press.

Saïd, S. 2006. "The Rewriting of the Athenian Past: From Isocrates to Aelius Aristides." In *Greeks on Greekness: Viewing the Greek Past Under the Roman Empire,* ed. D. Konstan and S. Saïd, 47–60. Cambridge: Cambridge Philological Society.

Schepens, G. 1977. "Historiographical Problems in Ephorus." In *Historiographia Antiqua: Commentationes Lovanienses in Honorem W. Peremans,* 95–118. Leuven: Leuven University Press.

Scibona, G. 1992. "Storia della Ricerca Archeologica." In *Bibliografia Topografica della Colonizzazione Greca in Italia e nelle Isole Tirreniche,* ed. G. Nenci and G. Vallet, 10:16–36. Pisa: Scuola normale superiore.

Scott, M. 2010. *Delphi and Olympia: The Spatial Politics of Panhellenims in the Archaic and Classical Periods.* Cambridge: Cambridge University Press.

Smith, C. F. 1952. *Thucydides: History of the Peloponnesian War,* bks. 5–6. Cambridge, MA: Harvard University Press.

Stadter, P. A. (ed.). 1973. *The Speeches in Thucydides: A Collection of Original Studies with a Bibliography.* Chapel Hill: University of North Carolina Press.

Stucchi, S. 1965. *L'Agora di Cirene,* vol. 1: *I Lati Nord ed Est della Platea Inferiore.* Rome: L'Erma di Bretschneider.

Tilley, C. 1994. *A Phenomenology of Landscape: Places, Paths and Monuments.* Oxford: Berg.

Too, Y. L. 1995. *The Rhetoric of Identity in Isocrates: Text, Power, Pedagogy.* Cambridge: Cambridge University Press.

Tsakmakis, A. 1995. *Thukydides über die Vergangenheit.* Tübingen: Gunter Narr.

Valenza Mele, N. 1977. "Hera ed Apollo nella colonizzazione euboica d'Occidente." *Mélanges d'archéologie et d'histoire de l'École Française de Rome* 89: 494–524.

Vallet, G. 1958. *Rhégion et Zancle: Histoire, commerce et civilisation des cités Chalcidiennes du détroit de Messine.* Paris: Boccard.

van Compernolle, R. 1950–51. "La fondation de Naxos et les sources littéraires: Contribution à l'histoire de la colonisation grecque en Sicile." *Bulletin de l'Institut Historique Belge de Rome:* 163–85.

van Compernolle, R. 1956. "Les dates de fondation des colonies Siciliotes: A propos d'un article récent." *L'Antiquité classique* 25: 100–105.

van Compernolle, R. 1959. *Etude de chronologie et d'historiographie Siceliotes: Recherches sur le système chronologique des sources de Thucydide concernant la fondation des colonies Siceliotes*. Brussels: Palais des Académies et Académia Belgica.

van Wees, H. 2002. "Herodotus and the Past." In *Brill's Companion to Herodotus*, ed. E. J. Bakker, I. J. F. de Jong, and H. van Wees, 321–49. Leiden: Brill.

Veronese, F. 2006. *Lo Spazio e la Dimensione del Sacro: Santuari Greci e Territorio nella Sicilia Arcaica*. Padua: Esedra.

Zahrnt, M. 2006. "Sicily and Southern Italy in Thucydides." In *Brill's Companion to Thucydides*, ed. A. Rengakos and A. Tsakmakis, 629–55. Leiden: Brill.

CHAPTER 3

Who's the Daddy? Contesting and Constructing Theseus' Paternity in Fifth-Century Athens

SUSANNE TURNER

Sometime after 475 BC, Theseus' bones came home to Athens. The Athenians were beginning to rebuild and transform their city and their self-image in the wake of victory against the Persians in 480/479; the unexpected successes on land and sea had not yet been forgotten, not least since the enemy had taken the battle to the city of Athens and sacked even the temples atop the Acropolis. Prior to the sack of Athens, the Delian League had been formed to continue the fight on Persian-held territories. According to collective memory, Theseus had himself taken an active part in war: Plutarch reports that Greek soldiers saw an apparition of Theseus fighting alongside them at Marathon, and Pausanias describes how his role in the battle was honored in paintings on the Stoa Poikile in the agora, erected around 460 BC.[1] Theseus was on his way to becoming—if he was not one already—an Athenian "national hero."[2] Athens, unlike so many other Greek cities, may have had no obvious *oikist*, but in Theseus, they had a *synoikist*—a hero to be celebrated for uniting the villages of Attika under Athens as political center and for introducing democracy.[3]

But this *synoikist* and "national hero" had, according to tradition, died in exile on Skyros. His body was discovered there and returned home by the Athenian general Kimon, who found himself in Skyros on campaign (Thuc. 1.98).[4] Spurred to search for the remains of the long-dead hero by an oracle from Delphi, he was guided by an eagle pecking at the ground. In that spot, says Plutarch, the "coffin of a great man [μεγάλου σώματος] was found, and a bronze spear, and a sword" (*Theseus* 36.2). What precisely he found is not entirely clear (a great man or a man of great size?); nonetheless, he took the heirloom back home to Athens. Accompanied by appropriate pomp and ceremony, the rediscovered bones were installed in the Theseion in the center of the city.[5] In a ritualized reburial, Theseus was returned to the ground from whence his ancestors came; the result must have been a transformation of Theseus cult in the city, from hero cult to tomb cult.[6] In the process, the bones of "Theseus" were also transformed, from anonymous skeleton to holy relics—and Theseus himself was reincorporated into the community and welcomed home in the spirit of forgiveness. Why Theseus was exiled in Skyros specifically is unclear, but according to the (later) story, Theseus had lost the support of his people, easily swayed by a nondemocratic faction, following his lust-filled kidnap of Helen and his abortive attempt to snatch Persephone from Hades—an adventure that resulted in the death of his fellow hero Perithoos and the abduction of his own mother at the hands of the Dioscuri.[7] The Athenians may have invested in Theseus as a (quasi-)founder and installed him in the agora, just as other cities did with their *oikists*, but they could never quite erase the less savory elements of his story.

In this chapter, I want to explore how Theseus was slotted into the mythic landscape of the newly empowered Athens by exploring the increased interest in stories regarding his paternity in the years following the return of his bones, evidenced in both text and image. In truth, the Athenians had to work quite hard to make Theseus belong in Athens because he was an outsider not only by death but also by birth. The "Athenian hero *par excellence*"[8] was born an outsider to a foreign woman, Aithra, in the Peloponnese.[9] Even worse, there was a question mark hanging over his paternity: his father might have been Aigeus, the king of Athens, or Poseidon, god of the deep, depending on which story was to be believed. It is striking not only that both versions of his pedigree, mortal and divine, gain a new precedence in the wake of the hero's return to Athens, but that both vase painters and poets treat the stories in different ways, suggesting that Theseus' genealogy was especially "good to think with," as the Athenians repaired and reconstructed their collective identity after the Persian crisis.

I begin by examining the patchwork of myths concerning Theseus' paternity, before focusing on how the competing claims of Poseidon and Aigeus were set into motion in the decades following Theseus' repatriation. Finally, I look—all too briefly—at the other side of his parentage by exploring the role of maternity claims in Theseus' Athenian backstory. My aim is to show that the myths of Theseus' dual paternity gain momentum at this historical moment precisely because they negotiate how and why Theseus belongs in fifth-century Athens, where kinship relations came under increasing scrutiny as the qualification for citizenship (most obviously through the restriction of citizenship to those with both citizen fathers and mothers in the middle of the century).

Narratives of Return: Recognition and Interpellation

Since Theseus was born outside Attica, the return journey of his bones to Athens in 475 BC was not this hero's first homecoming to the city of a people who sometimes called themselves Theseidai, or "people of Theseus."[10] According to Plutarch (*Theseus* 3), Aigeus, the king of Athens, was childless, so he inquired of Apollo at Delphi whether children lay in his future. The god answered in a riddling affirmative, warning him not to engage with the opposite sex until he was safely back home in Athens. But Aigeus sojourned at the palace of Pittheus, king of Troizen and father of Aithra. Pittheus understood the full intent of the oracle's prophecy, and, plying his guest with alcohol, he engineered a tryst between his daughter and the foreign king. Aigeus returned to Athens, leaving behind hidden tokens for the son he had conceived. Several years later, when that son, Theseus, was fully grown, he retrieved the hidden tokens (sword and sandals) and set out for Athens to meet his father and be recognized as heir to the throne, traveling in Aigeus' footsteps through the territory that he sought to inherit (Plut. *Theseus* 12).

Significantly, when the Athenians decorated their newly built Theseion, they invested their collective memories—perhaps somewhat surprisingly—in a rather different version of Theseus' paternity: the story that the god Poseidon had sired the Athenian hero.[11] According to Pausanias, the Theseion in Athens was located in the agora next to the gymnasium (Paus. 1.17.2). Archaeological remains of the building have not yet been identified, but we do have Pausanias' description of its decoration. It was Poseidon's paternity, not Aigeus', which was shown on the walls of the Theseion, alongside a Centauromachy and Amazonomachy celebrating Theseus' heroic exploits (Paus. 1.17.2–3). Pausanias, expressing concern that his readers might not know the scene, tells the story: on the sea voyage to Crete, King Minos insulted Theseus and challenged him to prove his paternity by recovering a ring from the deep. When Theseus reappeared, he had not just the ring but a golden wreath given to him by Amphitrite.[12] Pausanias' concerns may have been well founded because this story of Theseus as a son of Poseidon seems to have had a mixed reception in antiquity. For some ancient authors, Poseidon's parentage was not in doubt: Theseus, says Isocrates, was "reputedly the son of Aigeus, but in reality the progeny of Poseidon."[13] Plutarch, however, was less convinced: "A report was spread abroad by Pittheus that he was begotten by Poseidon"[14] because Poseidon was the patron deity of Troizen and, he implies, because Pittheus might thereby protect his daughter's honor.[15]

As these twisting tales of paternal claims indicate, myth was a fundamentally flexible medium that could be put to work in the present for various (and sometimes competing) ends.[16] Genealogy, moreover, was a useful mechanism for communities in the ancient world to lay claim to the past and to forge a collective identity in the present.[17] Genealogy was effective because it was enormously flexible; the family trees of the heroic and more recent past could be rewritten and reframed, expanded, or telescoped.[18] Genealogical myth negotiates the ties that bind a people together by positing a shared bloodline, framing collective identity through a model of reproductive relations that is reassuringly familiar.

Yet these two tales necessarily twist further in the retelling. My story so far is a pastiche, a construction; I have had to knit together the evidence of a fourth-century BC orator, a second-century AD biographer, and his contemporary travel writer to build a cohesive picture of the myths put to work in the second quarter of the fifth century BC. This is not, of course, an unfamiliar strategy; Claude Calame's masterful account of the structure underlying Theseus' myths is drawn by subtly combining a host of disparate sources to draw the bigger picture, and he teases out the ways in which questions about Theseus' paternity and legitimacy haunt so many of the episodes of his early life-story.[19] But it is also possible to look in more detail at the mobilization of Theseus' paternity in the fifth century by pitting contemporary textual and visual retellings of the story against one another: two odes by the lyric poet Bacchylides explore what happened when Theseus came to meet Poseidon and Aigeus; vase painters, too, experiment with the same myths. Theseus had played a role in Athenian mythmaking since the last quarter of the sixth century, when the stories of his defeat of the Minotaur and his travails against villainous opponents in the Attic countryside became popular on black-figure pottery.[20] And while Kimon may have cannily aligned himself with Theseus when he brought home the bones, one man's quest for self-aggrandizement does not explain the wider currency of the myths regarding his paternity. So how and why do the twin tales of Theseus' mortal and divine progenitors suddenly gain ground following the return of the bones and decoration of the Theseion? How far and to what effect is Theseus' posthumous return to Athens refigured as a repeat of his double journey in myth to meet his fathers?

To borrow a term from Judith Butler, Theseus is "interpellated" as (quasi-) legitimate son and heir when he faces up to his father(s). Butler argues that "interpellation," the act of naming or hailing, positions the subject within discourse in a regulatory and constitutive way. She argues that gendered interpellations begin from birth ("It's a boy!") and reveal the ways in which the subject is shaped and framed within kinship relations.[21] In Theseus' case, his paternity might be said to be performative, in the sense that it is produced and legitimated through the semi-formalized processes of recognition and naming. Gendered identity, argues Butler, is always in process and open-ended, actively produced rather than simply reflected in the acts that seem to put it on show. "Consider gender," she says, "as a *corporeal style*, as an 'act,' as it were, which is both intentional and performative, where '*performative*' suggests a dramatic and contingent construction of meaning."[22]

Athenian boys were formally and ritually "interpellated" as citizen sons from birth, officially accepted by their fathers as newborns and later when their paternity was examined and "performed" when they were registered in their father's phratry or to ensure that they were suitable for holding office.[23] But what was at stake for the Athenians in authorizing one myth of descent over another? In a world where paternity (in contrast to maternity) remained invisible and unverifiable, how and why did the myths of Theseus' generation prove useful to Athens (and to Theseus) at this moment in time? In the case of Theseus, recognition of his birthright is displaced onto a sort of proto-*dokimasia* when he encounters his twin fathers for the first time later in life. In the process, his eligibility—as a hero, as an Athenian—is measured and judged. As Calame emphasizes, the narrative of his legitimacy runs to the very heart of Theseus' story and his role in Athens.[24] Thus when Bacchylides and the now-nameless vase painters dramatized his competing claims to paternity, they were negotiating—in strikingly different ways, dependent upon how they chose to frame the meeting and its consequences—his very relevance to Athens and Athenian identity.

The Son of a God Theseus and Poseidon

The tondo of a red-figure *kylix* in Paris, dating to c. 500 BC, features a scene that indicates that the story of Theseus' divine paternity and his descent to the bottom of the ocean had a history long before it appeared on the walls of the Theseion (Fig 3.1).[25] The hero, clad in short chiton and with long wavy locks, is rather diminutive, dwarfed by the much larger and enthroned Amphitrite he reaches out to. Between them, watching over them, stands Athena, complete with a small Athenian owl cradled in her hand. The small Triton at Theseus' feet, pushed into the background behind Athena's skirts, and the dolphins at his back are not just an indication of the watery realm but also of Theseus' mode of transport. The emphasis on superhuman support, along with the larger size of the two goddesses, certainly underscores Theseus' mortality, but there is no Poseidon in this scene—the moment of Theseus' recognition

3.1. *Kylix* interior, showing Theseus with Amphitrite and Athena. Signed by Euphronios and attributed to Onesimos, c. 500 BC. Paris, Louvre G104. Photograph from Wikimedia Commons.

has been displaced on the figures of his divine stepmother and the patron of his mortal people, the Athenians. Indeed, Athena's presence with the central owl is an indication that his divine paternity has already been co-opted by Athenian mytho-poetic concerns; at his waist is the sword that indicates that the hero has already been recognized by Aigeus, its hilt peeking out from behind his body. Theseus' place at Athens may be secure, but his place with Poseidon has been sidestepped, since the god does not appear to greet his newfound son.

Theseus' divine parentage, then, should perhaps not be taken for granted even when the story of his journey to meet Poseidon is explicitly referenced, in text as well as in image. Bacchylides 17, which may be as early as 500 BC but which many scholars now date to the years following the establishment of the Delian League in 477, similarly holds back from straightforwardly introducing Theseus to the god of the deep.[26] The poem splits roughly into two halves: the first takes place on the surface of the water, on the ship that is taking the Athenian youths to Crete and carrying Theseus to his confrontation with the Minotaur, and focuses on a quarrel that erupts between the Athenian hero and King Minos; the second half takes place in the depths of the ocean, into which Theseus plunges headlong to prove his divine parentage. The narrative is set in motion by Minos' lust for one of the young Athenian maidens (8–20).[27] When Theseus rebukes him, Minos, son of Zeus, is enraged and challenges him to retrieve a ring that he hurls into the sea (20–66); clashing with words, the two heroes measure up their claims to divine parentage within a decidedly competitive frame.[28] Immortal birthrights apparently require external confirmation: an enraged Minos demands proof that Theseus is, as he claims, the son of a god and calls upon his own father Zeus, lord of the thunder, to send a "a fast-moving, flame-haired lightning bolt, a recognizable sign" (θοὰν πυριέθειραν ἀστραπὰν σᾶμ' ἀρίγνωτον, 55–57). Divine genealogy is figured as something that is not necessarily immediately recognizable in the heroic body but can certainly be made visible to all (πανδερκέα, 70) when the god in question consents to do so.

Theseus does not shy away from Minos' challenge. "He jumped, and the plain of the sea received him willingly" (ὄρουσε, πόντιόν τέ νιν δέξατο θελημὸν ἄλσος, 84–85). He is greeted by waiting dolphins who helpfully guide him into the depths (97–101). At his first encounter with divinity, Theseus' response is appropriately mortal: the sight of dancing Nereids terrifies him (101–3). As Bacchylides describes Theseus moving through the wonders of Poseidon's underwater realm, expectation grows—but, as was the case on the *kylix* in Paris, Theseus never meets his father and again is welcomed by the god's wife, ox-eyed

Amphitrite. In Poseidon's absence, she gives him gifts, adorning him with a
rosebud wreath and a purple cloak given to her by guileful Aphrodite (115–16).
These are gifts that insert Theseus into an economy of exchange that medi-
ates relations between the gods themselves but that also bestow upon him an
erotic allure that will allow him to best Minos in his own homeland, nodding
forward to his future seduction of Ariadne and turning him into what Shapiro calls "a kind of Archaic love-hero."[29]

Although Theseus fails to meet Poseidon in Bacchylides 17, he returns to
the surface in a climactic moment of epiphany with the glow of divine parentage about him.[30] In his absence, Minos has ordered the ship to continue on its
way, but the Athenian hero surprises the king by breaking water next to it.
He emerges from the deep, "a wonder to all" (θαῦμα πάντεσσι, 123) and un-
wetted (ἀδίαντος, 122). "The gifts of the gods were glowing around his
limbs" (λάμπε δ᾽ ἀμφὶ γυίοις θεῶν δῶρ᾽, 123–24). The verb used here, λάμπω, is
the same word used to describe the glowing divinity of the Nereids twenty
lines earlier (104). The ring long forgotten,[31] the proof of Theseus' divine parentage is written onto and under the surfaces of his body: he emerges from the
sea miraculously untouched by water and able, presumably, to breathe in the
depths. There is, it seems, no suspicion now that his is a merely mortal body.

Yet while Theseus' journey to his father's ocean palace has often been described as life-changing by commentators (who point to the initiatory implications of the narrative: he goes down mortal and comes up semidivine),[32] an
inherent ambiguity persists around the status of his relationship to Poseidon.
Bacchylides' narrative is structured like a rite of passage, with three stages: the
rite of separation (the challenge on the ship); the rite of transition (the journey
underwater); and the rite of aggregation (his reappearance).[33] At first glance,
Theseus seems to have undergone a significant change. But it might be useful
to invoke Butler's notion of the performative here, since she theorizes identities
and bodies as constitutive constructions that are produced through the acts
which seem to signify them.[34] In the course of the ode, Theseus is "interpellated" (by the others on the ship and, perhaps to a lesser extent, by the residents of Poseidon's underwater realm) as the son of a god—and it is precisely
when he is named and recognized as the son of a god that he *becomes* the son
of a god. It is only at the end of the ode that his inherited divinity is inscribed
on his body and recognized as such by the internal audience; he absorbs—or
dons?—a new masculine identity, the identity of son and hero.[35]

But performativity risks shading into mere performance in the sheer the-
atricality of his reappearance. For Butler, performative citation is produced in

and across time, requiring a series of acts—a process, not a one-off.[36] Here it is important that Theseus has never met his father in person, the one character whose interpellation carries the most significance. He is neither formally received by the god nor legitimated, and his paternal duties are displaced here onto the figure of the stepmother, Amphitrite.[37] At the very least, there is a sense that Theseus does not rank highly among the god's priorities, and thus his claim to divine paternity remains somewhat ambivalent.[38] Even the signs of his newly uncovered divine ancestry are ambiguous—where it is the limbs of the Nereids that glow with godhead (ἀπὸ γὰρ ἀγλαῶν λάμπε γυίων σέλας ὧτε πυρός, 103–5), it is Amphitrite's gifts that gleam *on* Theseus' limbs (ἀμφὶ γυίοις, 124).

Understanding Theseus' journey as initiatory might assume a fundamentally permanent change in the hero, but reading his new identity as a performative frame, then, prioritizes the inherent ambiguity of the narrative. Poseidon's claim to father Theseus is neither proved nor taken for granted in his visit to the ocean floor; rather, it is a claim that might be reaffirmed or reperformed at later points in Theseus' life. Understanding his dual claims to paternity as performative, moreover, also offers a means of reconciling the apparent absence of Poseidon here with the haunting presence of Aigeus in the background. It does this by framing the hero's identity as a process, one that stretches before the pivotal moment of his epiphanic reemergence and that goes beyond any initiatory explanation. A performative frame, in other words, has the potential to understand Theseus' dual paternities not as mutually exclusive but as mutually implicated in each other, as different positionings or identifications that might become more or less highly charged at different points in his story or different points in Athenian history.

The same theme of mutual interdependence between Aigeus and Poseidon continues even in those scenes that seemingly attempt to avoid ambiguity by showing immortal father and mortal son together on the sea floor. In the course of the 470s, vase painters began to freeze-frame the moment of reunion between father and son, most often showing them cementing their relationship by shaking hands, a gesture known as *dexiosis*.[39] Poseidon's godhead is usually easily identified, his trident and more mature stately stature marking him out from the youthful Theseus. On a column krater attributed to the Harrow Painter, for instance, Poseidon is resplendent in his decorated chiton and heavily draped himation; his trident breaks into the frieze of tongues above, in a graphic hint that his divinity cannot be contained by the frame (Fig. 3.2). Theseus wears a short *chitoniskos* and a fringed shawl, holding in his hand some unknown object (an apple? but why?); the wreath on his head connotes celebration and special status and has perhaps just been deposited there by the female figure behind him—most likely, Amphitrite.[40] The Doric column at the far left situates the encounter in Poseidon's palace at the bottom of the sea, his θεῶν μέγαρόν (Bacch. 17.100–101). Scenes like this one make the acknowledgment between father and son mutual, captured in the moment just before they properly clasp hands, standing near enough that their toes overlap, though the trident separates them. Moreover, Poseidon does not quite eclipse Aigeus here; Theseus wears at his waist a sword hung in a black scabbard, so that a symbol of Aigeus' prior recognition intrudes as it did on the

3.2. Column krater: Theseus and Poseidon, with onlookers. Attributed to the Harrow Painter, c. 470 BC. Cambridge, MA, Sackler Museum 1960.339. Reproduced with permission of the Harvard Arts Museums.

Paris *kylix*. Vase painters, then, are maintaining a subtle ambiguity even when they showcase Poseidon's paternity claims, while the addition of the sword also places the episode in a mythical timeline that stretches back into Theseus' past.

But the most elaborate example is a *kylix* in New York.[41] The tondo privileges the same moment as Bacchylides and the Paris cup, the greeting of Theseus by Amphitrite (Fig. 3.3). A young Theseus leans nonchalantly against a column, seemingly perfectly at home in the underwater palace. He wears the *chitoniskos* and fringed shawl again; but this time, the sword at his waist is pushed into the background. Amphitrite is seated and holds up a wreath, originally added in white paint now mostly lost. The scene on the outside, however, skirts to the end of the episode: Theseus is now in the company of his father Poseidon in a colonnaded hall, surrounded by witnesses (Fig. 3.4). He wears on his head the wreath that, in the tondo, Amphitrite was shown bestowing upon him. The scene is dominated by a large fishtailed Triton,

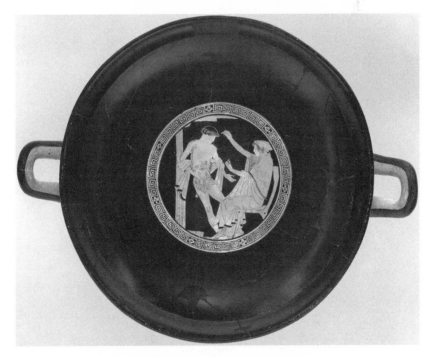

3.3. *Kylix* interior, showing Amphitrite with Theseus. Attributed to the Briseis Painter, c. 480 BC. The Metropolitan Museum of Art, Purchase, Joseph Pulitzer Bequest, 1953 (53.11.4). Photograph © The Metropolitan Museum of Art.

who holds on to the smaller Theseus while Poseidon points away in the opposite direction; here, the trident is directive, indicating that it is time for
Theseus to return.

The special relationship between father and son, indicated by the handshake, is absent, but the Triton functions as a linking device between the god
and the hero.[42] As Poseidon's "Man Friday of the deep,"[43] the Triton assumes all
the otherness of the god's marine realm. Poseidon's divinity is hidden behind
his anthropomorphic body, but the Triton's hybrid body, clothed on top and
scaled below, combines conflicting elements of human civilization and fishy
bestiality; the assistance that he gives to Theseus indicates that the Attic hero
does not belong on the ocean floor.[44] But this is Triton as the son of Poseidon
and Amphitrite,[45] quite a contrast in his excessive size and prominent crown to
the diminutive and sidelined Triton on the Paris *kylix*. This cup thus drama-
tizes what it is to be a son of Poseidon: to have two divine parents and to live
"in golden mansions beside his dear mother and lordly father" (Hesiod, *Theogony* 932–933)[46] on the ocean floor is to absorb the physical form of marine life.

3.4. *Kylix* exterior obverse (side A), showing Theseus and Triton, with Poseidon and
onlookers. Attributed to the Briseis Painter, c. 480 BC. The Metropolitan Museum
of Art, Purchase, Joseph Pulitzer Bequest, 1953 (53.11.4). Photograph © The
Metropolitan Museum of Art.

Theseus' heroic destiny, however, lies above ground. Why, then, did the Athenians endorse a paternity that placed their favorite hero outside any Athenian family tree and effectively bastardized him?[47] And why did they do so on the walls of his official cult building, no less, where we might expect them to emphasize his connections to Athens? Both ode and vase paintings have an interest in how Theseus' heroic status is confirmed and enhanced when Poseidon recognizes him as his son—enhanced, of course, because he becomes the son of a god.[48] By extension, Athens gains the divine sanction and support not only of a god that they have explicitly rejected in the past—when they chose Athena over Poseidon as patron of their city—but also that of a god of the sea. Adopting the son of Poseidon goes some way to healing the rift between Athens and the god that they scorned.

But there is perhaps more at stake here in light of the still-recent memories of the battle of Salamis. For with Poseidon as his father, Theseus inherits a mastery of the sea; Athens, via her national hero, thus highlights her own skills at seafaring and sea-fighting. In the years following the naval victory over Persia, such associations are particularly pointed.[49] As the son of Poseidon, Theseus becomes a figure in which Athenian naval power is virtually personified, even though his own great martial achievements take place on dry land. Indeed, just like the Athenians, Theseus overcomes a tyrannical overseas in the figure of Minos—a powerful mythical analogy for the defeated Persians.[50]

There are hints in Bacchylides' version, too, that the story could carry further political connotations, especially if the ode dates to the 470s and after the foundation of the Delian League in 477 BC. Perhaps Athenian thalassocracy and empire stand behind Theseus' conquest of Minos;[51] the designation of the youths on the ship not as Athenian but as Ionian (3) nods toward an Athenian desire to emphasize its own supposed colonial relationship with the Ionian cities of Anatolia.[52] In addition, the sheer strength of Athenian naval power is suggested, as Bacchylides explicitly contrasts Minos' famed skill at navigating the surfaces of the sea with Theseus' miraculous command of the deep. While Minos' knowledge is restricted to the πέλαγος (4) and the winds that propel a ship across the waves; but when Theseus dives, he is initiated into the πόντος (84–85, 94), the mysterious and dangerous underwater realm.[53]

Nonetheless, Bacchylides 17 was neither performed in Athens nor by Athenians; the poem ends with an address to Delian Apollo, and the celebratory songs of the Athenian youths at Theseus' return elide the mythical past into the present-time voices of a chorus from Ceos.[54] Any glorification of

Athens—and the theme seems particularly Athenian—is therefore displaced onto and "ventriloquized" by one of her "allies."[55] In addition, the performance of the ode at Delos, the symbolic center of Athens' captive league, is significant. From this perspective, divine paternity seems well placed to mediate Athenian power play abroad. Poseidon's claim to Theseus negotiates networks of Hellenic relations enacted and secured through maritime voyages, in an economy of power whose terms are set by (and in) Athens. The potential of Poseidon's parentage, in other words, was especially useful to an Athens looking to place herself on a world stage, beyond her own borders. Still, if Poseidon was convenient to the Athenians at home and especially abroad, why did the story of Aigeus' parentage gain a foothold during the same period? Why did Poseidon not displace Aigeus?

The Son of a King: Theseus and Aigeus

Although the Athenian mythmaking machine has much to gain by making Poseidon the procreator of Theseus, Aigeus is never quite erased from the picture. Aigeus' recognition functions as a precursor to Poseidon's, and mortal paternity is not canceled out by its divine counterpoint. Even in Bacchylides 17, for instance, the hero is introduced as the "descendant of Pandion" (15–16), father of Aigeus. Bacchylides also dramatized Theseus' encounter with his mortal father in another ode, playing with where Theseus came from for an Athenian audience and an Athenian ritual this time (although which festival remains unclear).[56] The dates for Bacchylides 18 are as fluid as those for 17, ranging from the 470s down to the 450s BC.[57] An earlier date would suggest that this ode, too, engages with the paternity on the Theseion—in the direction of mortality, rather than divinity.

The myth of Aigeus' paternity seems to predate the fifth-century sources— Aigeus is mentioned by Homer, although this may be a later Athenocentric addition.[58] However, Bacchylides tackles the story in a striking way, presenting a dialogue between Aigeus and a chorus of his subjects. A young man is on his way to Athens, killing every miscreant in his path, but his identity remains unknown to the internal characters. Bacchylides here plays with the fact that the external audience will recognize the signs that this is Theseus, on his way to be incorporated into the mytho-history of Athens. The dramatic dialogue begins with the city on alert. The chorus asks its king what to expect of the unknown man on his way: Is he an enemy with an army, or a robber? Aigeus replies by listing the unrecognized hero's "indescribable deeds" (18): he has killed Sinis, and the sow at Kremmyon, and Skiron, and defeated Kerkyron, and Prokoptas (Prokrustes) (19–30). But the king ends on a strong note of anxiety—"I fear in what way these things will end" (ταῦτα δέδοιχ ὅπᾳ τελεῖται, 30). He does not see the stranger as his son; Theseus reportedly carries "an ivory hilted sword" (48), but the king has not identified it as his own (yet). Once again, then, the moment of recognition is held off—and it is up to the external audience to "interpellate" him as his son instead. The strategy of focalizing the reaction to events through the Athenians showcases the uncertainty of their responses: only retrospectively will Theseus' deeds be characterized as heroic rather than threatening.

The temporal liminality of this reading—Bacchylides presents Theseus on the cusp of achieving an Athenian identity—converges in the figure of Theseus himself. Theseus is presented here as the "ephebe of ephebes."[59] As he treks through the wilderness of Attica, moving from the margin to the center, wearing the chlamys (54) that marks the Athenian ephebe,[60] he embodies the Athenian rite of passage for young men during which they spend two liminal years defending the marginal edges of Attica. Through his own personal *ephebia*, Theseus learns how to make war and how to be a man through his dangerous trials.[61] For those two years, the ephebes, like Theseus, become outsiders until they are reincorporated into the citizen body. Theseus-as-ephebe thus functions as a model for Athenian young men to follow—a protoephebe—but also finds his liminality exaggerated and exploited by the narrative context, in which Aigeus and his chorus set him outside the Athenian collective. In the course of his journey, he maps out the terrain of Athens, inserting himself and his achievements into the topography—performatively constructing the boundaries and extent of Athens itself in the process.[62] His journey also gives him a convenient opportunity to establish his relevance to contemporary Athenians, the ideal model of the Athenian versus barbarian Other (even while he remains an unknown Other himself).[63] In this sense, says Mills, "Theseus' birth outside of Athens is, in fact, more useful to his city than an Athenian birth would have been."[64]

Theseus, moreover, must learn how to be a man and how to be a good Athenian as he undergoes these tests of his heroism because he has had no fatherly example to follow. In his sheer dynamism, Theseus is already outperforming his Athenian father.[65] But there are hints that all is not as it seems or, as the *Oxford Classical Dictionary* has it, that his "claim to membership of the Athenian royal line is somewhat shaky"—and not just because Aigeus may be a rather late addition to the ruling family tree.[66] There are enough hints of divinity in the poem to trouble the story of mortal paternity dramatized here: the chorus claims that a god impels Theseus as he wreaks his punishments (40–41), and "from his eyes shines crimson Lemnian fire" (ὀμμάτων δὲ στίλβειν ἄπο Λαμνίαν φοίνισσαν φλόγα, 54–56).[67]

His opponents, too, are strange doubles of him. Theseus had a reputation for killing his opponents by turning their own methods of attack back upon them, but, more than that, Bacchylides describes Sinis, first in his list, as the son of Poseidon ("son of Lutaios the earth-shaker, son of Kronos," Κρονίδα Λυταίου σεισίχθονος τέκος, 21–22).[68] Here, too, what it might be to be the son of a god is explored; in this case, Theseus measures himself against his opposite, a negative counterexample of divine inheritance gone awry. It is perhaps particularly pointed that, in this ode, the distance between mythical past and present performance is closed down, since the ode was most likely performed by an Athenian chorus in an Athenian ritual and from the internal perspective of an Athenian community that cast Theseus as an unknown outsider. Bacchylides refigures Athenian opinions of their hero by acting out an alternative interpretation of his actions, and he does so in a context that holds off from acknowledging his Athenian-ness by postponing any recognition or direct confrontation of his paternity. What if, Bacchylides seems to ask, Theseus were neither Aigeus' son nor Athenian by birth?

As was the case with Poseidon, vase painters were more interested in the point of direct contact between Theseus and Aigeus, and they remained interested in the theme of Theseus' mortal paternity far longer than they did in the version of his immortal parentage.[69] The earliest example, a fragmentary *skyphos* in Paris attributed to the Brygos Painter, shows a beautifully groomed Theseus (in a costume and hairstyle almost identical to the one he wears on the New York cup; this one, though, is attributed to the Briseis Painter) shaking hands with an older, bearded figure.[70] The presence of spectators indicates that this is a public celebration of his status as son of a king. Aigeus holds the scepter of a mortal king, and Theseus is being wreathed, as in the Poseidon recognition scenes.

More often, however, vase painters removed the distraction of onlookers, focusing on the relationship between Theseus and Aigeus. The effects of age on Aigeus' mortal body are increasingly emphasized until he is white-haired on the latest example;[71] on a *pelike* in Cambridge, the sloping shoulders of the seated Aigeus, forced to look up at the standing Theseus, emphasize the youthful vitality of the son in comparison with the father (Fig. 3.5).[72] Two earlier pots show the young hero gleefully pulled into a welcoming embrace

3.5. *Pelike*, showing Theseus and Aigeus, c. 440–430 BC. Cambridge, Fitzwilliam Museum GR.25.1937. Photograph courtesy of the Fitzwilliam Museum.

(by Aigeus on an amphora in Cambridge; by a woman on a stamnos in Saint Petersburg);[73] over the course of the century, the distance between the two figures increases. Theseus is no longer represented wearing the short *chitoniskos* but instead is in the guise of a traveler, nude underneath his chlamys and wearing the petasos; on the *pelike*, he holds a tall walking stick, which creates a vertical dividing line separating him from Aigeus. Often, Theseus wears the all-important tokens of recognition—the sword at his waist and sandals laced up his calves[74]—but not always in clear view or visible; the viewer, like the king, is drawn into a process of identification predicated upon heavily loaded symbolic objects. Mortal paternity is worn on the body, rather than miraculously inscribed within it.

The model of Theseus' mortal paternity clearly had currency in Athens in the years following the return of the bones, both in addition to and in opposition to the divine story formalized on the Theseion. Where Theseus' divine paternity was put to work to negotiate international links enacted in an island context, Aigeus' legacy legitimates Theseus at home, suggesting that the story was not as useful in the international arena. Aigeus, in fact, would become the father of choice in fourth-century law-court speeches,[75] and vase painters continued to depict the theme long after they had stopped representing Poseidon. Where they bestowed a certain prominence on Poseidon by painting him especially on kraters and *kylikes*,[76] they painted Aigeus on a wider range of smaller pot shapes, not all necessarily associated with the symposium. Aigeus, in other words, appears more as a supporting figure than as the principal actor in Theseus' story. So what did Aigeus have to offer?

As a mortal king with an Athenian pedigree, Aigeus can stand in for contemporary Athens and Athenians, welcoming home their long-lost hero and already, perhaps, beginning to harbor dreams of ruling an empire. Indeed, Aigeus is far better suited to this domestic role than Poseidon. But Aigeus was also the very pretext upon which Theseus' claim to the Athenian throne and to Athenian identity rested. Without Aigeus, Theseus was an illegitimate bastard, an imposter in the royal line—a line that stretched back to the autochthonous origins of Athens. The fifth century was precisely the period in which Athenians began to formulate their conception of themselves as autochthonous. Over the course of the fifth century, the Athenians developed an autochthonous self-identity based upon their unique relation to their territory (born from the very earth beneath their feet) and their democratic politics (equality quite literally grounded in shared origins). These are powerful rhetorical ideas that are most clearly propounded in the fourth-century orations for the war dead.[77]

Autochthony, too, marks a particular Athenian relation to the past: every Athenian embodies the past through shared blood. Theseus' autochthonous status thus can be negotiated only through the bloodline that he inherits from Aigeus, hinting that the interest in his mortal paternity—refiguring his bones, in a sense, as relics of autochthony itself—marks the early seeds of this particular Athenian self-identity.[78] Poseidon may have been celebrated on the walls of the Theseion housing those bones. There was, as we have seen, an important complementarity and mutual dependency between Theseus' twin paternities— Claude Calame teasingly designates his enigmatic rebirth from the waves as an act of "autothalassie" that balances out his claims to autochthony.[79] Yet the evidence of the vase paintings seems to hint at sustained or even increasing interest in Aigeus (and decreasing interest in Poseidon) as ideas about Athenian autochthony were being conceptualized in ever more sophisticated ways.

Absent Fathers and Displaced Mothers

For Theseus, it seems that the invisibility of paternity was a useful device, allowing multiple allegiances to be mobilized in ways advantageous to the Athenians. Yet the very appearance of the theme of Theseus' paternity only highlights how both his potential fathers were remarkably absent for large parts of the hero's life story—sometimes, even in the retelling of their meeting. So what of the maternal figures in his mythography? What of Aithra, Athena, and Amphitrite? In many ways, thinking through the role of mother figures in Theseus' origins raises more questions than I can answer here. I will highlight the ways in which maternity plays its own role in the problem of how and why Theseus belongs in and to Athens.

Amphitrite, Poseidon's underwater wife, sometimes plays such a prominent role in the story of Theseus' recognition that she seems able to oust the god himself, and Theseus' paternity is rewritten as displaced maternity. This move has provoked much anxiety in the literature: Is Theseus re-gendered in the process of his aquatic dive?[80] As a stepmother, Amphitrite is perhaps a useful vehicle for the displacement of the types of ambivalent paternity that I have explored so far, since stepmothers have a fairly dire reputation in Greek myth. But she is also rewriting what it is to be a mythical stepmother, for Theseus had already encountered a paradigmatically evil stepmother in Athens in the figure of Medea.[81] Against the backdrop of Medea's murderous plottings, Amphitrite's welcome and kindness become rather loaded against Medea's example. In a complex process of repeated mirroring and transference, Amphitrite thus functions as a foil not just for Poseidon's lack of interest but also for Medea's enmity.[82] Once again, Theseus' tale twists into another series of doublings, this time focused on his other mothers.

Amphitrite, though, has a short-lived part to play in the script of Theseus' life, often playing a supportive role on the vases. In contrast, Theseus' biological mother, Aithra, steps into the spotlight on a rather different group of vases, in which she is pursued by Poseidon. The scenes are relatively formulaic, with Poseidon approaching from the left while a young Aithra runs, turning back to look at him. The scenes, however, vary in their choice of phallic substitute: a *lekythos* in Palermo shows Poseidon grabbing Aithra with one hand while he thrusts his trident at her stomach with the other, while a hydria in the British Museum shows him brandishing a dolphin at her.[83] This series of pots might also be best understood as exploring Theseus' paternity through not his recognition but his conception; vase painters footnote the hero even in his absence by representing the "seduction" of his mother in the manner of an erotic pursuit—and they do so in far greater numbers than they ever depicted father and son.[84]

In these scenes, Theseus' paternity is negotiated via the sexual rapacity of his divine father, but there are no equivalent scenes featuring Aigeus impregnating Aithra: only divine sexual prowess proves "good to think with." Yet this group of pots figure Aithra not so much as a mother but as a body; the reproductive and sexual potential of her femininity is harnessed by Athenian mythmaking in the name of Theseus.[85] The Athenian hero's identity is thus at stake even though he is absent, in the shape of a sexual fantasy appropriate for an all-male viewing context in the symposium; perhaps the implication is that Theseus inherits from Poseidon his prowess with the opposite sex. Yet these images court the risk that father (and son, that "kind of Archaic love hero") behave like Minos. That is, Poseidon's impregnation of Aithra is akin to the same sexual violence that spurs Theseus to meet his divine progenitor—thereby setting in motion yet another mirroring twist. Aithra is thus relegated to a reproductive rather than maternal role in her son's life, marginalizing her mothering role.[86]

Ultimately, Aithra is marginalized again by another deity when Theseus makes the journey to Athens, for there he comes under the protection of Athena. In this context, it is worth returning to the *kylix* in New York one last time, since it, too, carries a scene that shows Athena's personal commitment to this Attic hero and to his role in Athens (Fig. 3.6). On its other side, balancing Poseidon's palace, is a scene situated in Athens. Here, Theseus—again in a public context, with a host of spectators—is greeted not by Aigeus but by Athena. This scene is usually described as the return from Crete (and certainly, the gestures on display here are markedly different from those marking the Poseidon scene as a departure), although Neils has suggested that the prominence of the sword, which the hero has drawn, may indicate that this is his first appearance and recognition in the city.[87] In either case, the vase replaces Aigeus with Athena and thus avoids bringing the two versions of Theseus' paternity into direct dialogue with each other.

The result is that mortal paternity is refigured as divine maternity—and Athena is a useful goddess here, not just because she personifies Athens but because she invokes the divine origins of Athenian autochthony. It was Athena who spurred the desire of Hephaistos, resulting in the birth of the original autochthon, the baby Erichthonios, from the earth itself. Poseidon and Athena, moreover, are here represented as parental counterparts: Theseus' birth heals even discord between the gods, caused by the Athenian choice to

3.6. *Kylix*, exterior reverse (side B), showing Theseus and Athena with onlookers. Attributed to the Briseis Painter, c. 480 BC. The Metropolitan Museum of Art, Purchase, Joseph Pulitzer Bequest, 1953 (53.11.4). Photograph © The Metropolitan Museum of Art.

favor the virgin goddess over the sea god.[88] Probably more important is that when Theseus returns to Athens, he no longer has a mortal father to greet him. The Athenian "national hero," forgetting to sail the correct flag, caused his own father's suicide in what Sourvinou-Inwood calls "indirect patricide."[89] As a result, with Theseus on the throne, democracy was first introduced to Athens.[90] In this sense, Theseus' two fathers remained forever mutually exclusive; he is never the son of Aigeus and the son of Poseidon in the same time and space. And the very journey that occasioned his recognition as Poseidon's son also results in the death of Aigeus.

Conclusion

Theseus might seem a rather odd figure to include in this volume. He is no *oikist*, no founder of a city. Athens, unlike other cities, had no founder, for her inhabitants were autochthonous, born from the earth itself. Yet the fifth-century Athenians invested their collective energies in Theseus as they did in no other hero—and when they installed his newly found bones in the agora, in his very own Theseion, they elevated him to the status of *synoikist*. As they began to look at themselves with fresh eyes following the defeat of the Persians, Theseus became an integral part of their own (his-)story of who they were and where they had come from.

In this chapter, I have tried to show that, in the years after the bones came home, the competing versions of Theseus' paternity were one way in which Athenian audiences negotiated two facets of their identity: their special relationship to the land in which they lived, and their imperial success on sea. I have also sought to demonstrate that his paternity was useful in this context precisely because it was in doubt. Perhaps surprisingly, ancient authors and artists rarely contrasted Aigeus and Poseidon in the same context explicitly. Instead, they usually opted for one over the other—although sometimes, the alternative can be glimpsed in the background, as in Euripides' *Hippolytus*, where Artemis twice addresses Theseus as Aigeus' son even though the hero himself will see Poseidon's tragic actions at the end of the play as confirmation of his divine lineage.[91] Theseus' two fathers never eclipse each other but instead allow him to be mobilized in different ways—he can speak of different Athenian identities to different audiences in different contexts. Whether he is understood as a hero embedded in the locality or as an international adventurer with divine links on a Panhellenic scale, the stories of Theseus' paternity always set in motion a complex negotiation between mythical past and historical present. And, in a sense, the Athenian hero's paternal past was marked by its undecidability; it exists in the tension—the gap—between his two fathers.

NOTES

1. For Theseus fighting at Marathon, see Plut. *Theseus* 35, with Pritchett 1979: 24; Garland 1992: 54–57. For the *stoa poikile*, see Paus. 1.15.

2. "National hero": Agard 1928; Hurwit 1985: 314; Strauss 1993: 105; Calame 1990: 185–288 (ch. 4).

3. Mills 1997: 26: "The Athenians' belief that they were autochthonous precluded foundation myths of the usual kind, and so the *synoikist* of Attica will be a founding hero." Myth of *synoikism*: Thuc. 2.15; in fifth-century politics: Goušchin 1999. Plutarch, though, does describe him as *oikist* and proffers his story to be read alongside Romulus, founder of Rome: *Theseus* 1.2; Strauss 1993: 105.

4. For Kimon discovering the bones of Theseus on Skyros, see Plut. *Kimon* 8; Plut. *Theseus* 36; Paus. 3.3.7. For Kimon's campaign on Skyros more generally, see Thuc. 1.98.

5. Paus. 1.17; Plut. *Theseus* 36.2; Diod. Sic. 4.62.4.

6. Inauguration of the Theseia: Calame 1990: 154. Tomb cult vs. hero cult: Antonaccio 1993, 1994, 1995. On hero cult in Attica: Kearns 1989. Theseus cult: Christensen 1984; Ekroth 2010. Lack of cult places: Walker 1995: 20–21; Parker 1996: 169; cult places transferred to Herakles: Euripides, *Madness of Herakles* 1328–33.

7. Theseus' exile and death: Plut. *Theseus* 35; Paus. 1.17.6; Diod. Sic. 4.62.4 (with Athenian repentance as the motive for bringing back the bones); Apollodorus, *Epitome* 1.24. Theseus was not the only hero who found his bones relocated: Boedeker 1993 (on Orestes) and McCauley 1998 (on Hippodameia). On relics: Osborne 2010. On discovering bones: Mayor 2000; Boardman 2002: 33–43.

8. E.g., Neils 1987: 2; Boardman 1991: 87; Harding 2008: 50.

9. Plut. *Theseus* 3–4. Plutarch is the main literary source, with Apollodorus *Bibliotheca* 3.16 and *Epitome* 1.1–6 and Diod. Sic. 4.59.1. Plutarch drew heavily on the Atthidographers, the writers of local histories of Athens, recently translated and discussed by Harding 2008. The oracle: Euripides, *Medea* 674–87.

10. Aeschylus, *Eumenides* 1026.

11. Hyginus, *Fabulae* 37; Paus. 2.33.1; Diod. Sic. 4.59.1.

12. The painter, Mikon, may never have painted the entire story on that wall; Pausanias' text leaves the actual content of the painting somewhat ambiguous (does he describe the myth shown, or does he supplement it?). On this ambiguity: Castriota 1992: 60–61. Attempts to reconstruct the appearance of the paintings have stumbled on this third myth: Barron 1972; Woodford 1974.

13. Isocrates 10.18, tr. van Hook 1945.

14. Plut. *Theseus* 6.1, tr. Perrin 1914.

15. Plutarch (*Theseus* 6.1) claims that Aithra hid her pregnancy from Aigeus. There must also have been other versions of the story, probably where Aigeus and Aithra were married; see Kovacs 2008.

16. Uses and abuses of the mythical past in the present: Gehrke 2001 and Hobden 2007. See also the Introduction in this volume for further discussion on this point.

17. Hall 1997, 2002; Fowler 1998. Cf. Kowalzig 2007 on etiological myth.

18. Telescoping and family history: Thomas 1989.

19. Calame 1990. Beyond this key work, the bibliography on Theseus is vast and has often sought to identify a prominent individual as his "patron." Kimon: Vidal-Naquet 1986: 313; Castriota 1992: 61; Parker 1996: 168–70; Gouschin 1999. Peisistratos: Connor 1970; Tyrell and Brown 1991: 161–65. Cleisthenes: Kearns 1989: 116–17.

20. Theseus in early Athenian art: Neils 1987; Shapiro 1991, 1992; von den Hoff 2010.

21. Butler 1993: 7–8 and 121–24. Cf. Scafuro 1994, on the importance of witnessing in the production and proof of citizen identity in Athens.

22. Butler 2006: 190, original italics.

23. This happened first in the recognition ritual of the Amphidromia: Hamilton 1984; Golden 1986, and later in the phratry-focused ritual of the Apatouria.

24. Calame 1990: esp. 192–96.

25. Red-figure *kylix*, signed by Euphronios (potter) and attributed to Onesimos; Paris, Louvre G104. ARV^2 318.1, 1645, 318. *LIMC* 7 s.v. Theseus 36*.

26. Maehler (1997: 167–70; 2004: 174–76) judges Bacchylides to have invented the story, hence his suggestion of an early date. Date after 477 BC: Kowalzig 2007: 88; Wilson 2007: 178; Calame 2009: 171.

27. On the sexually transgressive nature of Minos' touch to the maiden's cheek, see Clark 2003.

28. On the heroes' clash as a "battle of genealogies," see Segal 1979: 27. On the measuring up of heroic lineage, see also Pieper 1972: 397–98. For the wider agonistic context, see Danek 2008.

29. "Archaic love hero": Shapiro 1991: 124, 128–29. See also Segal 1979: esp. 31–32. Role of Aphrodite: Brown 1991. But cf. Calame 1990: 96 and 198, who frames this episode as part of Theseus' initiation into adult sexuality but emphasizes that he is presented as defender of virginity here.

30. Epiphany: Kowalzig 2007: 89; Calame 2009: 172.

31. A detail that has often worried commentators, e.g., Stern 1967.

32. Segal 1979; Burnett 1985.

33. The structure of rites of passage: van Gennep 1960.

34. Butler 1993, 2006.

35. Father-son relationships: Strauss 1993; Shapiro 2003; Roisman 2005: esp. 41–46.

36. Clarified in Butler 1993: e.g., 12–13.

37. *Contra* Pieper 1972: 402, for whom Amphitrite proves Theseus' lineage from Poseidon.

38. Ambivalence: Walker 1995: 84–92.

39. *Dexiosis*: Davies 1985; Pemberton 1989.

40. See also *LIMC* Theseus 221–22.

41. Attributed to the Briseis Painter, c. 480 BC. New York, Metropolitan Museum 53.11.4. *ARV²* 406.7, *Addenda²* 232, *LIMC* 7 s.v. Theseus 219*.

42. Iconography of Triton: Glynn 1981: esp. 129.

43. Shapiro 1994: 119.

44. Harrison 2000: 273.

45. Hesiod, *Theogony* 930–33.

46. Hesiod, *Theogony* 932–33, tr. Most 2006.

47. Athenian laws against adultery and rape protected legitimate bloodlines in the non-mythical world; see Ogden 1997.

48. And echoes the divine paternity of his rival, Herakles: Shapiro 2003: 94. Zeus' ambivalent paternity: Mikalson 1986.

49. See, esp., Shapiro 1992 on the sudden prominence of the entire Cretan story in Athens in this period, which Shapiro attributes to Athens' defeat of Persia and her pursuit of a naval empire. Shapiro 1982; Mills 1997: 37–38.

50. Theseus as democratic anti-tyrant: Calame 1990: 219–23.

51. Castriota 1992: 60; Calame 1990: 424–29; Fearn 2007: 242. See also Giesekam 1977; van Oeveren 1999.

52. Kowalzig 2007: 102–10. See also Connor 1993, on changing Athenian constructions of their Ionian-ness.

53. Walker 1995: 85–86.

54. Calame 1990: 207; Fearn 2007: 242–56. Kowalzig (2007: 91–93) argues that Theseus' defeat of Minos is transformed into a victory that benefits all Greeks, not just Athenians.

55. "Ventriloquism": Wilson 2007: 179.

56. Maehler 2004: 189.

57. 460–450 BC: Maehler 2004: 190–91. 470s BC: Barron 1980.

58. Homer *Iliad* 1.265; Athenian additions: Walker 1995: 16–17.

59. "Ephebe of ephebes": Vidal-Naquet 1986: 112. On the initiatory and ephebe-like features of Theseus' story, see also Jeanmaire 1939: 227–383; Merkelbach 1973; Strauss 1993: 118–22; Walker 1995: 98–104.

60. Wind 1972: 518.

61. Liminality of ephebes: Vidal-Naquet 1986. Theseus' journey from ephebe to hoplite: Calame 1990: 187–92.

62. I thank one of the reviewers for this point. Politicization of the topography: Calame 1990: 420–24. Greek myth and landscape: Buxton 1994: 80–113. Parallel topography of Cretan adventure: Calame 1990: 224.

63. And defending Greek values: Calame 1990: 72.

64. Mills 1997: 21.

65. Strauss 1993: 110–11. Negative interpretations of Aigeus: Wind 1972; Strauss 1993: 116–18.

66. Arafat 1996: 1508. Harding 2008: 50: Aigeus "functions as little more than a foil to Theseus in the traditional tales."

67. Wind 1972: 513–14.

68. The epithet Lutaios refers to a Poseidon cult in Thessaly (Maehler 2004: 196). Doubling: Brelich 1956; Wind 1972: 513; Walker 1995: 97; Calame 1990: 188–89 and 233.

69. Fourteen examples of Theseus and Aigeus vs. four of Poseidon. Aigeus: *LIMC* 7 s.v. Theseus 156–69. Poseidon: *LIMC* 7 s.v. Theseus 219–22.

70. 475–470 BC. Paris, Louvre G195. *ARV*² 381.174, 368, *Addenda*² 227. *LIMC* 7 s.v. Theseus 156*. Shapiro (1994: 109–17) reads Bacchylides 18 alongside representations of Theseus' deeds instead of his recognition.

71. Neck amphora attributed to the Shuvalov Painter, 430–420 BC. Saint Petersburg, State Hermitage Museum ST1599. *ARV*² 1209.48, *Addenda*² 346. *LIMC* 7 s.v. Theseus 162*.

72. 440–430 BC. Cambridge, Fitzwilliam Museum GR.25.1937. *CVA* Cambridge, Fitzwilliam Museum 2, 58–59. *LIMC* 7 s.v. Theseus 160*.

73. Aigeus: c. 470 BC, attributed to the Painter of Louvre G231, Cambridge, Fitzwilliam Museum GR.21.1937, *ARV*² 580.2. *CVA* Cambridge, Fitzwilliam Museum 2, 57–58. *LIMC* 7 s.v. Theseus 157*. Woman: 470–460 BC, attributed to Hermonax, Saint Petersburg, State Hermitage Museum, ST1692, *ARV*² 484.15, *Addenda*² 248. *LIMC* 7 s.v. Theseus 158*.

74. So-called network sandals: Morrow 1985: 58; Harrison 2000: 276.

75. Strauss 1993: 110.

76. The symposium and its vases: Lissarrague 1990.

77. Rhetoric and development of Athenian autochthony: Rosivach 1987; Loraux 1986, 2000; Hall 1997: 53–56; Blok 2009; Rader 2009.

78. Shapiro (1998) argues that the early Erichthonius myths are evidence of belief in autochthony earlier than the literary evidence suggests; cf. Parker (1987: 193–98) on Erichthonius.

79. Calame 1990: 440.

80. E.g., Stern 1967.

81. Medea and Theseus: Plut. *Theseus* 12; Apollodorus *Epitome* 1.6; Ovid *Metamorphoses* 7.398–424. These textual sources may be late, but Sourvinou-Inwood (1979) argues that a series of perplexing vase scenes showing Theseus attacking a female figure with a sword should be understood as depicting Medea (although one identifies the female figure as Aithra: *LIMC* 1 s.v. Aithra 25–45—if these confusing scenes do depict Aithra as victim, we would see an otherwise unknown myth of maternal discord emerging at the same time as an interest in Theseus' paternity). On the trope of the "evil stepmother" in the ancient world, see Watson 1995: esp. 20–91.

82. Sourvinou-Inwood (1979: esp. 18–28) argues that the Theseus myth conditions a complex serious of displacements, in which Theseus should be expected to commit patricide but in fact kills Medea instead of Aigeus (who is later killed indirectly): the story of Theseus' paternity is characterized by its displacements.

83. Lekythos, attributed to Hermonax, c. 460 BC, Palermo, Museo Nazionale V672, *ARV*² 490.119, 1655, *Addenda*² 249. *CVA* Palermo, Museo Nazionale 1, 3.1.C.11. *LIMC* 1 s.v.

Aithra I 10*. *Hydria*, attributed to the Eucharides Painter, c. 470 BC, London, British Museum E174, *ARV*² 229.39, *Addenda*² 199. *CVA* London, British Museum 5, 3.1.C.13. *LIMC* I s.v. Aithra I 3*.

84. *LIMC* I s.v. Aithra I 1–12. The earliest scene (Basel, Art Market, *ARV*² 186.48, *Addenda*² 188. *LIMC* I s.v. Aithra I 1*) dates to the early fifth century, but the theme picks up around 480 BC. A hydria attributed to the Syleus Painter has name inscriptions (Rome, Vatican 16554, *ARV*² 252.47, *Addenda*² 203. *LIMC* I s.v. Aithra I 2*). Erotic pursuits: Stewart 1995; Cohen 1996. Their political potential: Arafat 1997.

85. Women and the reproduction of nations: Yuval-Davis 1997: 26–38.

86. A series of scenes that seem to show Theseus attaching his mother also emerge at this time, but their interpretation is too complex to do justice to here. If they *do* show Aithra and Theseus (and Sourvinou-Inwood has tried to explain the "Aithra" figures as "Medea"), they exhibit an interest in maternal discord at precisely the same time as vase painters explore paternal concord. *LIMC* I s.v. Aithra I 25–43; discussion and bibliography: Sourvinou-Inwood 1979.

87. Departure: e.g., Harrison 2000: 271. Arrival: Neils 1987: 97.

88. Or expands Poseidon's power? Calame 1990: 257–58.

89. Sourvinou-Inwood 1979: 21.

90. Calame 1990: 259–60.

91. Euripides, *Hippolytus* 1431: 1283–84. Paternity in *Hippolytus*: Ebbott 2003: 85–108. Theseus as king: Davie 1982. Theseus in tragedy: Mills 1997. Only fragments of Euripides' *Aigeus* survive, but it seems to have hinged upon the drama of recognition: Strauss 1993: 111. The single vase that might show both Poseidon and Aigeus together with Theseus probably features Pittheus instead; amphora attributed to the Oinanthe Painter, 480–460 BC, London, British Museum E264. *ARV*² 579.1, *Addenda*² 262. *CVA* London, British Museum 3, 3.1.C.5. *LIMC* 7 s.v. Theseus 31*. Pittheus: Neils 1987: 106.

REFERENCES

Agard, W. R. 1928. "Theseus: A National Hero." *Classical Journal* 24 (2): 84–91.

Antonaccio, C. M. 1993. "The Archaeology of Ancestors." In *Cultural Poetics in Archaic Greece*, ed. C. Dougherty and L. Kurke, 46–70. Cambridge: Cambridge University Press.

Antonaccio, C. M. 1994. "Contesting the Past: Hero Cult, Tomb Cult, and Epic in Early Greece." *American Journal of Archaeology* 98 (3): 389–410.

Antonaccio, C. M. 1995. *An Archaeology of Ancestors: Tomb Cult and Hero Cult in Early Greece.* Lanham, MD: Rowman & Littlefield.

Arafat, K. W. 1996. "Theseus." In *The Oxford Classical Dictionary.* 3rd ed., ed. S. Hornblower and A. Spawforth, 1508–9. Oxford: Oxford University Press.

Arafat, K. W. 1997. "State of the Art—Art of the State: Sexual Violence and Politics in Late Archaic and Early Classical Vase-Painting." In *Rape in Antiquity*, ed. S. Deacy and K. F. Pierce, 97–122. London: Duckworth.

Barron, J. P. 1972. "New Light on Old Walls: The Murals of the Theseion." *Journal of Hellenic Studies* 92: 20–45.

Barron, J. P. 1980. "Bakchylides, Theseus and a Wooly Cloak." *Bulletin of the Institute of Classical Studies* 27 (1): 1–8.

Blok, J. H. 2009. "Gentrifying Genealogy: On the Genesis of the Athenian Authochthony Myth." In *Antike Mythen: Medien, Transformationen und Konstructionen*, ed. U. Dill and C. Walde, 251–75. Berlin: De Gruyter.

Boardman, J. 1991. "The Sixth-Century Potters and Painters of Athens and Their Public." In *Looking at Greek Vases*, ed. T. Rasmussen and N. Spivey, 79–102. Cambridge: Cambridge University Press.

Boardman, J. 2002. *The Archaeology of Nostalgia: How the Greeks Re-Created Their Mythical Past*. London: Thames & Hudson.

Boedeker, D. 1993. "Hero Cult and Politics in Herodotus: The Bones of Orestes." In *Cultural Poetics in Ancient Greece*, ed. L. Kurke and C. Dougherty, 164–77. Cambridge: Cambridge University Press.

Brelich, A. 1956. "Theseus e i suoi avversari." *Studi e materiali di storia delle religione* 27: 136–41.

Brown, C. G. 1991. "The Power of Aphrodite: Bacchylides 17, 10." *Mnemosyne* 44 (3–4): 327–35.

Burnett, A. P. 1985. *The Art of Bacchylides*. Cambridge, MA: Harvard University Press.

Butler, J. 1993. *Bodies That Matter: On the Discursive Limits of "Sex."* New York: Routledge.

Butler, J. 2006. *Gender Trouble: Feminism and the Subversion of Identity*. 3rd ed. New York: Routledge.

Buxton, R. 1994. *Imaginary Greece: The Contexts of Mythology*. Cambridge: Cambridge University Press.

Calame, C. 1990. *Thésée et l'imaginaire athénien*. Lausanne: Payot.

Calame, C. 2009. "Apollo in Delphi and in Delos: Poetic Performances Between Paean and Dithyramb." In *Apolline Politics and Poetics*, ed. L. Athanassaki, R. P. Martin, and J. F. Miller, 169–97. Athens: European Cultural Centre of Delphi.

Castriota, D. 1992. *Myth, Ethos and Actuality: Official Art in Fifth-Century Athens*. Madison: University of Wisconsin Press.

Christensen, K. A. 1984. "The Theseion: A Slave Refuge at Athens." *American Journal of Ancient History* 9 (1): 23–32.

Clark, C. 2003. "Minos' Touch and Theseus' Glare: Gestures in Bakkylides 17." *Harvard Studies in Classical Philology* 101: 129–53.

Cohen, A. 1996. "Portrayals of Abduction in Greek Art: Rape or Metaphor?." In *Sexuality in Ancient Art*, ed. N. B. Kampen, 117–35. Cambridge: Cambridge University Press.

Connor, W. R. 1970. "Theseus in Classical Athens." In *The Quest for Theseus*, ed. A. C. Ward, 143–74. London: Pall Mall.

Connor, W. R. 1993. "The Ionian Era of Athenian Civic Identity." *Proceedings of the American Philosophical Society* 137 (2): 194–206.

Danek, G. 2008. "Heroic and Athletic Contest in Bacchylides 17." *Wiener Studien* 121: 71–83.

Davie, J. N. 1982. "Theseus the King in Fifth-Century Athens." *Greece and Rome* 29 (1): 25–34.

Davies, G. 1985. "The Significance of the Handshake Motif in Classical Funerary Art." *American Journal of Archaeology* 89 (4): 627–40.

Ebbott, M. 2003. *Imagining Illegitimacy in Classical Greek Literature*. Lanham, MD: Lexington.

Ekroth, G. 2010. "Theseus and the Stone: The Iconographic and Ritual Contexts of a Greek Votive Relief in the Louvre." In *Divine Images and Human Imaginations in Ancient Greece and Rome*, ed. J. Mylonopoulos, 143–69. Leiden: Brill.

Fearn, D. 2007. *Bacchylides: Politics, Performance, Poetic Tradition*. Oxford: Oxford University Press.

Fowler, R. L. 1998. "Genealogical Thinking: Hesiod's *Catalogue*, and the Creation of the Hellenes." *Proceedings of the Cambridge Philological Society* 44: 1–19.

Garland, R. 1992. *Introducing New Gods*. London: Duckworth.

Gehrke, H.-J. 2001. "Myth, History, and Collective Identity: Uses of the Past in Ancient Greece and Beyond." In *The Historian's Craft in the Age of Herodotus*, ed. N. Luraghi, 286–313. Oxford: Oxford University Press.

Giesekam, G. 1977. "The Portrayal of Minos in Bacchylides 17." *Papers of the Liverpool Latin Seminar*: 237–52.

Glynn, R. 1981. "Herakles, Nereus and Triton: A Study of Iconography in Sixth Century Athens." *American Journal of Archaeology* 85 (2): 121–32.

Golden, M. 1986. "Names and Naming at Athens: Three Studies." *Echos du monde classique* 30: 245–69.

Gouschin, V. 1999. "Athenian Synoikism of the Fifth Century BC, or Two Stories of Theseus." *Greece and Rome* 46 (2): 168–87.

Hall, J. M. 1997. *Ethnic Identity in Greek Antiquity*. Cambridge: Cambridge University Press.

Hall, J. M. 2002. *Hellenicity: Between Ethnicity and Culture*. Chicago: University of Chicago Press.

Hamilton, R. 1984. "Sources for the Athenian Amphidromia." *Greek, Roman and Byzantine Studies* 25 (3): 243–51.

Harding, P. 2008. *The Story of Athens: The Fragments of the Local Chronicles of Athens*. London: Routledge.

Harrison, E. B. 2000. "Eumolpos Arrives in Athens." *Hesperia* 69 (3): 267–91.

Hobden, F. 2007. "Imagining Past and Present: A Rhetorical Strategy in Aeschines 3, *Against Ctesiphon*." *Classical Quarterly* 57 (2): 490–501.

Hurwit, J. 1985. *The Art and Culture of Early Greece, 1100–480 BC*. Ithaca, NY: Cornell University Press.

Jeanmaire, H. 1939. *Couroi et Courètes: Essai sur l'éducation spartiate et les rites d'adolescence dans l'antiquité hellénique*. Lille: Bibliothèque de l'Université.

Kearns, E. 1989. *The Heroes of Attica*. Institute of Classical Studies Bulletin Supplement 57. London: Institute of Classical Studies.

Kovacs, D. 2008. "And Baby Makes Three: Aegeus' Wife as Mother-to-Be of Theseus in Euripides' *Medea*." *Classical Philology* 103 (3): 298–304.

Kowalzig, B. 2007. *Singing for the Gods: Performances of Myth and Ritual in Archaic Greece.* Oxford: Oxford University Press.

Lissarrague, F. 1990. *The Aesthetics of the Greek Banquet: Images of Wine and Ritual.* Tr. A. Szegedy-Maszak. Princeton, NJ: Princeton University Press.

Loraux, N. 1986. *The Invention of Athens: The Funeral Oration in the Classical City.* Tr. A. Sheridan. Cambridge, MA: Harvard University Press.

Loraux, N. 2000. *Born of the Earth: Myth and Politics in Athens.* Tr. S. Stewart. Ithaca, NY: Cornell University Press.

Maehler, H. 1997. *Die Lieder des Bakchylides,* vol. 2: *Die Dithyramben und Fragmente.* Leiden: Brill.

Maehler, H. 2004. *Bacchylides: A Selection.* Cambridge: Cambridge University Press.

Mayor, A. 2000. *The First Fossil Hunters.* Princeton, NJ: Princeton University Press.

McCauley, B. 1998. "The Transfer of Hippodameia's Bones: A Historical Context." *The Classical Journal* 93 (3): 225–39.

Merkelbach, R. 1973. "Der Theseus des Bakchylides (Gedicht für ein attisches Epheben-fest)." *Zeitschrift für Papyrologie und Epigraphik* 12: 59–62.

Mikalson, J. D. 1986. "Zeus the Father and Heracles the Son in Tragedy." *Transactions of the American Philological Association* 116: 89–98.

Mills, S. 1997. *Theseus, Tragedy and the Athenian Empire.* Oxford: Clarendon.

Morrow, K. 1985. *Greek Footwear and the Dating of Sculpture.* Madison: University of Wisconsin Press.

Most, G. W. 2006. *Hesiod. Theogony, Works and Days, Testimonia.* Cambridge, MA: Harvard University Press.

Neils, J. 1987. *The Youthful Deeds of Theseus.* Rome: Bretschneider.

Ogden, D. 1997. "Rape, Adultery and Protection of Bloodlines in Classical Athens." In *Rape in Antiquity,* ed. S. Deacy and K. F. Pierce, 25–41. London: Duckworth.

Osborne, R. 2010. "Relics and Remains in an Ancient Greek World Full of Anthropomorphic Gods." *Past and Present,* supplement 5: *Relics and Remains:* 56–72.

Parker, R. 1987. "Myths of Early Athens." In *Interpretations of Greek Mythology,* ed. J. Bremmer, 187–214. London: Croom Helm.

Parker, R. 1996. *Athenian Religion: A History.* Oxford: Clarendon.

Pemberton, E. G. 1989. "The Dexiosis on Attic Gravestones." *Mediterranean Archaeology* 2: 45–50.

Perrin, B. 1914. *Plutarch. Lives: Theseus and Romulus; Lycurgus and Numa; Solon and Publicola.* Cambridge, MA: Harvard University Press.

Pieper, G. W. 1972. "Conflict of Character in Bacchylides' Ode 17." *Transactions of the American Philological Association* 103: 395–404.

Pritchett, W. K. 1979. *The Greek State at War,* vol. 3: *Religion.* Berkeley: University of California Press.

Rader, R. 2009. "'And Whatever It Is, It Is You': The Autochthonous Self in Aeschylus' *Seven Against Thebes*." *Arethusa* 42 (1): 1–44.

Roisman, J. 2005. *The Rhetoric of Manhood: Masculinity in the Attic Orators*. Berkeley: University of California Press.

Rosivach, V. J. 1987. "Autochthony and the Athenians." *Classical Quarterly* 37 (2): 294–306.

Scafuro, A. C. 1994. "Witnessing and False Witnessing: Proving Citizenship and Kin Identity in Fourth-Century Athens." In *Athenian Identity and Civic Ideology*, ed. A. L. Boegehold and A. C. Scafuro, 156–98. Baltimore: Johns Hopkins University Press.

Segal, C. 1979. "The Myth of Bacchylides 17: Heroic Quest and Heroic Identity." *Eranos* 77: 23–37.

Shapiro, H. A. 1982. "Theseus, Athens, and Troizen." *Archäologischer Anzeiger*: 291–97.

Shapiro, H. A. 1991. "Theseus: Aspects of the Hero in Archaic Greece." In *New Perspectives in Early Greek Art*, ed. D. Buitron-Oliver, 123–39. Hanover, NH: University Press of New England.

Shapiro, H. A. 1992. "Theseus in Kimonian Athens: The Iconography of Empire." *Mediterranean Historical Review* 7 (1): 29–49.

Shapiro, H. A. 1994. *Myth into Art: Poet and Painter in Classical Greece*. London: Routledge.

Shapiro, H. A. 1998. "Autochthony and the Visual Arts in Fifth-Century Athens." In *Democracy, Empire, and the Arts in Fifth-Century Athens*, ed. D. Boedeker and K. Raaflaub, 127–52. Cambridge, MA: Harvard University Press.

Shapiro, H. A. 2003. "Fathers and Sons, Men and Boys." In *Coming of Age in Ancient Greece: Images of Childhood from the Classical Past*, ed. J. Neils, 85–111. New Haven, CT: Yale University Press.

Sourvinou-Inwood, C. 1979. *Theseus as Son and Stepson: A Tentative Illustration of the Greek Mythological Mentality*. Institute of Classical Studies Bulletin, supplement 41. London: Institute of Classical Studies.

Stern, J. 1967. "The Structure of Bacchylides' Ode 17." *Revue belge de philologie et d'histoire* 45 (1): 40–47.

Stewart, A. 1995. "Rape?." In *Pandora: Women in Classical Greece*, ed. E. Reeder, 74–90. Princeton, NJ: Princeton University Press.

Strauss, B. S. 1993. *Fathers and Sons in Athens: Ideology and Society in the Era of the Peloponnesian War*. London: Routledge.

Thomas, R. 1989. *Oral Tradition and Written Record in Classical Athens*. Cambridge: Cambridge University Press.

Tyrell, W. B., and F. S. Brown. 1991. *Athenian Myths and Institutions: Words in Action*. New York: Oxford University Press.

van Gennep, A. 1960. *The Rites of Passage*. Tr. M. B. Vizedom and G. L. Caffee. London: Routledge & Kegan Paul (original edition 1907).

van Hook, L. 1945. *Isocrates*, vol. 3. London: Heinemann.

van Oeveren, C. 1999. "Bacchylides Ode 17: Theseus and the Delian League." In *One Hundred Years of Bacchylides*, ed. I. Pfeijffer and S. Slings, 31–42. Amsterdam: VU University Press.

Vidal-Naquet, P. 1986. *The Black Hunter: Forms of Thought and Forms of Society in the Greek World.* Tr. A. Szegedy-Maszak. Baltimore: Johns Hopkins University Press.

von den Hoff, R. 2010. "Media for Theseus, or: The Different Images of the Athenian Polis-hero." In *Intentional History: Spinning time in Ancient Greece,* ed. L. Foxhall, H.-J. Gehrke, and N. Luraghi, 161–88. Stuttgart: Franz Steiner.

Walker, H. J. 1995. *Theseus and Athens.* New York: Oxford University Press.

Watson, P. A. 1995. *Ancient Stepmothers: Myth, Misogyny and Reality.* Leiden: Brill.

Wilson, P. 2007. "Performance in the *Pythion*: The Athenian Thargelia." In *The Greek Theatre and Festivals: Documentary Studies,* ed. P. Wilson, 150–82. Oxford: Oxford University Press.

Wind, R. 1972. "Myth and History in Bacchylides Ode 18." *Hermes* 100 (4): 511–23.

Woodford, S. 1974. "More Light on Old Walls: The Theseus of the Centauromachy in the Theseion." *Journal of Hellenic Studies* 94: 158–65.

Yuval-Davis, N. 1997. *Gender and Nation.* London: Sage.

CHAPTER 4

The Founder's Shrine and
the Foundation of Ai Khanoum

RACHEL MAIRS

De Delphes a l'Oxus

They haven't seen for centuries such lovely gifts in Delphi
as those that had been sent to them by both of the two brothers,
the rival Ptolemaic kings. But after they'd received them,
the priests began worrying about the oracle.
They'll need all their experience—how to compose astutely:
which of the two, of such as these two, will have to be offended.
So they hold a meeting secretly at night
To talk about the family affairs of the Lagidae.

But look, the envoys are back. They bid goodbye.
They are returning to Alexandria, they say, and they
don't want an oracle at all. And the priests hear this with joy
(and as it is well understood, they keep the splendid presents),
but they are at the same time completely bewildered,
not understanding what this abrupt indifference means.
For they don't know that yesterday the envoys received grave news.
The oracle was pronounced in Rome; it was there the deal was made.

Constantine P. Cavafy, "Envoys from Alexandria"[1]

Delphi was rarely, if ever, a significant power broker in the political affairs of the Hellenistic kingdoms. The historical circumstances of the foundation of most "new" cities of the Hellenistic East also left little room for a Delphic connection in their foundation narratives. Delphi and its oracle are conspicuously absent from what "histories" we have of these cities' foundations or of later traditions concerning them.[2] Rather than colonies sent out by cities of the Aegean with oracular sanction, these Alexandrias, Seleuceias, and Antiochs (or Apameas, Berenices, and Arsinoes) were notionally the creations of the royal dynasties of Graeco-Macedonian origin that achieved political power in the eastern Mediterranean from the late fourth century BC. Many of these "new" eponymous Hellenistic city foundations were, in fact, accretions onto existing settlements, but the act of renaming them and reshaping their urban landscape gave them new, Greek foundation myths.

The ancient name of the city of Ai Khanoum, in eastern Bactria (modern northeastern Afghanistan), is not known. Various attempts have been made to claim it as an Alexandria or as a Eukratideia, named for the Graeco-Bactrian king Eukratides. I will discuss these modern "foundation myths" in the concluding part of this chapter. The first part of my discussion will consider whether Delphi and its oracle held symbolic significance in the life of the Hellenistic city of Ai Khanoum and whether Delphi came to play a role in the city's narratives of its own foundation. The evidence that allows us to approach this question at all is archaeological and epigraphic: Ai Khanoum does not appear in any ancient narrative source. A structure within the central complex of official buildings at Ai Khanoum has been identified, plausibly, as the shrine of the city's founder. In this shrine, one of the very few Greek inscriptions from the site was discovered; it bears the text of the Delphic maxims and an additional statement that these had been copied down carefully at Delphi itself and brought here to the *temenos* of Kineas (the putative founder). This suggests that the citizens of Ai Khanoum, in the first part of the third century BC, were aware of Delphi's existence and its importance to Greek culture and identity and that they saw the shrine of the city's founder as an appropriate place to state a Delphic connection. I will not argue that the inhabitants of third-century Ai Khanoum considered their city to be a Delphic foundation in the conventional sense, a colony sent out from Greece upon oracular consultation; the inscription does not claim this. But renovations to the city's urban fabric during the course of the third century—and the changing position of the inscription stone itself within the shrine sanctuary—suggest that the notion of a connection with Delphi became bound up in public discourse with the assertion of Greek identity and with the city's ideological "myth" of its origins.

Ai Khanoum and Hellenistic Bactria

Bactria, marginal and marginalized, has tended to be positioned outside the mainstream of scholarship on the Hellenistic world because of its geographical distance from the Greek states of the Mediterranean littoral and because of the relative dearth of written sources, whether these be literary, epigraphic, or documentary (Fig. 4.1).[3] Even identifying the precise geographical boundaries of ancient Bactria, as Achaemenid province or as Graeco-Bactrian state, is rather difficult. Although some ancient and modern historians treat the river Oxus (modern Amu-darya) as the boundary between Bactria and Sogdiana, Bactria is bound together by the Oxus, not divided by it.[4] This can be seen most clearly in terms of material culture. The political frontier between Bactria and Sogdiana seems sometimes to have been close to the river, but more often a good distance to the north, in the mountains of the watershed

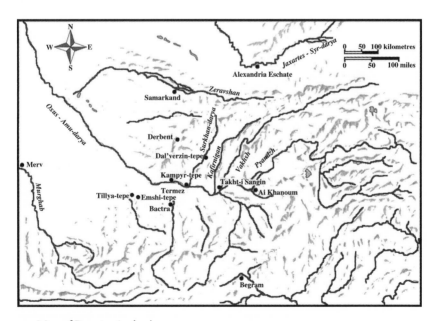

4.1. Map of Bactria. Author's own.

between the Oxus and the Zeravshan.[5] "Archaeological Bactria" as a region therefore corresponds roughly to the catchment area of the middle-upper river Oxus, the present-day borderlands of Afghanistan and Tajikistan/ Uzbekistan, taking in some level of control over the resources (minerals, pasturage) of its mountainous hinterland. Ai Khanoum lies in eastern Bactria, at the junction of the Oxus with a southern tributary, the Kokcha. Its location, as will be discussed below, gave it control over an agricultural plain and the products (in particular, lapis lazuli) of the Badakshan mountains.[6] Ai Khanoum, which was excavated from 1964 to 1978, is published in the series *Fouilles d'Aï Khanoum*, consisting at present of nine volumes.[7] There are, however, many features that make the site's publication, and subsequent analyses of its material, problematic.[8] I will give special attention to issues of chronology in my discussion of the shrine of Kineas and its inscription (see below).

Despite what frequently appears in print (including in the Barrington Atlas), we have little or no firm evidence on the ancient names of even the most important excavated sites of Hellenistic Bactria-Sogdiana, such as Ai Khanoum and Takht-i Sangin (site of the "Temple of the Oxus").[9] The recent emergence of documentary texts of various periods from Bactria in Aramaic (Achaemenid–early Hellenistic), Greek (Hellenistic), and Bactrian (Kushan) offers the possibility that it may one day be possible to relate the place names mentioned in these to locations on the ground, but the data available at present are not sufficient for this.[10] The circumstances of the "foundation" of the excavated Hellenistic-period sites in the region are also difficult to disentangle. Many will have started out as "Alexander foundations"—but what this generally amounts to in Bactria is a garrison or "refounded" town in the vicinity or directly on the site of a preexisting, well-established settlement.[11]

Given the lack of literary or historical evidence—and still less, *local* literary or historical evidence—for the ancient name of Ai Khanoum, its foundation, and the place that this occupied in the city's own traditions, it might seem an unpromising subject for a discussion about foundation myths and civic and cultural identity. But some questions about the foundation of Ai Khanoum can be approached productively, using the available archaeological and epigraphic evidence, without second-guessing too much the motives and self-identifications of its Hellenistic-period citizens. The first concerns the *temenos* of Kineas in the heart of the city's complex of public buildings, containing the shrine of the city's founder and the Delphic inscription introduced above. I would like to contrast this early third-century literal and figurative enshrinement of the city's Greek colonial origins with the archaeological evidence for significant Achaemenid and Bronze Age settlement and economic exploitation of the region. The evidence for such settlement in the city's hinterland is very well documented, even if it has been somewhat neglected in modern scholarship, in contrast to the more celebrated remains of the city. I will also suggest that the city-site of Ai Khanoum itself is almost certain to have borne an Achaemenid settlement and an early post-Achaemenid settlement of the late fourth century BC. While the "Greek settlement" of Ai Khanoum represented a significant departure from earlier foundations and likely brought new local power structures and systems of economic exploitation, the archaeological survey evidence indicates a broad continuity in population and in administration.

Although we have little evidence for any oral histories or dominant views of the foundation of Ai Khanoum among its Hellenistic-period citizens, the issues I will discuss also highlight "competing myths" in several senses. The archaeological survey data from Ai Khanoum's hinterland demonstrate the long history of settlement and centralized management of the district and its resources. The introduction of a Graeco-Macedonian (military) settler population, however, represents some kind of departure, and this settler population and their descendants likely drew their notions of their identity, civic and cultural, from this new foundation, rather than from the long local history that preceded it.[12] With reference to the shrine of Kineas, I will argue that an initial structure of the late fourth century—perhaps built at the time of Kineas' death, or perhaps a small shrine that predates his death and was adapted to contain his tomb—was enlarged and renovated in the first part of the third century as part of a wider remodeling of the city's whole architectural program and simultaneously reconfiguring or reinforcing common notions about its civic identity. I will suggest that the commissioning of the inscription of Delphic maxims belongs to this later program of renovation, in the second, third, or subsequent generations of the Greek city, rather than to the shrine's initial phases, and that it therefore represents a recasting of the city's "foundation myth" with the addition of a Delphic connection, albeit a tenuous one. I would also suggest, tentatively, that this later "Greek" generation of Ai Khanoum, which must have been the product of extensive intermarriage with local populations, will have felt some need to make just such a statement and reinforcement of their Greek colonial identity. Finally, the modern attempts to discover Ai Khanoum's ancient name, or clarify who actually founded the site and when, compete with one another as well as struggling with the reluctance of the historical sources to give us any story of the foundation (and, indeed, subsequent history) of Ai Khanoum.

Ai Khanoum and Eastern Bactria

The city of Ai Khanoum, the architectural remains of which I will discuss in greater detail in the following section, was placed in some much-needed geographical and chronological context by the implementation, from 1974 to 1978, of a field survey project in eastern Bactria, with its focus on the immediate agricultural hinterland of the city (the "plaine d'Aï Khanoum" or "plaine de Dasht-i Qala"). The results of this survey revealed much about the nature and extent of long-term settlement and irrigation in the region—such as its dense Bronze Age occupation—and the economic and agricultural foundations upon which Ai Khanoum was built.[13]

The settlement history of the region is, as demonstrated by the survey, of considerable chronological depth and its connections with regions beyond eastern Bactria long-standing.[14] The major fortified site in the vicinity of Ai Khanoum before the Macedonian conquest was some three kilometers to the north, at Kohna Qala (the "Ville Ronde"), a citadel on the left bank of the Oxus with two concentric surrounding walls, which are still visible on satellite photographs. Its earliest occupation dates to the period when Bactria was a Persian satrapy. Evidence for such Iron Age or Achaemenid settlement occurs across the survey area as a whole. The survey teams found that river courses and climatic conditions did not appear to have altered appreciably over the periods investigated and that canals tended to follow the lines of earlier irrigation channels as a matter of course. The plain of Ai Khanoum does appear to have experienced an intensification in irrigation works and increase in population corresponding to the period of the Greek settlement, but this built upon preexisting systems of land management of some complexity, which required a degree of central planning and organization of labor for their maintenance. Some Achaemenid Aramaic documents, part of the central archive of the satrap at Bactra (the provincial capital of Bactria), recently given a preliminary publication, reveal the wide reach and efficiency of the administration of Bactria under the Achaemenids.[15] Some of these documents will be discussed in my conclusion.

Among the advantages and attractions of the site of Ai Khanoum—as well as the reasons that eastern Bactria held such importance to the Indus civilization, the Achaemenids, and the Greeks—are control over routes of trade, invasion, and pastoral transhumance, both north and south of the Oxus, by river and on land; the proximity of the mountains of Badakshan, the only exploited source of lapis lazuli in the ancient world (some seventy-five kilograms of unworked blocks of lapis lazuli were found in the Treasury at Ai Khanoum)[16] and of other precious metals and minerals; the agricultural potential, with irrigation, of the flatland between the rivers and the hills; and various natural protuberances that might readily be fortified, such as the Ai Khanoum "citadel" and "acropolis" as well as the "Ville Ronde" to the north. Lapis lazuli occurs from a very early period in regions far from Bactria and appears to be a key reason for the establishment of the Indus civilization outpost at Shortughai.[17]

Given the evidence of such extensive earlier occupation and exploitation of resources in the city's hinterland and the site's strategic advantages, some Achaemenid settlement was likely on the site of the later Hellenistic city at Ai Khanoum.[18] The substantial renovations that the city underwent during its Graeco-Bactrian occupation (discussed in the following section) and the relative lack of excavation and survey on the acropolis and citadel (the areas with the greatest strategic advantages) mean that substantial material traces of any such Achaemenid occupation have not been uncovered. Possibly, some architectural elements of the Hellenistic city are reused pieces from its predecessor.[19]

As for the actual circumstances of the city's Hellenistic foundation—scholarly debates on which I will discuss below—all we can do is point to the historical evidence on the Graeco-Macedonian military settlements left in the region by Alexander,[20] even though Ai Khanoum is not among the settlements and garrisons mentioned by the Alexander historians (for example, Bactra: Arrian 3.29.1; Marakanda: Arrian 4.5.2, Curtius 7.6.10; Peukelaotis: Arrian 4.28.6; Alexandria Eschate: Arrian 4.4.1). Some common, and significant, themes among these foundation stories are that they are garrison settlements of de-mobbed Greek and Macedonian soldiers, often implanted in the citadels of existing towns or fortified places, alongside existing settlements and populations: the verb *sunoikizein* is used on several occasions to refer to the mixed local-Greek character of the settlements. These very first "colonies," as might be expected, have not been traced archaeologically. Probably they cannot be, or at least cannot be materially differentiated from the earlier settlements to which they adhered. Any substantial architectural remains of "Greek" presence are later, and they reflect the establishment of a more permanent colonial community. The initial settlers seem to have hoped and expected to be able to leave Bactria; on two occasions, they revolted and attempted to return west. These revolts were suppressed bloodily by Alexander and his successors.[21] Their remnants, along with subsequent generations, were forced, or were committed, to stay.

Several points suggest that the later "origin myths" of the Graeco-Bactrian population will have been more or less those of the Alexander historians, who, despite their references to the longer settlement history and mixed population of the garrison-settlements, still regard them as foundations of Alexander. Alexander had some ideological importance to the subsequent "Greek" rulers of Bactria. Around the second quarter of the second century BC, the Graeco-Bactrian king Agathocles reproduced the image of Alexander in his series of "pedigree coins," which trace his political lineage.[22] An ivory carving from Takht-i Sangin depicts a possible Alexander-Heracles wearing a lion-skin headdress.[23] It may also be argued that Alexander, or his immediate successors in the East, is the only likely candidate as a founder figure for both individual settlements in Bactria and the Graeco-Bactrian state as a whole. Unlike other regions of the Hellenistic world—such as Egypt, where open communications and opportunities for jobs and land encouraged ongoing Greek immigration throughout the Hellenistic period—Bactria probably had a cessation of any incoming, fresh settler population by the mid-third century BC, at the latest. The external political relations and internal configuration of Bactria-Sogdiana from the late fourth to the late third century BC are difficult to disentangle, but they all point to a decisive political break between Bactria and the other Hellenistic states to the west by the mid-third century. Lerner argues persuasively that the key period for Graeco-Bactrian, as for Parthian, autonomy from the Seleucid Empire was the mid-third century, when the Third Syrian War (c. 246–241 BC) and the war between Seleucus II and Antiochus Hierax (c. 240 to before 236 BC) effectively prevented the Seleucids from asserting their authority over the increasingly powerful and independent Diodotids.[24] The Graeco-Macedonian "colonial" population of Bactria could therefore point to common founder figures among Alexander, his Successors, and his generals and satraps in Bactria, but not to any more recent founder from the Greek world to the west. Although it therefore seems likely that Alexander played some important role in the Greek inhabitants of Ai Khanoum's concept of who they were and where they came from, the lack of epigraphic reference to or artistic representation of Alexander at

Ai Khanoum means that this is unfortunately as far as this argument can proceed.

Kineas and His *Temenos*: Ai Khanoum and Delphi

In addition to an extramural necropolis, the city of Ai Khanoum had two mausoleums within its walls (Fig. 4.2). Both consisted of vaults containing multiple burials, topped by a small shrine. The earliest of these two mausoleums is in the sanctuary of Kineas, the city's probable founder. The second mausoleum has received comparatively little attention and has not been published fully

4.2. Plan of Ai Khanoum. Author's own.

in the incomplete series *Fouilles d'Aï Khanoum*. It dates to the mid-third century BC.[25] The construction of an impressive family tomb with a stone vault within the walls of the city, at a time when Bactria was asserting its independence from the Seleucid Empire and Ai Khanoum was undergoing substantial renovations, suggests the tomb of a powerful local dynasty, perhaps the family of a governor, whose fortunes were on the rise in a newly autonomous Bactria.

The tomb-shrine in the sanctuary of Kineas is earlier than this second mausoleum by some decades, and the question of precisely how much earlier it is has implications for the date and nature of the foundation of the Hellenistic city at Ai Khanoum and for possible evolutions in the foundation myths of its citizens. This tomb took the form of a small chapel or shrine, set on a raised platform within a walled enclosure.[26] Four individuals were buried underneath this chapel, two in stone sarcophagi and two in wooden coffins. The main burial was the earliest and was linked to the upper room through an aperture and a conduit to receive liquid offerings poured down into the coffin. No other burials were given this kind of provision for cult offerings; it therefore seems likely that this individual was the one in whose honor the shrine was constructed and that the others were his family. Since, as will be discussed below, the earliest construction phases of this monumental tomb with its shrine date back to the very beginning of the life of the city, even if Kineas was not the founder of Ai Khanoum, he was certainly a very prominent early citizen.

The inscription states that one Klearchos had copied down the famous sayings of wise men from Delphi and had brought them here to be set up in the *temenos* of Kineas. A small sample of these wise sayings is preserved on the left-hand side of the inscription. The preserved portion of the inscription was the socketed base of a larger stone text that survives only in small fragments, only one of which bears further legible text:

[. . .]
ε[ὐλόγει πάντας]
φιλόσοφ[ος γίνου]
[. . .]

Ἀνδρῶν τοι σοφὰ ταῦτα παλαιοτέρων ἀνάκει[τα]ι
ῥήματα ἀριγνώτων Πυθοῖ ἐν ἠγαθέαι·
ἔνθεν ταῦτ[α] Κλέαρχος ἐπιφραδέως ἀναγράψας
εἴσατο τηλαυγῆ Κινέου ἐν τεμένει.

Παῖς ὢν κόσμιος γίνου,
ἡβῶν ἐγκρατής,
μέσος δίκαιος,
πρεσβύτης εὔβουλος,
τελευτῶν ἄλυπος.

[. . .] speak well of everyone; be a lover of wisdom [. . .][27]
These wise sayings of men of old, the maxims of renowned men, are enshrined in the holy Pytho [i.e., at Delphi]. There, Klearchos copied them conscientiously, and set them up here in the sanctuary of Kineas, blazing them from afar.

As a child, be well-behaved; as a young man, self-controlled; in middle age, be just; as an elder, be of good counsel; and when you come to the end, be without grief.

Although discussions of this inscription (the fundamental study is Louis Robert's 1968 article "De Delphes à l'Oxus") have emphasized the connection between Delphi and Greek colonization, this inscription is not the foundation story of a colony sent out with oracular sanction or endorsement, and we have no evidence that this kind of Delphic foundation myth existed for Ai Khanoum at all. The actual mechanisms of the foundation of the various Greek garrison-settlements in Central Asia have been discussed above. The question is whether we should consider the Hellenistic-period city and citizens of Ai Khanoum to have had any notion of this archaic and classical Greek model of Delphi-sanctioned colonization and whether the Delphic connection in the inscription from the *temenos* of Kineas was as resonant for them in this regard as it is for us. I would argue cautiously that it was, but that the third- and second-century inhabitants of Ai Khanoum can only have been very aware of what kind of Greek colony they were not.

Although the inscription from the *temenos* of Kineas makes a connection between Delphi and the city's *oikist*—if this is what Kineas was—the reader is under no illusion that this connection was direct. Kineas did not go to Delphi; Klearchos did. And we are not told that Klearchos consulted the oracle but that he copied the maxims. Nor are we told that his original business at Delphi had anything to do with Ai Khanoum, whatever later use its citizens made of the notes he took there. Robert proposed to identify the Klearchos of the inscription with the philosopher Klearchos of Soloi, a pupil of Aristotle who had eastern interests, and this identification has passed into the literature

more or less without further examination.[28] If this was the historical Klearchos of Soloi, this would put the date of his hypothetical tour of the East and
visit to Ai Khanoum in the final two decades of the fourth century BC or
perhaps the beginning of the third. This would, in turn, have obvious implications for our understanding of the date of the foundation of the Greek city
and for the date at which the Delphic maxims were initially received there,
whatever their later use in the remodeled shrine of Kineas in the course of the
third century BC. But as it has more recently been stated with refreshing di-
rectness, we know nothing of who this Klearchos truly was, and there is nothing
to support the view that he was the historical Klearchos of Soloi, or that the
philosopher Klearchos even traveled in the East.[29] The Klearchos of the inscription from the *temenos* of Kineas should be, until we gain evidence to the contrary, a citizen of Ai Khanoum, and his visit to Delphi fits within the growing
body of evidence that third-century Bactria remained in constant interaction
with the western Hellenistic world.

As it happens, the shrine of Kineas is one of the few institutions at Ai
Khanoum whose architectural history can plausibly be traced back to the
late fourth century BC. The architectural form of the shrine, like that of the
city's major temple,[30] with its stepped podium, is another connection to a
hypothetical Achaemenid-period settlement on the site of the later Ai Khanoum, a settlement that, I would argue, must have existed. I restrict my
remarks here to the shrine and its chronology relative to the structures surrounding it. Ai Khanoum was not a planned settlement constructed according to a grid plan but underwent a couple of major phases of construction
and renovation between the early third and mid-second century BC. The
shrine of Kineas is in the heart of the lower city, within a complex of public
buildings accessed through a monumental set of propylaea and behind the
city's main temple. But the shrine predates all these structures in their excavated forms.[31] The position of the shrine also seems to have had some influence on the layout of the city's administrative quarter, in its form of the first
half of the third century, where the approach to the main courtyard visibly
turns to "avoid" the shrine.[32]

Lerner's 2003–4 article "Correcting the Early History of Ay Kanom"
aims to straighten out the relative chronology of Ai Khanoum's various institutions and their internal periodization, with particular attention to ceramic
sequences established subsequent to the initial published reports. My remarks
here are confined to a few points about the architectural phases of the shrine
of Kineas, and the date and changing physical position of the inscription.[33]

The crucial period for our purposes is that of Stage II of the shrine of Kineas, contemporary to Ceramic Period IV. This is conventionally dated to c. 260–220 BC, with a proposed revision by Lerner to c. 210–170 BC.[34] Stage II was the period at which an initial structure of the late fourth century BC, atop the three-stepped podium derivative of Achaemenid architecture, was completely renovated and given a new terrace and a much more spacious shrine—and an inscription of Delphic maxims. This renovation coincided with a vast architectural program throughout the city, including the construction of the great courtyard of the neighboring administrative quarter and several other buildings. The stone of the inscription was found reused as a pedestal in Stage IV of the shrine, with the inscribed face turned in toward the wall.

Lerner argues against Robert's (1968) dating of the inscription to the first quarter of the third century on several grounds, including that the paleographical criteria used by Robert are not sufficiently precise. I would prefer still to give considerable weight to paleographical dating criteria, especially now that the Aramaic and Greek documentary texts from Bactria—which may be dated according to royal names and dating formulas—demonstrate that Bactrian cursive hands were all but identical to contemporary hands from documents found in Egypt.[35] The association of the inscription with the building program of Stage II, however, still throws up problems, and I do not propose to relocate this to the early third century in order to follow Robert's dating. A date toward the mid-third century would, however, both accommodate Robert's paleographical analysis and accord with the established dating of Ceramic Period IV to c. 260–220 BC. My limited acquaintance with the ceramic record does not permit me to engage more actively in the debate between the high and low chronologies for Period IV; I refer the reader to the sources already cited for further discussion.

The precise, absolute date of the inscription and of the building program in which it assumed a prominent role is not crucial to my argument. More important is that both date to after the initial "foundation" of the Greek city of Ai Khanoum over its Achaemenid predecessor and after the first phase of the founder's shrine. This renovation represented an occasion on which the city took the opportunity to give new prominence to, and a possible new twist on, the life of its founder and the early life of the city, at a time when the city as a whole was subject to a remodeling of its urban landscape (and at which it presumably had the prosperity to finance this remodeling). The inscription was not a direct product of the foundation but a product of new ways of viewing the foundation.

Previous analyses of the shrine of Kineas and its inscription of Delphic maxims have owed much to the better-documented cases of archaic and classical Greek colonies, where the consultation of the Delphic oracle often figures prominently in foundation myths. As noted above, the circumstances of the foundation of Ai Khanoum were very different from those of such earlier colonies sent out by Greek cities in the Mediterranean (it will have begun its life as a Graeco-Macedonian garrison in an existing settlement), and the Delphic inscription from Ai Khanoum does not outline any account of the city's origins in which the Delphic oracle played a part. If this inscription represents a later addition to the preexisting founder shrine, however, it is possible that some Delphic connection was constructed as an accretion onto an existing foundation myth and that this happened only after the first generation of the city's Greek colonists had died. Here, we find another reason to make the Klearchos of the inscription a citizen of Ai Khanoum and not the philosopher of the late fourth century. For Klearchos of Soloi to have brought the Delphic maxims to Ai Khanoum, these would need to have been recorded and handed down in some other form before they were carved into the inscription in the *temenos* of Kineas decades later. A more agnostic approach to the identity of Klearchos liberates us from these chronological restrictions, and we are free to suppose that the journey to Delphi and the commissioning of the inscription were not so widely separated in time. Klearchos' journey may not have been solely or principally an Ai Khanoum "embassy" to Delphi in origin or in reception, but back at Ai Khanoum, his personal copying of the maxims could have been regarded as a kind of consultation by proxy, an attempt to give the founder—and his foundation—a connection with Delphi that they did not have in any literal sense.

Mints and Monograms

Material from the *temenos* of Kineas feeds into another debate on the foundation, status, and ancient name of Ai Khanoum. This particular argument draws on evidence for the location of a mint at Ai Khanoum; for the association of a particular monogram with this mint; and for the deduction of the ancient name of Ai Khanoum from this monogram.

The sarcophagus of the earliest, principal burial at the shrine (of the late fourth or early third century BC) was sealed with burned bricks, many of which bear a monogram consisting of a circular frame containing a delta-like triangle with a semicircle on its base.[36] This same monogram appears on a series of silver coins struck around 285–280 BC in a Bactrian workshop by Antiochus in the name of his father, Seleucus, and in his own name as viceroy of the eastern provinces of the Seleucid Empire.[37]

On the face of it, the identification of these two monograms offers an opportunity to deduce the ancient name of Ai Khanoum, or to say something about its position under the Seleucids, but it is doubtful that the monogram on the coins relates specifically to Ai Khanoum. That Ai Khanoum was the location of a mint has been argued from finds of bronze flans at the site,[38] but it was not the principal royal mint of Bactria.[39] There is no evidence for the minting of silver coinage, such as that which bears the relevant monogram, at Ai Khanoum; and the issues with the monogram occur more widely across Bactria. The majority, if not all, must still be attributed to a main royal mint at Bactra.[40] As for the appearance of the monogram in question on the bricks from the main burial at the shrine of Kineas, we are not in a position to say much about what these represent. The cautious argument presented by Bernard in the initial volume of *Fouilles d'Aï Khanoum*[41] is still about as far as we can reasonably take this material. Bernard suggests that the monogram represents an official in charge of brick production. He mentions the flans and evidence that coins were minted at Ai Khanoum, and he then tentatively postulates a connection between the brick and the coin marks. The presence of this mark—one made up of simple geometric shapes or letters, on different media, of different dates—does not presuppose any real connection between them.

It seems unlikely that the monogram represents the name of the city itself, even if it were the case that it derived from a mint or other authority at Ai Khanoum. One might read a delta and an omega, but these do not allow us to reconstruct a plausible name. Narain suggests a Dionysopolis, possibly later renamed Diodoteia or Diodotopolis.[42] There is no evidence for a Dionysopolis in the region, and Diodotid rule in Bactria, from the mid-third century, postdates the main burial in the shrine of Kineas and, of course, Antiochus' vice-regency and minting activities in the region. We do not know if we should be reading the monogram alphabetically; but if we should be doing so, we do not know whether we should be looking for the name of a person or of a place.

The brick and coin marks, in conclusion, do not lead us toward finding a name for Ai Khanoum or toward establishing its political status in the early third century. What this debate does illuminate rather well is the nature of

the modern search—often desperate—for a foundation myth and civic identity for Ai Khanoum.

"Alexandria Oxeiana": Modern Foundation Myths

As a coda to my discussion of the processes by which Ai Khanoum was
founded and of how its foundation was conceptualized by its later citizens,
I would like to consider some modern scholarly foundation myths of Ai Khanoum. I do not mean to suggest by my use of the term "myth" that these
constructions are utterly fantastical, but they are drawn up in the face of very
limited evidence and deserve to be problematized. In identifying Ai Khanoum as an "Alexandria," more is at stake than simply discovering its ancient
name. Naming it as an eponymous Graeco-Macedonian foundation may im-
pose certain preconceptions about what—politically, culturally—this means.[43]
As I hope the archaeological evidence has demonstrated, Ai Khanoum was
never a new, planned Greek colonial city of the same kind as Alexandria-by-
Egypt and as perhaps few, if any, of the eastern Alexandrias ever were. We
have no direct evidence that Ai Khanoum was an Alexandria, a Seleuceia, an
Antiocheia, or a Eukratidia; and we have no evidence that Alexander, Seleucus, or Antiochus was ever present at the site. The only figure in the city's
very early history whom we know by name is Kineas, and even his position
and identity are elusive. Ai Khanoum remains, for the present, the only ex-
tensively excavated major Bactrian settlement site of the Hellenistic period.
This has given it an undue prominence in the scholarly literature—it was an
important regional center of eastern Bactria, but this is all—and meant that
the details of its foundation and the question of its ancient name(s) have sometimes been argued with more enthusiasm than care.

There are no definite references to a city on the site of Ai Khanoum by
any Greek or Roman historian, and there are no inscriptions from the site itself that give its ancient name. Schlumberger's early hope that the excavations
might resolve this question remains unrealized.[44] Nevertheless, there have been
various attempts to identify the city, in its Hellenistic form, as an eponymous
foundation of Alexander, Seleucus, or Antiochus, or to argue that it was later
named after the Graeco-Bactrian king Eukratides.[45] The archaeological evidence, as already discussed, indicates that the earliest elements of the "Greek"
city were constructed in the late fourth century on the site of a probable Achaemenid predecessor.[46] This indicates that Hellenistic Ai Khanoum had its

origins in a garrison established by either Alexander, his generals, or one of his immediate successors, on the site or in the neighborhood of an Achaemenid regional center. Ai Khanoum may later have been renamed after King Eukratides, in the first half of the second century BC.[47]

Unlike other cities in Bactria that may more plausibly be identified as Alexandrias on the basis of the topographical information in the historical accounts of Alexander's campaigns in the region, the case that Ai Khanoum was a named Alexandria is not an especially strong one.[48] Bosworth has proposed that in 328 BC, Alexander conquered eastern Bactria, an itinerary not given in the extant histories, and crossed the river Oxus not far from Ai Khanoum, which he may have noted or marked as a likely settlement site.[49] Bernard suggests, more plausibly, that the site received attention from one of Alexander's officers and may have been garrisoned, receiving further attention under Seleucus and/or Antiochus.[50] Given the site's natural strategic position and the evidence for a late fourth-century occupation, this seems not unreasonable; there is no need to make it in addition an "Alexandria." The site will already have had a local name, to which it probably continued to be referred by the local, and perhaps even Greek, inhabitants of the city and district.[51]

Other attempts to find the ancient name of Ai Khanoum use the information given in Claudius Ptolemy's chapter on Sogdiana (6.12.5–6), particularly his reference to two cities called Alexandria Oxeiane and Oxeiana. Rapin suggests that these are Termez and Takht-i Sangin;[52] Bernard says that they are Termez and Ai Khanoum.[53] Numerous problems arise in using Ptolemy's account as evidence in this way, not least that we cannot be sure that he is even referring to two different cities. Leriche's review of the question is more skeptical and cautious about the value of Ptolemy as a source for the ancient name of Ai Khanoum, or any other city on the Oxus.[54] Any such approach depends upon history and archaeology each supplying us with a complete list of places and a good index of their relative importance, and having these two equivalent lists match up with each other. It is extremely doubtful that the accuracy of Ptolemy's testimony or the current state of the archaeological evidence permits us to do this. Our ancient sources on Bactrian geography mostly postdate the fall of the Greek kingdom of Bactria in the mid-second century BC; none of their authors knew the region personally, and their priorities are very different.[55]

In sum, despite competing views of the question, we cannot identify the ancient name of Ai Khanoum, Greek or local. The one hope that we might one day be able to do so comes from the new documentary material from Bactria: Aramaic documents of the Achaemenid and very early Hellenistic periods[56] and Greek documents of the Hellenistic period.[57] The Greek documents offer the possibility of identifying at least one Bactrian town,[58] and the Aramaic offer still better data.[59] None of these place names may be identified with Ai Khanoum, but future discoveries of documents may yield useful information. For now, all we can say from the archaeological data is that the first substantial Hellenistic foundation at Ai Khanoum was probably a garrison of one of Alexander's generals or satraps left at an important existing regional center, which was consolidated and possibly significantly expanded and developed under the Seleucids.

Achaemenid and Hellenistic Bactria: Business as Usual?

Although the Alexander historians may suggest the creation of new foundations in Central Asia—and although present-day scholars may be keen to identify these as "Alexandrias"—what the archaeological evidence shows is that, whatever changes there were in the scale and nature of settlement and resource exploitation in the Hellenistic period, there was little or no fresh colonization of areas and sites with no previous occupation. Ai Khanoum is no exception to this rule, as can be seen from the excellent evidence for the longer-term settlement history of the plain surrounding it and possibly also the city-site itself.[60]

As is the case with many of the political and economic structures of the Hellenistic world, any Alexandrian gloss given by ancient or modern commentators to the foundation or origins of cities such as Ai Khanoum is a fiction and obscures, perhaps purposefully, their Achaemenid history. In the late fourth century BC, immediately following Alexander's conquests in the region, the implantation of Greek garrison-colonies brings no observable change in material culture or administrative practices. Aramaic-literate administrators switch seamlessly from dating their everyday documents by Darius to dating them by Alexander:

Column l, 1: On the 15th of Sivan, year 7 of Alexander
2: the King. Disbursement of barley from: Vakhshudata, the barley-supplier
3: in Ariavant.[61]

Bactria is open for business as usual. But did the Graeco-Macedonian settler population of Bactria, in their first generation, or subsequently, consider this to be the case? In addition to the shrine of Kineas and its inscription, other elements in the architectural program of the city of Ai Khanoum suggest that its inhabitants had a sense of themselves as a colonial community and that Alexander's conquests and their settlement in the region represented some kind of historical break. Structures such as the theater and gymnasium, along with aspects of the Greek epigraphic record of the Hellenistic Far East as a whole, hint that the Greek colonists and their descendants may be protesting their Greekness too much.[62]

The mid-third century BC is a watershed in Ai Khanoum's view of its own origins and position. I do not think that events in this period imply rejection of any earlier traditions of the city's foundation—the direct replacement of an Alexander narrative with a Delphi narrative—but new strands came to be incorporated. This is a period when even the very youngest members of the first generation of the Greek settlement will have long died, giving way to the second and third, and stories about the city's foundation will have passed from primary testimony into oral tradition, with all the possibilities for creative license that this implies. In this case at least, I argue that foundation narratives increased in political and cultural importance over time and that the generational transition from pioneer-founders who had some Greek or Macedonian homeland to those whose only experience was of the colony is an especially sensitive moment. Delphi has a special association with Greek colonization, but it is also symbolic of the Greek world and a common Greek identity.

Although we lack any written foundation myth for Ai Khanoum and do not even know its ancient name, this model may be supported by the archaeological and epigraphic evidence from eastern Bactria. While significant settlement in the city's hinterland predates even the very first Graeco-Macedonian remains of the late fourth century BC by many centuries, Ai Khanoum underwent a substantial building program contemporary to Ceramic Period IV, of the mid-third century BC, by the standard chronologies. Many questions about the shrine of Kineas, its history and relative and internal chronologies, remain to be satisfactorily resolved. The retention of the shrine and its continuing importance through this period is one thing, but I would also suggest that this importance was reinforced and reimagined, both by the integration of the shrine into the urban fabric of the city's central complex and by the renovation and enlargement of the shrine itself. The remodeling of the shrine and the city, as well as the introduction or new prominence of the Delphic maxims—and their tenuous connection to Greek colonization, a connection that Ai Khanoum's citizens can only have been very aware

did not amount to a "Delphic foundation" in any conventional sense—
therefore represented an occasion on which the first Bactrian-born generations of the Greek settlement reimagined or reinvented myths about their
colonial origins, their Greekness, and their civic identity. The fate of the inscription in Stage IV of the construction—disassembled and reused, its inscribed face toward the wall—also perhaps suggests that this myth held the
imagination of its creators for only a limited time.

NOTES

I would like to thank Naoíse Mac Sweeney and the two anonymous reviewers for
their helpful comments and suggestions.

1. C. P. Cavafy, "Envoys from Alexandria" (1918), in *The Collected Poems*, tr. Evan-
gelos Sachperoglou (Oxford: Oxford University Press, 2007).

2. Note, e.g., the almost complete absence of Delphi in the city foundations discussed in Cohen 2006. See also Cohen 2013.

3. The very few passages in ancient Greek or Latin works that make more than passing reference to Bactria are collected in Appendix D to Holt 1999.

4. See Leriche 2007: 124–25, on disagreements in the Greek and Roman historians.

5. Rapin 2003b; Rapin et al. 2006.

6. The archaeological literature on Hellenistic Bactria and adjacent regions is sur-
veyed in Mairs 2011.

7. Paris: De Boccard 1973–92.

8. These are discussed by Fussman 1996; Lerner 2003–4.

9. Litvinskii and Pichikyan 2000; Litvinskij and Pičikjan 2002. See also Bernard
1974 on the ancient names of Kandahar.

10. Shaked 2003; Grenet 1996; index to Sims-Williams 2000.

11. On Alexander in Bactria, see Holt 1988; Bernard 1990.

12. On identity and the urban landscape at Ai Khanoum, see Mairs 2013.

13. The results of the survey were published in three final volumes: Gentelle 1989;
Lyonnet 1997; Gardin 1998. Satellite photographs of the plain today reveal intensive modern agricultural exploitation and settlement (to view on Google Earth, enter the coordi-
nates 37°10'24"N 69°24'49"E).

14. The late third- to early second-millennium site of Shortughai, discovered by the
survey team in 1975 around twenty-one kilometers northeast of Ai Khanoum, and excavated 1976–79, was a commercial outpost of the Indus civilization: Francfort 1989. Further
connections with the Indus civilization may be documented in the material culture of the
region throughout the Chalcolithic and Bronze Ages: Lyonnet 1977; Lyonnet 1981; Francfort
1985; Jarrige 1985. The Bronze Age irrigation of eastern Bactria is discussed by Gardin 1984,

with a useful summary of practical and methodological issues in English, and pre-Hellenistic sites, including fortifications, in Gardin 1981, 1995.

15. Shaked 2004.

16. Bernard and Francfort 1978: 9; Rapin 1992: 50, pl. 100.2.

17. See, e.g., Bavay 1997 on lapis in predynastic Egypt.

18. On the evidence for such a settlement, see Bernard and Francfort 1978: 12–14. On Alexander and Ai Khanoum, Bernard 1982. On local pre-Hellenistic traditions of craftsmanship, from the materials at Ai Khanoum, see Guillaume 1985.

19. Bernard 1967: 316.

20. Seleucus and Antiochus also gave some attention to the region in the late fourth and early third centuries BC.

21. Holt 1988.

22. Holt 1984.

23. Litvinskii 2001: tab. 71; Pitschikjan 1992: Abb. 41.

24. Lerner 1999: 30–31.

25. On the stratigraphy of this mausoleum, see Francfort and Liger 1976: 32–33.

26. Bernard 1973; material summarized in Grenet 1984: H8. See also Mairs 2007: 118–21, on the shrine of the city's founder as a focus for civic and religious identity within the new city.

27. Text: Robert 1968; Canali De Rossi 2004, *IK Estremo Oriente* 182–84. For a "reconstruction" of the inscription with the complete text of the Delphic maxims—almost all of it in square brackets—see Canali De Rossi 2004; *IK Estremo Oriente* 183.

28. Holt 1999: 37–47, traces the imagined journey of Klearchos, providing a description of cities along the route, and eventually of Ai Khanoum itself, which retains its merits even if the identification of the philosopher is incorrect.

29. Lerner 2003–4: 393–94.

30. Mairs 2013.

31. See Bernard in Bernard and Francfort 1978: 12–15, on the earliest excavated strata of the city's various institutions.

32. Bernard 1973: 102.

33. See further Lerner 2003–4: 383–90.

34. Lerner 2003–4: 295; Lerner's argument pays especial attention to the "Megaran bowl" forms discussed in Gardin 1985.

35. See, e.g., Clarysse and Thompson 2007: 273–74; Shaked 2004: 12.

36. Schlumberger and Bernard 1965: 654, fig. 37.

37. Discussed in Bernard 1973: 9, 85–86, 88, 104–7, pl. 97a and b.

38. Bernard 1969: 355 and fig. 27; Bernard 1985: 83–84. See also Le Rider 1987: 240, on the evidence for early minting activity at Ai Khanoum.

39. Bopearachchi 1994: 514.

40. Bernard 1973: 9; Bernard and Guillaume 1980: 18–19; Bernard 1985: 39–40; Narain 1986.

41. Bernard 1973.

42. Narain 1986.

43. I am grateful to Naoíse Mac Sweeney for this point.

44. Schlumberger and Bernard 1965: 601–2.

45. Fussman 1996: 246, discusses the limitations of various attempts by the excavators to establish the city's name and the circumstances of, and reasons for, its foundation.

46. See Bernard, "Le nom de la ville grecque du Tepe Ai Khanoum," in Bernard and Francfort 1978: 12–15, for an institution-by-institution survey of the evidence.

47. Rapin 2003a; Rapin 2005: 146–47 (cf. "Eukratideia" in Strabo 11.11.2).

48. See, e.g., the discussion of Leriche 2002 on Termez as a possible Alexander foundation.

49. See Bernard 1982's response to Bosworth 1981.

50. Bernard in Bernard and Francfort 1978: 13–15.

51. Rapin 2003a considers one such possible local name.

52. Rapin 2003a.

53. Bernard and Francfort 1978: 4–5.

54. Leriche 2007: 121–22.

55. See further discussion in Leriche 2007: 122–24.

56. Shaked 2004; Naveh and Shaked 2012.

57. Rea et al. 1994; Bernard and Rapin 1994; Rapin 1996; Clarysse and Thompson 2007.

58. Grenet 1996.

59. Shaked 2003.

60. For a wider Bactrian perspective on this issue, see Leriche 2007 on long-term occupation and "rhythms" of settlement in Bactria, as well as Greek use of preexisting settlements and fortifications.

61. C4 [Khalili IA 17], 8 June 324 BC: Shaked 2004.

62. See, e.g., the discussion in Mairs 2008.

REFERENCES

Bavay, L. 1997. "Matière première et commerce à longue distance: Le lapis-lazuli et l'Égypte prédynastique." *Archéo-Nil* 7: 79–100.

Bernard, P. 1967. "Deuxième campagne de fouilles d'Aï Khanoum." *Comptes-rendus de l'Académie des inscriptions et belles-lettres*: 306–24.

Bernard, P. 1969. "Quatrième campagne de fouilles à Aï Khanoum (Bactriane)." *Comptes-rendus de l'Académie des inscriptions et belles-lettres*: 313–55.

Bernard, P. 1974. "Un problème de toponymie antique dans l'Asie centrale: Les noms anciens de Qandahar." *Studia Iranica* 3: 171–85.

Bernard, P. 1982. "Alexandre et Aï Khanoum." *Journal des Savants* 2: 125–38.

Bernard, P. 1985. *Fouilles d'Aï Khanoum IV: Les monnaies hors trésors, questions d'histoire gréco-bactrienne.* Paris: Diffusion de Boccard.

Bernard, P. 1990. "Alexandre et l'Asie centrale: Reflexions à propos d'un ouvrage de F. L. Holt." *Studia Iranica* 19: 21–38.

Bernard, P. (ed.). 1973. *Fouilles d'Aï Khanoum I (Campagnes 1965, 1966, 1967, 1968).* Paris: Diffusion de Boccard.

Bernard, P., and H.-P. Francfort. 1978. *Études de géographie historique sur la plaine d'Aï Khanoum (Afghanistan).* Paris: Éditions du Centre National de la Recherche Scientifique.

Bernard, P., and O. Guillaume. 1980. "Monnaies inédites de la Bactriane grecque à Aï Khanoum (Afghanistan)." *Revue Numismatique* 22: 9–32.

Bernard, P., and C. Rapin. 1994. "Un parchemin gréco-bactrien d'une collection privée." *Comptes-rendus de l'Académie des inscriptions et belles-lettres*: 261–94.

Bopearachchi, O. 1994. "L'indépendence de la Bactriane." *Topoi Orient-Occident* 4: 513–19.

Bosworth, A. B. 1981. "A Missing Year in the History of Alexander the Great." *Journal of Hellenic Studies* 101: 17–39.

Canali De Rossi, F. 2004. *Iscrizioni dello Estremo Oriente Greco: Un Repertorio.* Inschriften griechischer Städte aus Kleinasien 65. Bonn: Habelt.

Clarysse, W., and D. J. Thompson. 2007. "Two Greek Texts on Skin from Hellenistic Bactria." *Zeitschrift für Papyrologie und Epigraphik* 159: 273–79.

Cohen, G. M. 2006. *The Hellenistic Settlements in Syria, the Red Sea Basin, and North Africa.* Berkeley: University of California Press.

Cohen, G. M. 2013. *The Hellenistic Settlements in the East from Armenia and Mesopotamia to Bactria and India.* Berkeley: University of California Press.

Francfort, H.-P. 1985. "Tradition harappéenne et innovation bactrienne à Shortughaï." In *L'archéologie de la Bactriane ancienne: Actes du Colloque franco-soviétique, Dushanbe (U.R.S.S.), October 27–November 3, 1982,* ed. M.S. Asimov et al., 95–104. Paris: Éditions du Centre National de la Recherche Scientifique.

Francfort, H.-P. 1989. *Fouilles de Shortughaï: Recherches sur l'Asie centrale protohistorique.* Paris: Mission archéologique française en Asie centrale.

Francfort, H.-P., and J.-C. Liger. 1976. "L'hérôon au caveau de pierre." In Paul Bernard et al., "Fouilles d'Aï Khanoum (Afghanistan): Campagne de 1974." *Bulletin de l'École Française d'Extrême Orient* 63: 5–51.

Fussman, G. 1996. "Southern Bactria and Northern India Before Islam: A Review of Archaeological Reports." *Journal of the American Oriental Society* 116: 243–59.

Gardin, J.-C. 1981. "The Development of Eastern Bactria in Pre-Classical Times." *Purātattva: Bulletin of the Indian Archaeological Society* 10: 8–13.

Gardin, J.-C. 1984. "Canal Irrigation in Bronze Age Eastern Bactria." In *Frontiers of the Indus Civilization (Sir Mortimer Wheeler Commemorative Volume),* ed. B. B. Lal and S. P. Gupta, 311–20. New Delhi: Indian Archaeological Society and Indian History and Culture Society.

Gardin, J.-C. 1985. "Les relations entre la Méditerranée et la Bactriane dans l'antiquité, d'après des données céramologiques inédites." In *De l'Indus aux Balkans: Recueil à la mémoire de Jean Deshayes*, ed. J.-L. Huot, M. Yon, and Y. Calvet, 447–60. Paris: Éditions Recherche sur les Civilisations.

Gardin, J.-C. 1995. "Fortified Sites of Eastern Bactria (Afghanistan) in Pre-Hellenistic Times." In *In the Land of the Gryphons: Papers on Central Asian Archaeology in Antiquity*, ed. A. Invernizzi, 83–105. Florence: Le Lettre.

Gardin, J.-C. 1998. *Prospections archéologiques en Bactriane orientale (1974–1978) 3: Description des sites et notes de synthèse.* Paris: Éditions Recherche sur les Civilisations.

Gentelle, P. 1989. *Prospections archéologiques en Bactriane orientale (1974–1978) 1: Données paléogéographiques et fondements de l'irrigation.* Paris: Éditions Recherche sur les Civilisations.

Grenet, F. 1984. *Les pratiques funéraires dans l'Asie centrale sédentaire: De la conquête grecque à l'Islamisation.* Paris: Éditions du Centre national de la recherche scientifique.

Grenet, F. 1996. "Ασαγγωρνοις, Ασκισαγγοραγο, Sangchârak." *Topoi* 6: 470–74.

Guillaume, O. 1985. "Contribution à l'étude d'un artisanat bactrien pré-hellénistique." In *L'archéologie de la Bactriane ancienne: Actes du Colloque franco-soviétique, Dushanbe (U.R.S.S.), October 27–November 3, 1982*, ed. M. S. Asimov et al., 257–67. Paris: Éditions du Centre national de la recherche scientifique.

Holt, F. L. 1984. "The So-Called 'Pedigree Coins' of the Bactrian Greeks." In *Ancient Coins of the Graeco-Roman World: The Nickle Numismatic Papers*, ed. W. Heckel and R. Sullivan, 69–91. Waterloo, Ontario: Wilfrid Laurier University Press.

Holt, F. L. 1988. *Alexander the Great and Bactria: The Formation of a Greek Frontier in Central Asia.* Leiden: Brill.

Holt, F. L. 1999. *Thundering Zeus: The Making of Hellenistic Bactria.* Berkeley: University of California Press.

Jarrige, J.-F. 1985. "Les relations entre l'Asie centrale méridionale, le Baluchistan et la vallée de l'Indus à la fin du 3e et au début du 2e millénaire." In *L'archéologie de la Bactriane ancienne: Actes du Colloque franco-soviétique, Dushanbe (U.R.S.S.), October 27–November 3, 1982*, ed. M. S. Asimov et al., 106–18. Paris: Éditions du Centre national de la recherche scientifique.

Leriche, P. 2002. "Termez fondation d'Alexandre?." *Journal Asiatique* 290: 411–15.

Leriche, P. 2007. "Bactria, Land of a Thousand Cities." In *After Alexander: Central Asia Before Islam*, ed. J. Cribb and G. Herrmann, 121–53. Oxford: Oxford University Press.

Le Rider, G. 1987. "Monnaies d'Aï Khanoum." *Revue Numismatique* 236–44.

Lerner, J. D. 1999. *The Impact of Seleucid Decline on the Eastern Iranian Plateau: The Foundations of Arsacid Parthia and Graeco-Bactria.* Stuttgart: Franz Steiner.

Lerner, J. D. 2003–4. "Correcting the Early History of Ay Kanom." *Archäologische Mitteilungen aus Iran und Turan* 35–36: 373–410.

Litvinskii, B. A. 2001. *Храм Окса в Бактрии (Южный Таджикистан). Том 2: Бактрийское Вооружение в Древневосточном и Греческом Контексте [The Temple of the Oxus in Bactria (Southern Tadzhikistan)*, vol. 2: *Bactrian Arms in the Ancient Eastern and Greek Context].* Moscow: Vostochnaya Literatura.

Litvinskii, B. A., and I. R. Pichikyan. 2000. *Эллинистический Храм Окса в Бактрии (Южный Таджикистан). Том 1: Раскопки, Архитектура, Религиозная Жизнь* [*The Hellenistic Temple of the Oxus in Bactria (Southern Tadzhikistan)*, vol. 1: *Excavations, Architecture, Religious Life*]. Moscow: Vostochnaya Literatura.

Litvinskij, B. A. (=Litvinskii, B. A.), and I. R. Pičikjan (=I. R. Pichikyan). 2002. *Taxt-i Sangin, der Oxus-Tempel: Grabungsbefund, Stratigraphie und Architektur*. Mainz: Philipp von Zabern.

Lyonnet, B. 1977. "Découverte de sites de l'âge du bronze dans le N.E. de l'Afghanistan: Leurs rapports avec la civilisation de l'Indus." *Annali dell'Istituto Orientale di Napoli* 37: 19–35.

Lyonnet, B. 1981. "Établissements chalcolithiques dans le Nord-Est de l'Afghanistan: Leurs rapports avec les cultures du Bassin de l'Indus." *Paléorient* 7: 57–74.

Lyonnet, B. 1997. *Prospections archéologiques en Bactriane orientale (1974–1978)*, vol. 2: *Céramique et peuplement du Chalcolithique à la conquête Arabe*. Paris: Éditions Recherche sur les Civilisations.

Mairs, R. 2007. "Ethnicity and Funerary Practice in Hellenistic Bactria." In *Crossing Frontiers: The Opportunities and Challenges of Interdisciplinary Approaches to Archaeology*, ed. H. Schroeder et al., 111–24. Oxford: Oxford University School of Archaeology.

Mairs, R. 2008. "Greek Identity and the Settler Community in Hellenistic Bactria and Arachosia." *Migrations and Identities* 1: 19–43.

Mairs, R. 2011. *The Archaeology of the Hellenistic Far East: A Survey. Bactria, Central Asia and the Indo-Iranian Borderlands, c. 300 BC–AD 100*. Oxford: BAR Archaeopress.

Mairs, R. 2013. "The 'Temple with Indented Niches' at Ai Khanoum: Ethnic and Civic Identity in Hellenistic Bactria." In *Cults, Creeds and Contests: Religion in the Post-Classical City*, ed. R. Alston, O. M. van Nijf, and C. Williamson, 8–111. Leuven: Peeters.

Narain, A. K. 1986. "The Greek Monogram (X) and Aï Khanoum—the Bactrian City." *Numismatic Digest* 10: 4–15.

Naveh, J., and S. Shaked. 2012. *Aramaic Documents from Ancient Bactria (Fourth Century B.C.E.) from the Khalili Collections*. London: Khalili Family Trust.

Pitschikjan, I. R. (=I. R. Pichikyan) 1992. *Oxos-Schatz und Oxos-Tempel: Achämenidische Kunst in Mittelasien*. Berlin: Akademie.

Rapin, C. 1992. *Fouilles d'Aï Khanoum VIII: La trésorerie du palais hellénistique d'Aï Khanoum, l'apogée et la chute du royaume grec de Bactriane*. Paris: Diffusion de Boccard.

Rapin, C. 1996. "Nouvelles observations sur le parchemin gréco-bactrien d'Asangôrna." *Topoi* 6: 458–69.

Rapin, C. 2003a. "Le nom antique d'Aï Khanoum et de son fleuve." In *De l'Indus à l'Oxus: Archéologie de l'Asie centrale. Catalogue de l'exposition*, ed. O. Bopearachchi, C. Landes, and C. Sachs, 115. Lattes: Musée de Lattes.

Rapin, C. 2003b. "Les Portes de Fer de Derbent: Histoire d'une frontière." *Au fil des routes de la soie, chemins d'étoiles, invitations à l'itinérance* 11: 148–56.

Rapin, C. 2005. "L'Afghanistan et l'Asie centrale dans la géographie mythique des historiens d'Alexandre et dans la toponymie des géographes gréco-romains: Notes sur la route d'Herat à Begram." In *Afghanistan: Ancien carrefour entre l'est et l'ouest*, ed. O. Bopearachchi and M.-F. Boussac, 143–72. Turnhout: Brepols.

Rapin, C., et al. 2006. "Les recherches sur la region des Portes de Fer de Sogdiane: Bref état des questions en 2005." *История материальнои культуры Узбекистана* 35: 91–112.

Rea, J., R. C. Senior, and A. S. Hollis. 1994. "A Tax Receipt from Hellenistic Bactria." *Zeitschrift für Papyrologie und Epigraphik* 104: 261–80.

Robert, L. 1968. "De Delphes à l'Oxus: Inscriptions grecques nouvelles de la Bactriane." *Comptes-rendus de l'Académie des inscriptions et belles-lettres*: 416–57.

Schlumberger, D., and P. Bernard. 1965. "Ai Khanoum." *Bulletin de Correspondance Hellénique* 89: 590–657.

Shaked, S. 2003. "De Khulmi à Nikhšapaya: Les données des nouveaux documents araméens de Bactres sur la toponymie de la région (IVe siècle av. n. è.)." *Comptes-rendus de l'Académie des inscriptions et belles-lettres*: 1517–35.

Shaked, S. 2004. *Le satrape de Bactriane et son gouverneur: Documents araméens du IVe s. avant notre ère provenant de Bactriane*. Paris: De Boccard.

Sims-Williams, N. 2000. *Bactrian Documents from Northern Afghanistan*, part 1: *Legal and Economic Documents*. Oxford: Oxford University Press.

CHAPTER 5

Alexander, Agathos Daimon, and Ptolemy: The Alexandrian Foundation Myth in Dialogue

DANIEL OGDEN

Most of the contributions to this volume consider the significance of dialogues internal to foundation myths. They exploit the similarities between variants to expose ideologies central to cities' self-images; or they exploit the differences between variants to expose structural tensions within the cities. This chapter looks, by contrast, at a foundation myth that—initially, at any rate—seems to have been quite unitary, as indeed one might have expected from a state created and ruled autocratically. However, it was from the outset engaged in harmonious dialogues with external myths and institutions, and it derived much of its meaning and force from them. The myth in question is that of the foundation of Alexandria and Alexander's slaying of the Agathos Daimon (Agathodaimon) serpent in connection with it. This drew upon the old Greek city foundation myths, with their motifs of animal guides and serpent slayings, to tell the Alexandrians that their city was the equal of the old cities and to confer legitimacy and dignity upon it. It spoke with a range of serpent myths surrounding the figure of Alexander in such a way as to tell the Alexandrians that Ptolemy was the true heir to his city. It spoke with native Egyptian traditions of the god Šaï, to tell the city's Egyptian inhabitants that it was, for good or ill, under the protection of one of their own. It spoke—presumably, despite Ptolemy—with the foundation myths of Antioch and Seleuceia in Pieria to confer legitimacy and dignity upon those cities as well. And in due course, with light revision, it spoke with Christian tradition, to give the Christians, too, a gratifying and legitimating involvement, of sorts, in the city's creation.[1]

The Foundation Myth

The foundation myth is first attested rather late, in the earliest recoverable version of the *Alexander Romance*, c. AD 300.[2] However, much of the material in this version of the *Romance* is evidently of early Hellenistic vintage, our myth among it. The narrative tells how Alexander's architects had marked out the projected city to extend between the rivers Drakōn ("serpent") and Agathodaimon[3] (the latter being the name given to the Canopic branch of the Nile in several inscriptions and in the *Geography* of Claudius Ptolemy).[4] Then:

> They began to build Alexandria from the Middle plain and so the place took on the additional name of "Beginning," on account of the fact that the building of the city had begun from that point. A serpent [*drakōn*] that was in the habit of presenting itself to people in the area kept frightening the workmen, and they would break off their work upon the creature's arrival. News of this was given to Alexander. He gave the order that on the following day the serpent should be killed wherever it was caught. On receipt of this permission, they got the better of the beast when it presented itself at the place now called the Stoa and killed it. Alexander gave the order that it should have a precinct there, and buried the serpent. And he gave the command that the neighborhood should be garlanded in memory of the sighting of Agathos Daimon. He commanded that the soil from the digging of the foundations should all be deposited in one particular place, and even up until this day a large hill is there to be seen, called the "Dung Heap." When he had laid the foundations for most of the city and measured it out, he inscribed five letters, alpha, beta, gamma, delta, epsilon: alpha for "Alexander," beta for "king," gamma for "scion," delta for "of Zeus" and epsilon for "founded this unforgettable city." Beasts of burden and mules were at work. When the foundations of the heroon had been laid down <he set [the stele on which he had inscribed the letters] on a pillar>.[5] There leaped out from it a

large host <of snakes>, and, crawling off, they ran into the four[?] houses that were already there. Alexander, who was still present, founded the city and the heroon itself on the 25th Tybi. From that point the door-keepers admitted these snakes to the houses as Agathoi Daimones. These snakes are not venomous, but they do ward off those snakes that do seem to be venomous, and sacrifices are given to the hero him-self <, as serpent-born>. They garland their beasts of burden and give them a holiday since they helped in the foundation of the city by carrying loads. Alexander ordered that the guardians of the houses be given wheat. They took it and milled it and made porridge[?] and gave it to the snakes in the houses. The Alexandrians preserve this custom until today. On the 25th Tybi they garland their beasts of burden, make sacrifice to the Agathoi Daimones that look after their houses and make them gifts of porridge.

Alexander Romance 1.32.5–13 A ~ §§ 86–88 Armenian

The public cult of Agathos Daimon described here was almost certainly es-tablished during the reign of the first Ptolemy, and we may assume that a mythology, which presumably resembled this one in broad outline, was de-veloped for the serpent at the same time. This is because the Agathos Daimon serpent was integrated into the Alexander Aegiochus statue type that was developed in c. 320–300 BC and (eventually) decorated Alexander's tomb in Alexandria. In this statue, Alexander wore an aegis decorated with a small *gorgoneion*, or Gorgon head; in his right hand, he held a spear; in his left, he held a *palladion*, a small statuette of the goddess Athene. The original statue is attested by eighteen copies in various states of repair—statues, statuettes, and cameos—all, where provenance is known, deriving from Egypt. In two severely damaged copies, one in the Louvre's Collection Lambros-Dattari, the other a cruder one in the new Museo Bíblico y Oriental in León (Spain), Alexander's leg is supported by a tree trunk around which winds a serpent.[6] Despite its vestigial attestation, the serpent presumably did feature in the original. This is further suggested by the Aegiochus' strong allusions to Phi-dias' famous *chryselephantine* (gold and ivory) Athena Parthenos statue for the Athenian Parthenon, allusions supported by the featured *palladion*. The Parthenos statue, too, wore the aegis and held a spear and a female statu-ette—in this case, of Nike, Victory. And nestling under the Parthenos' shield was a magnificent protective serpent, be it the anguiform Erictho-nius or the *oikouros ophis* ("house-guarding snake") that supposedly lived on the acropolis, much as Agathos Daimon was the protective spirit of the city of Alexandria.[7] As with the heroes of old Greece, so with Agathos Daimon: his death marks the end of his mythical narrative but the commencement and justification of his career as a supernatural protective presence in his land.

Dialogue with the Old Greek Foundation Myths

The tale broadly aligns with a traditional Greek story type in which the founder of a city is somehow guided to its site by an animal. We think of the crows that guided settlers to Cyrene, Magnesia, and (appropriately) Coraces ("crows"); the cow that guided Ilus to Ilium; the mouse that guided settlers to Argilos; the fish and the boar that guided settlers to Ephesus; the wolves and the sheep that they were eating that guided Athamas to Athamantia; and the metaphorical "goat," the fig with hanging vine tendrils, that led settlers to the site of Tarentum.[8] The motif is also found in some of the multifarious foundation myths of Macedon. According to these, the founder figure, be it Archelaus, Caranus, or Perdiccas, was led to the site of Aegae by goats (*aiges*).[9] Indeed, Alexander himself, according to a later version of the *Alexander Romance*, founded Cilician Aegae in the fashion of the Macedonian founder figure, after routing the Persians in a night battle in which he had panicked them by driving goats at them with torches tied to their horns.[10] If it seems odd, in this connection, that the Agathos Daimon serpent should only appear at the site of Alexandria once the Macedonians have already started to build their city, let us not forget that they had first chosen to site it between the rivers named Drakōn and Agathodaimon.

The tale also salutes old Greek traditions that derive foundations of cities from the slaying of a serpent—a serpent that is tightly associated with a water source and that is duly memorialized afterward.[11] The prime example is Kadmos' foundation of Thebes in connection with the slaying of the Serpent of Ares. The canonical myth was already established by the fifth century BC. Kadmos was guided to the site of Thebes by another animal guide, a heifer. Wishing then to sacrifice the animal, he sent men to fetch water from an adjacent spring, Dirce. But this was the preserve of the Serpent of Ares, which killed the men. Kadmos killed the serpent, in turn, by dashing a rock against its head. According to Euripides, at any rate, some sort of cult was established in honor of the slain serpent, based in a precinct (*sêkos*). Intriguingly, Cadmus was himself eventually transformed into a serpent in Illyria, alongside his wife Harmonia.[12]

Another example is to be found in the myth that Antoninus Liberalis takes over from Nicander's second-century BC *Heteroioumena* (*Metamorphoses*). This tells how Alcyoneus slew the apparently anguiform (snake-shaped) Sybaris or Lamia at Delphic Crisa on Mount Cirphis by throwing her down the mountainside. As her body dashed against the rocks, it disappeared, and a spring—Sybaris again—appeared in its place. And it was in the name of this spring that the Locrians then founded the city of Sybaris in Italy. The motifs of water source, foundation, and memorialization are explicit, if partly indirect.[13] The resonances between the Theban foundation myth and the Alexandrian one are several: both foundations are rooted in the killing of a serpent strongly identified with a water source, both result in the foundation of cult for the serpent (*drakōn*), and both founder-slayers are themselves, curiously, ultimately identified with serpents. In the *Romance* narrative, Alexander is described as serpent-born (of which more anon) and confusingly projected as a hero in this regard, alongside the heroized serpent that he has slain. We are inclined to wonder whether Ptolemy was projecting Alexandria as a compensatory foundation for Alexander's destruction of Thebes. For what it is worth, the *Suda* mentions, without elaboration, that Agathos Daimon also had a *heroon* in Thebes.[14] But however outlandish the Macedonian and Greek settlers found their new Egyptian environment, the myth reassured them that their city was born in a similar fashion to those of the old Greek world.

The *Romance* narrative casts Alexander as a dragon slayer, but as a dragon-slaying story fit for Alexander, it is admittedly less than satisfactory: the serpent in question appears to be more of a nuisance than an ultimate peril; the hero of the story does not even encounter it in person but superciliously delegates the task of slaying to a nameless group of builders. Perhaps a more dynamic narrative has been deflated with an element of rationalization in this version of the *Romance*. Alexander had to wait until a later version of the *Romance*, known to us only from the seventh-century AD Syriac translation of the Greek original, to get or to recover the full-blown dragon fight that was his due. This dragon, which he encounters near Indian Prasiace, sucks down oxen whole. Alexander destroys it by feeding it ox hides restuffed with gypsum, pitch, lead, and sulfur.[15] This story was then taken

up into the c. AD 1000 Persian version of the *Romance* incorporated into Ferdowsi's *Shahnameh*.[16]

Dialogue with the Myths of Alexander's Other Serpents

The Agathos Daimon myth also entered into dialogue with the myths of the
other great serpents in the Alexander tradition, almost certainly at Ptolemy's
behest.[17] Two of these other serpent myths are, significantly, strongly tied to
Ptolemy. First, in a well-known passage, Arrian gives us an intriguing insight
into Ptolemy's own account of Alexander's march to Siwah. While all others,
he tells us, Aristobulus included, had told that Alexander's army had been
rescued from the Western Desert by a pair of crows, Ptolemy had given instead
a pair of talking serpents (*drakontes*).[18] Second, Clitarchus, who worked in Ptolemy's own Alexandria and is now believed to have published soon after 310
BC, recorded the tale of the serpent (*drakōn*) that appeared to Alexander in a
dream during the siege of Indian Harmatelia and told him how to heal the
dying Ptolemy, the favorite for whom the king was deeply grieving, with the
help of a local herb.[19]

The most striking serpent myth associated with Alexander is that referred
to in passing in the *Romance* narrative above and best known from Plutarch,
that in accordance with which he was actually sired by a gigantic serpent (*drakōn*
again). The cases of the Siwah and Harmatelia serpents invite us to suppose
that this myth, too, was sponsored, if not actually invented, by Ptolemy. The
earliest direct attestation of the serpent-siring myth comes only with Cicero's
On Divination, of 45–44 BC, although it is important to note that he here
identifies Alexander's siring serpent with the healing serpent of Harmatelia.[20]
But we probably have an indirect indication of the myth's currency closer to
Ptolemy's own age. It was almost certainly the subject of the secret of Alexander's birth that Olympias supposedly entrusted to him only as he set out on
campaign and that Plutarch tells us was spoken of by Eratosthenes (c. 285–194
BC).[21] When the ghost of Silius Italicus' Pomponia tells Scipio that he was
serpent-sired, the information is similarly presented as the final revelation
from mother to son of a long-kept secret.[22]

It seems that Ptolemy or his agents contrived to develop a network of striking serpent-themed myths around Alexander, to the greater glory of Ptolemy
himself, his land of Egypt, and his city of Alexandria. The Harmatelia myth
advertised Alexander's great affection for Ptolemy. In combination with the

siring myth, it presented Ptolemy as quasi-brother to Alexander: as the marvelous serpent had given life to Alexander, so it had given new life to Ptolemy. Given that marvelous serpents, too, had manifested themselves to save Alexander and his army in the Western Desert and so celebrate his bond with the land of Egypt, and that another again, our own Agathos Daimon, had manifested itself at his foundation of Alexandria to celebrate his bond with the city, who could doubt that Ptolemy was the rightful heir to Alexander's splendid Egyptian patrimony?[23]

Dialogue with Native Egyptian Gods

It has been contended that the myth of Agathos Daimon's killing also saluted Egyptian prototypes, and so spoke equally to native Egyptians from the first. It has, for example, been argued that it salutes the type of Egyptian myths of dynastic establishment, as instantiated in the tale of the victory of Ammon-Ra over the Apophis serpent or in that of Horus over Seth-Typhon.[24] Unfortunately, the comparanda seem too vague to be immediately compelling.

But that the figure of Agathos Daimon did speak to native Egyptians from an early stage is demonstrated by their ready embrace of him in his identification with their own serpent deity Šaï, god of destiny. Manetho, the native Egyptian priest of Heliopolis under the second Ptolemy (r. 282–246 BC), undertook to explain Egypt's history in Greek for the benefit of its new masters. The relevant fragment of his *History of Egypt* incorporates the principal Egyptian gods, some under their *interpretatio Graeca* (Hellenized) names, into a mythical first dynasty of pharaohs, and Agathos Daimon is already among them, in second place, no less: Hephaestus, Agathos Daimon, Helios, Cronus, Osiris and Isis, Typhon, Horus, Ares, Anubis, Heracles, Apollo, Ammon, Tithoes, Sosos, Zeus. By this stage, accordingly, Agathos Daimon had been identified with Šaï, and an admittedly philhellene Egyptian was happy to embrace the identification.[25] Rather more striking is the message conveyed by the famous *Oracle of the Potter*. This text, probably third-century BC in origin, perhaps second, is a unique piece of native Egyptian–derived propaganda against the Ptolemies' Macedonian regime, originally composed in Demotic but, ironically, surviving only in Greek. This oracle, which imagines itself to have been issued at the time of Alexandria's foundation, prophesies that Agathos Daimon will abandon the city that is currently being built for the native Egyptian city of Memphis. In other words, it seems, Alexandria will be deprived of its protecting deity. So by this stage, rather less philhellene Egyptians were also accepting the identification of Agathos Daimon with Šaï, and more particularly accepting his role as patron and protector of Alexandria and seemingly seeking to appropriate him in this role for their own Memphis.[26] This sort of thinking seems to have inspired a tale reported by Cassius Dio, according to which the portents that followed the fall of Alexandria to Octavian included the manifestation of a huge serpent with a loud hiss: Agathos Daimon on his way out, or perhaps threatening to leave?[27]

Given the success of the identification of Agathos Daimon with Šaï, we may wonder about his origins. Was he essentially a Greek god offered to (among others) the Egyptians, or was he essentially an Egyptian god appropriated by the Greeks and Macedonians? The answer turns upon the thorny issue of whether the Greek Agathos Daimon, whom the classical comic poets had known chiefly as a protector of domestic stores and sponsor of their enjoyment, and to whom Timoleon had dedicated his house, had an anguiform identity before he came to Alexandria, or acquired it only upon his arrival.[28] If he did already have such an identity, it would seem that his identification with Šaï was convenient and compelling, and an opportunity seized. If he did not, it would seem that the Agathos Daimon of the myth was rooted in Šaï in the first instance, who was then made accessible for Greek and Macedonian consumers by a less compelling identification with their own hitherto humanoid-only Agathos Daimon.

It must be admitted from the first that there is no certain evidence of a direct nature for Agathos Daimon's conceptualization as an anguiform prior to his arrival in Alexandria. Some hold that we find Agathos Daimon represented as a serpent in a single pre-Ptolemaic (or effectively pre-Ptolemaic) image, the relief dated to the fourth century from Boeotian Eteonos, now in Berlin: a man leading a small boy by the hand offers a cake to a large bearded serpent that emerges from a cave.[29] But the image does not carry the god's name, and the serpent could as well be Zeus Meilichios or another anguiform manifestation of Zeus.[30] A unique votive relief dated to the fourth century from Mytilene (now in the Samos Museum) is perhaps the best candidate for a pre-Ptolemaic image of Agathos Daimon in serpent form, though the case is far from secure. A rampant snake coils upon a rock and is approached by three adoring male worshipers. Against the rock lies a caduceus, with its own entwining-snakes motif. The caduceus, which properly belongs to Hermes, is one of a range of attributes given to the serpentine Agathos Daimon on the coinage of Roman Egypt from the reign of Nero onward.[31] The earliest certain representation of Agathos Daimon as a serpent from the old Greek world is, alas, post-Ptolemaic in date and conception. It is also the finest extant image of him to survive from antiquity. It is found in a Hellenistic relief from a private house on Delos. A huge bearded serpent coils over a draped altar flanked by two cornucopia-holding humanoid figures who wear calathos head-dresses and who seemingly merge Isis and Agathe Tyche (Good Fortune), on the one hand, and Sarapis and Agathos Daimon, on the other. In other words, Agathos Daimon appears simultaneously in two guises (as Asclepius and Hygieia regularly do in their iconography).[32]

There are, in fact, only two certainly pre-Ptolemaic images of Agathos Daimon, and both represent him in humanoid form. First, a relief of the late fourth century BC found to the east of the Parthenon is dedicated to "Agathos Daimon and Agathe Tyche." Below the inscription, a male bearded figure holds a cornucopia and is accompanied by two female figures.[33] Second, a broken relief from Thespiae of the last quarter of the fourth century BC carries the dedication "Hagestrotos, Timokrateia, Ptoilleia, Empedonika, to Agathos Daimon" and shows a bearded, avuncular, seated figure being approached by two worshipers. He holds a cornucopia, and an eagle sits beneath his throne.[34]

In pairing Agathos Daimon with Agathe Tyche, these images seemingly bestow upon the god a wider province—namely, that of good fortune in general—than is evident from the literary sources of the same age, a province that prepares him well for the role he is to undertake in Alexandria.[35] Despite the absence of serpent imagery, these two humanoid reliefs paradoxically constitute the strongest indication we have that Agathos Daimon was, on occasion, conceptualized as a serpent in the pre-Ptolemaic Greek world. This is because the syndrome of these humanoid reliefs corresponds closely with those of the later fourth-century BC humanoid reliefs of Zeus Meilichios, Zeus Ktesios, and, above all, Zeus Philios, all of whom enjoyed parallel iconographic careers as serpents. Two images of Zeus Philios are of particular interest: the c. 347 BC Aristomache relief in which Zeus Philios is given both Agathos Daimon's traditional cornucopia and his traditional consort Agathe Tyche;[36] and the 324–322 BC *Eranistai* relief, the remains of which preserve an eagle sitting beneath the throne, which coincides so well in this respect with the Thespian relief of Agathos Daimon.[37] Given the tight similarities between the representation-syndromes of these gods, a never-anguiform Agathos Daimon is rather harder to account for than a sometime-anguiform one.

A thought game also suggests that Agathos Daimon was an anguiform before he came to Egypt. If the origin of the Alexandrian god was indeed in Šaï, why was a never-hitherto-anguiform Agathos Daimon chosen to serve as his *interpretatio Graeca*, in preference to the Greek anguiform sponsors of good luck and household prosperity that were thriving in this age, not least Zeus Meilichios himself? So Agathos Daimon was, we conclude, in origin essentially a Greek god offered to the Egyptians, but one taken up by them with striking alacrity.

Dialogue with the Foundation Myths of Antioch and Seleuceia in Pieria

At a later stage, as we shall see, the Agathos Daimon myth, duly modified, was to speak to another constituency in Alexandria: its Christians. But let us first consider its possible impact upon a pair of external—and strongly rival—cities: the two great Seleucid capitals of Antioch and Seleuceia in Pieria. As we have seen, Ptolemy seems to have constructed his foundation myth for Alexandria around the Agathos Daimon serpent and its rivers before 300 BC. This was the year in which Seleucus founded Antioch and Seleuceia. For these cities too the Seleucids in their turn developed foundation myths that were similarly built around the motifs of river and serpent (*drakōn*), albeit in a more elaborate, symbolically and typologically complex, fashion.[38] It is hard to believe that these myths did not constitute, at least in part, a response to the Ptolemaic myth.

It is now held that the myth of Zeus' battle with the primeval serpent (*drakōn*) Typhon, in which the god destroyed him with his thunderbolts, effectively originated in an *interpretatio Graeca* of a mythical battle between a storm god and a sea serpent that had been located since the age of the Hurrians on ancient Syria's (modern Turkey's) towering Mount Kasios, now the Jebel Aqra. For the Hurrians, who had known the mountain as Hazzi (probably the origin of the Greek name Kasios), the storm god in question had been Teshub, and the dragon Hedammu. For the Hittites, he had been Tarhunna, and the dragon Illuyankas. For the Canaanites, for whom the mountain was Sapuna, the storm god in question had been Baal-Sapon, and he had been victorious over Yam and Lotan (the biblical Leviathan), the sea serpents that were embodiments of chaos.[39]

At some point—presumably, early in the Seleucid era—the river Orontes, the great waterway that flowed beneath Kasios and linked, more or less, the two new cities of Antioch and Seleuceia in Pieria, was identified with the serpent.

The Augustan Strabo preserves the tale that the Orontes' riverbed was created when Zeus hurled his thunderbolts down on Typhon. As Typhon fled, he cut the highly serpentine riverbed with his writhing coils, before releasing its source into it as he finally dived down into the earth. The river initially took Typhon's name for its own. The Christian chronographer John Malalas, writing in the fifth or sixth century AD, was to say that the river actually had four names in all: Orontes, Drakōn ("Serpent"), Typhon, and Ophites ("Snake River").[40]

The fourth-century AD Pausanias of Antioch records a tale about Perseus and the Orontes in which the hero typologically reenacts his father Zeus' battle against Typhon. The river Orontes, at this point called the Drakōn, flooded disastrously, and Perseus advised the local Iopolitans to pray. In answer to their prayers, a ball of fire came down from heaven and dried up the flood. Like his father Zeus before him, Perseus, famous destroyer of anguiform monsters (the Gorgons, the sea monster sent against Andromeda), fought the dragon river with fire from the sky. Perseus then founded a sanctuary "Of the Immortal Fire" for the Iopolitans, and took some of the heavenly fire back to Persia, the land named after him, and there taught the Persians to revere it, appointing trustworthy men to tend the flame, to whom he gave the name "magi." In other words, he founded the Zoroastrian religion.[41]

The foundations of Antioch and Seleuceia in Pieria were associated—indirectly, at least—with these great dragon slayings by a myth fashioned to identify Seleucus typologically with Zeus and Perseus in his acts of foundation. John Malalas tells how, as Seleucus was sacrificing to Zeus on Mount Kasios and asking where he should found his city, the god's own eagle seized part of the sacrifice and dropped it in Pieria, where Seleucus accordingly went on to found the first of the two cities. He gave thanks for the foundation by sacrificing to Zeus Keraunios ("of the Thunderbolt") in the sanctuary founded by Perseus. He then sacrificed to Zeus again at nearby Antigoneia to ask whether he should adopt Antigonus' city and rename it or found a new one elsewhere. Again, an eagle seized meat from the altar and dropped it on Mount Silpios, so signifying that a new city should be built there. As Malalas tells us, Seleucus chose the exact site for the new city, Antioch, beside the great Drakōn river, now the Orontes, in such a way as to avoid the torrents that came down from the mountain.[42] The fourth-century AD Libanius had already made it clear that the meat seized by the Antioch eagle took the specific form of flaming ox thighs.[43] The symbolic equivalence of the flaming ox thigh and the thunderbolt is made clear in Syrian coinage of the imperial

period, long after the disappearance of the Seleucids, where highly similar series of reverses issued under Marcus Aurelius show eagles bearing either lightning bolts or ox thighs in parallel configurations.[44] In his founding of Seleuceia
and Antioch, therefore, Seleucus is projected as a third conqueror of the
Drakōn river. He metaphorically masters it with his pair of city foundations
but also gets the better of it by avoiding the paths of its torrents. Though he
does not deploy thunderbolts or heavenly balls of fire directly against the river,
he is guided to his mastering foundations by Zeus, who drops thunderbolt-
like flaming ox thighs down from the sky, reminiscent of the weapons he had
used in his primeval battle.

It is curious that the Seleucids should have calqued Ptolemaic imagery in
developing a serpent-river myth for themselves, for all that they were able to
connect that myth with indigenous myths of great antiquity from their own
realm. That they chose to do so in preference to developing a wholly independent imagery must say something of the compelling and immediate power of
Ptolemy's myth. In this respect, as in others, the Seleucids seem to have been
playing catch-up with the Ptolemies.

A Later Dialogue with Christians, and Perhaps
Something Earlier

And so to the Christians. The latter part of the *Romance*'s Agathos Daimon
narrative constitutes an etiology of the private cult practice of (supposedly)
feeding friendly "Agathos Daimon" house snakes. The practice is first attested
in a fragment of Phylarchus, whose history finished in 219 BC with the death of
Cleomenes II of Sparta. He speaks of the Egyptians keeping asps in their
houses: these come when called by a snap of the fingers to receive gifts of barley
in wine and honey, retreating at a second snap (Phylarchus' designation of the
Agathos Daimon snakes as asps, as opposed to anti-asps, is unique).[45] Plutarch
subsequently gives us a vignette of two Egyptian neighbors fighting for possession of a luck-bringing Agathos Daimon snake that they find in the road.[46]

Christian tradition preserves a tale related to this latter part of the *Romance*'s story, in that it also has Alexander presiding over the introduction
into Alexandria of good snakes that attack bad snakes. A third-century AD
pseudo-Epiphanian narrative survives in two versions of its own and is reflected
in better, though not perfect, condition in the seventh-century AD *Chronicon
Paschale*. The three texts differ from one another only by variation in what

they—quite confusingly—omit. The following translation merges them to produce an almost fully intelligible story:

> Jeremiah was of Anathoth, and he died in Daphnae in Egypt when he was stoned to death by the local people. He was laid to rest in the region of the Pharaoh's palace, because the Egyptians held him in honor, since he had done them good service. For he prayed for them, and the asps left them alone, as did the creatures of the waters, which the Egyptians call *menephōth* and the Greeks call crocodiles, which were killing them.[47] The prophet prayed and the race of asps was averted from that land, as were the attacks of the creatures from the river. Even to this day the faithful pray in the place he lay, and by taking earth from the site of his tumulus they heal bites inflicted upon people, and many avert even the creatures in the water. We heard from some old men, descendants of Antigonus and Ptolemy, that Alexander the Macedonian visited the tomb of the prophet and learned the mysteries pertaining to him. He transferred his remains to Alexandria, and arranged them, with all due honor, in a circle. The race of asps was thus averted from that land, as similarly were the creatures from the river. And thus he threw in [sc. inside the circle] the snakes called *argolaoi*, that is "snake-fighters" [*ophiomachoi*], which he had brought from Peloponnesian Argos, whence they are called *argolaoi*, that is, "right-hand-men [*dexioi*] of Argos." The sound they make is very sweet and of all good omen.
>
> [Epiphanius] *De prophetarum et obitu*
> ~ first recension, p. 9, Schermann
> ~ second recension, pp. 61–62, Schermann
> ~ *Chronicon Paschale*, p. 293, Dindorf[48]

The final sentences remain slightly enigmatic but appear to mean that Alexander took Jeremiah's deterrent remains from Daphnae and arranged them in a circle around the city of Alexandria, presumably by distributing the limbs or, more probably, by sprinkling a fine line of cremation ash: the latter would recall the tradition found first in Strabo that Alexander had first marked out the circle of Alexandria for his architects by sprinkling a line of barley meal (which was then devoured by birds—more animal guides—in an act of good omen).[49] Snakes (and crocodiles) outside the circle were thus prevented from entering it. He then threw his other snake-fighting *argolaoi* snakes inside the circle (evidently, they could not pass through it any more than any other snakes could), where they will have destroyed the bad snakes marooned inside it, and taken their place. Jeremiah was, it seems, a Saint Patrick avant la lettre and is associated with the phenomenon known to folklorists (in consequence of Saint Patrick) as "Irish earth," that of the soil of certain places being repellent to certain venomous creatures and an antidote to their venoms, which is well attested elsewhere in Graeco-Roman culture, at least from the age of the elder Pliny in the first century AD onward.[50] The Jeremiah tale also salutes a familiar motif of ancient snake-control stories, that of the deployment of a "magic circle" against them, as in the tale of a Thessalian witch's battle against the *hieros ophis* ("sacred snake") attributed to Aristotle.[51]

Like the *Romance*'s myth, this one accounts for the arrival, alongside Alexander, of a host of good snakes in Alexandria, which we may assume were to be identified with those that became the object of private cult: we note the *Romance*'s contention that its Agathoi Daimones "are not poisonous, but they do ward off those snakes that do seem to be poisonous": these, clearly, are "snake-fighters," too. The tale also efficiently salutes the Argeads' and thereby the Ptolemies' claim to derive their stock ultimately from Argos.[52] The motif of Alexander's physical transporting of the *argolaoi* serpents from Argos further salutes the Greek traditions of cult transfer associated with the greatest anguiform god of the all, Asclepius. Numerous glorious accounts, inscriptional and literary, survive from the later fourth century BC onward describing this god's journey to a new cult site in the form of a massive, benign serpent (*drakōn, draco*). The particularly splendid accounts of Asclepius' passage from Epidaurus to Rome describe a journey that supposedly took place in 292 BC, shortly after, as it would seem, the development of the notion of Alexander's encounter with Agathos Daimon.[53] It is noteworthy too that the ancient variety of snakes particularly associated with the sanctuaries of Asclepius, the kindly and healing *pareias* (probably *Elaphe quatuorlineata*, the four-lined snake), had a reputation for attacking vipers.[54]

It is hard to believe that the Jeremiah material as we have it, with its motif of martyrdom, antedates the Christian era (nice as it would have been to imagine that this was a variant of the foundation legend designed at an early stage to engage and include Hellenistic Alexandria's large Jewish population). The story's function, in the form we have it, is no doubt to install a figure of Christian interest at the heart of the foundation of Alexandria for the gratification and validation of its Christian inhabitants. However, it is possible that the basic tale is older and that Jeremiah has supplanted another marvelous figure. The motif of the transfer of a great man's remains from the land of Egypt proper to Alexandria is strikingly reminiscent of Ptolemy's historical transfer of Alexander's own body from Memphis to Alexandria.[55] On this basis, it may be that the tale was developed as a typological justification for Ptolemy's transfer and therefore, presumably, developed by or for the Ptolemaic dynasty. Another possibility is that the story originated actually as a more direct reimagining of Ptolemy's historical transfer of Alexander's body, with Alexander accordingly in Jeremiah's role and Ptolemy himself in Alexander's. It is unlikely, however, that any original story relating to Alexander's body subjected it to dispersal in the fashion of Jeremiah's, given that it famously lay intact inside his Alexandrian tomb, up until the point at which Octavian broke off its nose.[56] Either way, the original tale would, gratifyingly, have found a way, directly or indirectly, of bringing Ptolemy where he must have aspired to be and indeed where he frankly deserved to be: close to the heart of an Alexandrian foundation myth.

The Alexandrian foundation myth spoke to the new city's Greek and Macedonian settlers and to native Egyptians alike. If it did not immediately speak to the city's third great constituency, the Jews, it did eventually speak, with Jewish imagery, to its subsequent Christian inhabitants. The serpent imagery that it invoked embraced together the figure of Alexander with that of Ptolemy, the city of Alexandria with Egypt, and the men with the land. The myth's immediate and compelling impact is best demonstrated by the Seleucids' adoption and adaptation of its imagery for the mythical underpinning of their rival capitals.

NOTES

1. For Agathos Daimon in general, see Harrison 1912: 277–316; Cook 1914–40: vol. 2, part 2: 1125–29; Ganschinietz/Ganszyniec 1918, 1919; Jakobsson 1925: esp. 151–75; Rohde 1925: 207–8 n. 133; Tarn 1928; Taylor 1930; Dunand 1969, 1981, with bibliography; Fraser 1972: 1:209–11, with associated notes; Quaegebeur 1975: 170–76 and passim; Mitropoulou 1977: 155–68; Pietrzykowski 1978; Sfameni Gasparro 1997; Jouanno 2002: 75–76, 105–8; Stoneman 2007: 532–34; Stoneman 2008: 56–58.

2. This earliest extant recension of the *Alexander Romance*, α, is recovered from a single Greek MS ("A"), reporting a badly corrupt and lacunary account of it, and an Armenian translation of a rather better account of it.

3. *Alexander Romance* 1.31.7 (A).

4. See *OGI* no. 672, with further references ad loc.; Claudius Ptolemy *Geography* 4.5.

5. This and other angle-bracketed portions are supplied for the corrupt and lacunary A MS from the Armenian translation; for a full English translation, see Wolohojan 1969. The β recension has a slightly more elaborate tale: when the gatehouse to the shrine was being built, a huge, ancient tablet full of letters fell out of it, and it was out of this that the snakes emerged. Presumably, the notion was that a piece of ancient Egyptian masonry was being reused. But this tablet full of letters would seem to be a doublet of the tablet that Alexander has just inscribed with his own five letters.

6. For the Louvre copy, see Schwarzenberg 1976: 235 with fig. 8; Stewart 1993: 247; Stoneman 2007: 533. I thank Prof. Victor Alonso Troncoso for drawing the León statuette to my attention.

7. See Stewart 1993: 248–50 for the Athena Parthenos comparison. Paus. 1.24.5 speculated that her snake was Ericthonius. The *oikouros ophis*: Hdt 8.41; Ar. *Lys.* 758–59 with schol.; Phylarchus *FGrH* 81 F72 = Photius *Lexicon* s.v. οἰκουρὸν ὄφιν; Plut. *Themistocles* 10; *Etymologicum Magnum* s.v. Ἐρεχθεύς. Gourmelen 2004: 346–47 contends that the Parthenos' snake actually represented both of these.

8. Cyrene: Callimachus *Hymn* 2.65–66. Magnesia: *I.Magnesia* 46 = *FGrH* 482 F3. Coraces: Demon *FGrH* 327 F7; Aristotle F496 Rose. Ilium: Apollodorus *Bibliotheca* 3.12.3. Argilos: Heraclides of Pontus *FHG* ii p. 224 F42; Stephanus of Byzantium s.v. Ἄργιλος. Ephesus: Creophylus *FGrH* 417 F1 at Athenaeus 361d–e. Athamantia: Apollodorus *Bibliotheca* 1.9.2. Tarentum: Dionysius of Halicarnassus 19.1–2. For animal guides in general, see Schmid 1947: 94–101.

9. Archelaus: Hyginus *Fabulae* 219 (summarizing Euripides *Archelaus*); Dio Chrysostom 4.70–72. Caranus: Justin 7.1.7–7.2.1 (from Trogus; perhaps ultimately from Theopompus); schol. Clement of Alexandria *Protrepticus* 2.11, incorporating Euphorion FF38a–b + 1182 Powell = F35 Lightfoot. Perdiccas: Diod. Sic. 7.16.

10. *Alexander Romance* 2.23 (β).

11. For dragon-slaying traditions at foundation sites in the Greek world, see Trumpf 1958.

12. Pherecydes F22ab, 88 Fowler; Eur. *Phoen.* 238, 638–48, 657–75, 818–21, 931–41, 1006–12 (for the cult), 1060–66, 1315 (all with schol.), *Bacchae* 1330–39, 1355–60; Hellanicus FF1a, 51, 96, 98; Fowler; Palaephatus 3–4; Apollonius *Argonautica* 3.1176–90; Ovid *Metamorphoses* 3.28–98 (the most expansive account); Apollodorus *Bibliotheca* 3.4.1–2, 3.5.4; Hyginus *Fabulae* 6, 148, 178, 274.4; Paus. 9.10.5; Philostratus *Imagines* 1.18; etc. For the iconography of the episode, see *LIMC* Harmonia 1–7, Hesperie 1(?), Kadmos i 7–47.

13. Antoninus Liberalis *Metamorphoses* 8. Although the monster's form is not explicitly described, other lamia monsters in Greek literature are described as part anguiform, e.g., Philostratus *Life of Apollonius* 4.25; Dio Chrys. *Orations* 5 (where comparanda tell us that the monster in question is a lamia, even though the term is withheld). For *lamiai* in general, see Rohde 1925: 590–95; Fontenrose 1959: 44–45, 100–104, 119–20; Scobie 1983: 25–29; Boardman 1992; Burkert 1992: 82–87; Johnston 1999: 161–202 (the last with care). Furthermore, up until the fight itself, the distinctive Alyconeus tale is the close doublet of

the tale of Menestratus of Thespiae at Paus. 9.26.7–8, where the monstrous opponent is explicitly stated to be a serpent (*drakōn*).

14. *Suda* s.v. Ἀγαθοῦ Δαίμονος.

15. *Syriac Alexander Romance* 3.7 (recension δ). For text and translation, see Budge 1889, with the relevant portion at 102–3. It is possible that this dragon fight is ultimately derivative of the Agathos Daimon narrative: Ogden 2012.

16. Ferdowsi *Shahnameh* C1331–34. Khaleghi-Motlagh 1988– will be the standard edition of the text when complete. Tr. Davis 2006: 506–8; Warner and Warner 1912: 6:148–53.

17. For more comprehensive arguments and evidence on this subject, see Ogden 2009a, 2009b, 2011: 7–56.

18. Arrian *Anabasis* 3.3.4–6, incorporating Ptolemy *FGrH* 138 F8. It is usually believed that Ptolemy compiled his history toward the end of his reign: See Roisman 1984. Arrian's observation is borne out by the remnants of it that survive. All other sources give us crows, with the serpents being preferred only here, in association with Ptolemy's version. Strabo C814 = Callisthenes *FGrH* 124 F14, Diod. Sic. 17.49.5, Curtius 4.7.15, Plut. *Alexander* 27, *Itinerarium* 21 (crows, but acknowledging the variant of serpents).

19. Diod. Sic. 17.103.4–8; Curtius 9.8.22–28: coincidence between these authors normally entails that Clitarchus is their ultimate source.

20. Cicero *On Divination* 2.135, Livy 26.19.7–8, Trogus as reflected in Justin 11.11.2–5, Plut. *Alexander* 2–3, Ptolemy son of Hephaistion at Photius *Library* no. 190 (148a; Ptolemy wrote either in the Neronian-Flavian or the Trajanic-Hadrianic one: *Suda* s.vv. Ἐπαφρόδιτος and Πτολεμαῖος, respectively).

21. Eratosthenes *FGrH* 241 F28 *apud* Plut. *Alexander* 2–3.

22. Silius Italicus *Punica* 13.636: *quando aperire datur nobis, nunc denique disce*, "Learn it at last, now that I am permitted to reveal it."

23. However, other gigantic serpents found their way into the early Alexander tradition, seemingly without help from Ptolemy. Writing by 309 BC at the latest, Alexander's "chief helmsman of the fantastic," Onesicritus of Astypalaea, told that the Indian king Abisares had regaled Alexander with tales of a pair of gigantic serpents (*drakontes*), one 140 cubits, the other eighty cubits in length: *FGrH* 134 16a–c.

24. The case is made by Merkelbach 1977: 36–38. Apophis: *P. Bremner-Rhind*, reproduced in photographs at Budge 1910 pl. i–xix; tr. *ANET* 6–7. Nigidius Figulus p. 123, 8 Swoboda records that Seth-Typhon was killed in the Memphite temple in which the pharaohs were crowned.

25. Manetho *FGrH* 609 F3; cf. Quaegebeur 1975: 174–75; Dunand 1969: 37; Dunand 1981: 277.

26. *P.Oxy.* 2332 lines 51–53: κατά τε ὁ ἀγαθὸς / δαίμων καταλείψει τὴν κτιζομένην πόλειν καὶ ἀ/πελεύσεται εἰς τὴν θεοτόκον Μέμφειν καὶ ἐξερημώσηται. For this text, see Tarn 1928: 215; Fraser 1972: 1:683–84.

27. Cassius Dio 51.17.4–5: καί τις δράκων ὑπερμεγέθης ἐξαίφνης σφίσιν ὀφθεὶς ἀμήχανον ὅσον ἐξεσύρισε.

28. The comic fragments are collected at Athenaeus 692f–693e. Timoleon: Plut. *Moralia* 542e, καὶ τὴν οἰκίαν Ἀγαθῷ Δαίμονι καθιερώσας.

29. *LIMC* Agathodaimon no. 6. Harrison 1912: 283 and Dunand 1981 ad loc. take this to be an image of Agathos Daimon. Cook 1914–40: vol. 2, part 2: 1151–52 and Mitropoulou 1977: 135 take it to be Zeus Meilichios, and the superficial resemblance of this relief to the fourth-century Attic Zeus Meilichios reliefs is indeed strong.

30. For Zeus Meilichios, see the testimonia and discussion at Jameson et al. 1993: 81–103, 132–41; Lalonde 2006: 103–20. For his iconography, see Cook 1914–40: vol. 2, part 2: 1091–1160; Mitropoulou 1977: 112–55.

31. Mytilene relief: Mitropoulou 1977: 178–80 (with fig. 92). Coins: *LIMC* Agathodaimon nos. 31, 35. See Dunand 1969: 36; Dunand 1981: 281.

32. *LIMC* Agathodaimon no. 3; cf. Fraser 1972: 2:356–57 n. 164; Mitropoulou 1977: 164–65; Dunand 1981: 278, 280.

33. *LIMC* Agathodaimon 4; cf. Mitropoulou 1977: 159–60 no. 1 (with fig. 79). There is insufficient evidence to associate Mitropoulou 1977: 159–61 no. 2 (fig. 80) with Agathos Daimon.

34. *IG* vii 1815 = *LIMC* Agathodaimon 2; cf. Mitropoulou 1977: 161–62 no. 3 (with fig. 81).

35. For the pairing, see Bonnechere 2003: 234 n. 42.

36. Copenhagen Ny Carlsberg Glyptothek 1558 = *IG* ii² 4627 = Harrison 1912: 312, fig. 90, Harrison 1922: 355, fig. 106; Cook 1914–40: vol. 2, part 2:1162, fig. 970 = Mitropoulou 1977: 102–3 no. 6 and fig. 42.

37. Athens National Museum no. 8738 = *IG* ii² 2935 = Mitropoulou 1977: 99–100 no. 1 (with fig. 39). For the particular relevance of the iconography of Zeus Philios to Agathos Daimon, see Dunand 1981: 280.

38. In biblical and classical contexts, the term "typology" is used to denote the study of prefigurative myths.

39. The case laid out here is adumbrated at West 1997: 303–4 and argued in expansive detail by Lane Fox 2008: 255–73. Teshub against Hedammu: text at Siegelova 1971; tr. Haas 2006: 153–56 (German). Tarhunna against Illuyankas: texts at Beckman 1982; tr. Hoffner 1998: 10–14. Baal-Sapon against Yam and Lotan: text at Smith 1994, at KTU 1.1–3 = CTA 1–3; tr. Caquot et al. 1974 (French). Apollodorus *Bibliotheca* 1.6.3 (c. AD 100) is the earliest extant Greek source actually to locate the battle between Zeus and Typhon on Mount Kasios, although Pindar *Pythians* 1.15–28, 8.15–16, F92 Snell-Maehler locates it in the adjacent Cilicia, just across the gulf of Issus from Mount Kasios.

40. Strabo C750–51; cf. Paus. (Periegetes) 8.29, John Malalas *Chronicle* 197 Dindorf.

41. Pausanias of Antioch *FHG* 4:467–68, F3 = John Malalas *Chronicle* 37–38 Dindorf. In other contexts, we may wish to note, the Greeks deployed Agathos Daimon as the *interpretatio Graeca* of the Zoroastrian "Good Principle," Spenta Mainyu/ Ahura Mazda: Diod. Sic. 1.94; cf. Ganschinietz 1918: 39.

42. John Malalas *Chronicle* 198–200 Dindorf.

43. Libanius *Orations* 11.85–88.

44. Dieudonné 1929 with plate ii (iv). Note, esp., 16 (eagle with thigh) and 18 (eagle with thunderbolt).

45. Phylarchus *FGrH* 81 F27 = Aelian *Nature of Animals* 17.5.

46. Plut. *Moralia* 755e.

47. Perhaps the starting point for the attribution such powers to Jeremiah is Jer. 8:17, where God, speaking through the prophet, threatens plagues of venomous, biting serpents resistant to charming.

48. For the Epiphanius recensions, see Schermann 1907. Brief discussion at Stoneman 1994, 2007: 533; Stoneman 2008: 57. A yet more confusingly contracted version of the narrative is found at *Suda* s.v. ἀργόλαι and [Zonaras] *Lexicon* s.v. ἀργόλαι; note also *Suda* s.vv. Ἰερεμίας, Ὀστᾶ Γιγάντων, Ὄφις.

49. Strabo C792, Plut. *Alexander* 26.

50. Pliny *Natural History* 3.11 (Ebesus; so, too, Pomponius Mela 2.7), 5.7 (Galata), 37.54 (Sicily, including the *achate*), Dioscorides 5.113 (Lemnian earth an emetic for poisons), Galen *De simplicium medicamentorum temperamentis ac facultatibus* xii.169 Kühn (Lemnian earth cures poisonous snakebites in general), Philostratus *Heroicus* 6.2 (Lemnian earth cures Philoctetes), Aelian *Nature of Animals* 5.2 (Crete), 5.8 (Astypalaea). See Hasluck 1909–10 for the Greek material; Krappe 1941, 1947, with a great many parallels, for the wider folkloristic belief.

51. [Aristotle] *Mirabilia* 845b; cf. Lucan 9.915–37, Lucian *Philopseudes* 11–13.

52. Curtius 9.8.22; Paus. 1.6.2, 1.6.8; *Alexander Romance* 3.32 (A); unpublished Ptolemaic inscription at Errington 1990: 265 n. 6 (Ἡρακλείδας Ἀργεάδας).

53. Livy 29.11.1 and *Periocha* 11; Ovid *Metamorphoses* 15.622–744; Valerius Maximus 1.8.2; Pliny *Natural History* 29.72; Arnobius *Against the Gentiles* 7.44–48; Augustine *City of God* 3.17; Claudian *On the Consulship of Stilicho* 3.171–73; [Aurelius Victor] *De viris illustribus* 22.1–3; Latin *Anthology* 1.2.719e.1–7; Q. Serenus Salmonicus *Liber medicinalis* prooemium 1–10.

54. Harpocration s.v. Παρεῖαι ὄφεις, incorporating Hyperides F80 Jensen.

55. Diod. Sic. 18.28; Strabo C794; Curtius 10.10.20. However, Paus. 1.7.1 attributes the transfer to Philadelphus. Discussion at Saunders 2006: 49–62.

56. Suetonius *Octavian* 2.18; Cassius Dio 21.16.

REFERENCES

Beckman, G. 1982. "The Anatolian Myth of Illuyanka." *Journal of the Ancient Near Eastern Society* 14: 11–25.

Boardman, J. 1992. "Lamia." *LIMC* 6 (1): 189.

Bonnechere, P. 2003. *Trophonios de Lébadée: Cultes et mythes d'une cité béotienne au miroir de la mentalité antique.* Leiden: Brill.

Burkert, W. 1992. *The Orientalizing Revolution.* Cambridge, MA: Harvard University Press.

Budge, E. A. W. 1889. *The History of Alexander the Great, Being the Syriac Version of the Pseudo-Callisthenes*. Cambridge: Cambridge University Press.

Budge, E. A. W. 1910. *Facsimiles of Egyptian Hieratic Papyri in the British Museum*. London: British Museum.

Caquot, A., M. Sznycer, and A. Herdner. 1974. *Textes ougaritiques* I: *Mythes et légendes*. Paris: Cerf.

Cook, A. B. 1914–40. *Zeus: A Study in Ancient Religion*. 3 vols. Cambridge: Cambridge University Press.

Davis, D. (tr.). 2006. *Albolqasem Ferdowsi: Shahnameh, the Persian Book of Kings*. New York: Penguin.

Dieudonné, A. 1929. "Les monnaies grecques de Syrie au Cabinet des Médailles." *Revue numismatique* 15–26.

Dunand, F. 1969. "Les representations de l'Agathodémon: À propos de quelques bas-reliefs du Musée d'Alexandrie." *Bulletin de l'Institut français d'archéologie orientale* 67: 9–48.

Dunand, F. 1981. "Agathodaimon." *LIMC* I (I): 277–82.

Errington, R. M. 1990. *A History of Macedonia*. Berkeley: University of California Press.

Fontenrose, J. 1959. *Python: A Study of the Delphic Myth and Its Origins*. Berkeley: University of California Press.

Fraser, P. M. 1972. *Ptolemaic Alexandria*. 3 vols. Oxford: Clarendon.

Ganschinietz/Ganszyniec, R. 1918. "Agathodaimon." *Paulys Real-Encyclopädie der classischen Altertumswissenschaft*, supplement 3: 37–59.

Ganschinietz/Ganszyniec, R. 1919. *De Agatho-daemone*. Warsaw: Prace Towarzystwa Naukowego Warszawskiego.

Gourmelen, L. 2004. *Kékrops, le roi-serpent: Imaginaire athénien, représentations de l'humain et de l'animalité en Grèce ancienne*. Paris: Les Belles Lettres.

Haas, V. 2006. *Die hethitische Literatur: Texte, Stilistik, Motive*. Berlin: De Gruyter.

Harrison, J. 1912. *Themis*. Cambridge: Cambridge University Press.

Harrison, J. 1922. *Prolegomena to the Study of Greek Religion*. Cambridge: Cambridge University Press.

Hasluck, F. W. 1909–10. "Terra Lemnia." *Annual of the British School at Athens*: 220–31.

Hoffner, H. A. 1998. *Hittite Myths*. 3rd ed. Atlanta: Scholars Press.

Jakobsson, O. 1925. *Daimon och Agathos Daimon*. Lund: Akademisk avhandling.

Jameson, M. H., D. R. Jordan, and R. D. Kotansky. 1993. *A Lex Sacra from Selinous*. Greek, Roman and Byzantine Studies Monographs II. Durham, NC: Duke University Press.

Johnston, S. I. 1999. *Restless Dead: Encounters Between the Living and the Dead in Ancient Greece*. Berkeley: University of California Press.

Jouanno, C. 2002. *Naissance et métamorphoses du Roman d'Alexandre: Domaine grec*. Paris: CNRS.

Khaleghi-Motlagh, D. (ed.). 1988–. *Abu al-Qasim Firdawsi: Shahnameh (The Book of Kings)*. 8+ vols. New York: Bibliotheca Persica.

Krappe, A. H. 1941. "Irish Earth." *Folk-Lore* 52: 229–36.

Krappe, A. H. 1947. "St Patrick and the Snakes." *Traditio* 5: 323–30.

Lalonde, G. 2006. *Horos Dios: An Athenian Shrine and Cult.* Leiden: Brill.

Lane Fox, R. 2008. *Travelling Heroes: Greeks and Their Myths in the Epic Age of Homer.* London: Penguin.

Merkelbach, R. 1977. *Die Quellen des griechischen Alexanderromans.* Zetemata 9. 2nd ed. Munich: C. H. Beck.

Mitropoulou, E. 1977. *Deities and Heroes in the Form of Snakes.* 2nd ed. Athens: Pyli.

Ogden, D. 2009a. "Alexander's Snake Sire." In *Alexander and His Successors: Essays from the Antipodes,* ed. P. Wheatley and R. Hannah, 136–78. Claremont, CA: Regina.

Ogden, D. 2009b. "Alexander, Scipio and Octavian: Serpent-Siring in Macedon and Rome." *Syllecta Classica* 20: 31–52.

Ogden, D. 2011. *Alexander the Great: Myth, Genesis and Sexuality.* Exeter: University of Exeter Press.

Ogden, D. 2012. "Sekandar, Dragon-Slayer." In *The Alexander Romance in Persia and the East,* Ancient Narrative Supplementum 15, ed. R. Stoneman, K. Erikson, and I. Netton, 277–94. Groningen: Barkhuis.

Pietrzykowski, M. 1978. "Sarapis-Agathos Daimon." In *Hommages à M. J. Vermaseren: Études préliminaires aux religions orientales dans l'Empire romain 68*: 3:959–66. Leiden: Brill.

Quaegebeur, J. 1975. *Le dieu égyptien Shaï dans la religion et l'onomastique.* Orientalia Lovaniensia Analecta no. 2. Leuven: Peeters.

Rohde, E. 1925. *Psyche.* London: Routledge and Kegan Paul (tr. from the 8th German ed.).

Roisman, J. 1984. "Ptolemy and His Rivals in His History of Alexander the Great." *Classical Quarterly* 34: 373–85.

Saunders, N. J. 2006. *Alexander's Tomb.* New York: Basic Books.

Schermann, T. 1907. *Prophetarum vitae fabulosae.* Leipzig: Teubner.

Schmid, P. B. 1947. *Studien zu griechischen Ktisissagen.* Freiburg: Paulus.

Schwarzenberg, E. 1976. "The Portraiture of Alexander." In *Alexandre le Grand: Image et réalité,* ed. E. Badian, 223–67. Geneva: Fondation Hardt.

Scobie, A. 1983. *Apuleius and Folklore: Toward a History of ML3045, AaTh567, 449A.* London: Folklore Society.

Sfameni Gasparro, G. 1997. "Daimon and Tyche in the Hellenistic Religious Experience." In *Conventional Values of the Hellenistic Greeks,* Studies in Hellenistic Civilisations 7, ed. P. Bilde et al., 67–109. Aarhus: Aarhus University Press.

Siegelova, J. 1971. *Appu-Märchen und Hedammu-Mythos.* Wiesbaden: Harrassowitz.

Smith, M. S. 1994. *The Ugaritic Baal Cycle. Vetus Testamentum* supplement 55. Leiden: Brill.

Stewart, A. 1993. *Faces of Power: Alexander's Image and Hellenistic Politics.* Berkeley: University of California Press.

Stoneman, R. 1994. "Jewish Traditions on Alexander the Great." *Studia Philonica Annual* 6: 37–53.

Stoneman, R. (ed. and tr.). 2007. *Il romanzo di Alessandro.* Milan: Mondadori.

Stoneman, R. 2008. *Alexander the Great: A Life in Legend.* New Haven, CT: Yale University Press.

Tarn, W. W. 1928. "The Hellenistic Ruler-Cult and the Daemon." *Journal of Hellenic Studies* 48: 206–19.

Taylor, L. R. 1930. "Alexander and the Serpent of Alexandria." *Classical Philology* 25: 375–78.

Trumpf, J. 1958. "Stadtgründung und Drachenkampf (Exkurse zu Pindar, Pythien 1)." *Hermes* 86: 219–57.

Warner, A. G., and E. Warner (tr.). 1912. *The Sháhnáma of Firdausí*. 9 vols. London: Routledge.

West, M. L. 1997. *East Face of Helicon*. Oxford: Oxford University Press.

Wolohojian, A. M. (tr.). 1969. *The Romance of Alexander the Great by Pseudo-Callisthenes*, tr. from the Armenian version. New York: Columbia University Press.

CHAPTER 6

Figuring Rome's Foundation on the Iliac Tablets

MICHAEL SQUIRE

Although much of this volume has focused on stories about (broadly defined) "Greek" civic origins, Roman foundation myths evidently operated in no less complex and multifaceted ways. Whatever Rome's "original" origins, different legends have long been manipulated and exploited—by Republican leaders, by Roman emperors, and, indeed, by more contemporary political dictators. Exactly when did Rome come into being? Who was responsible? And where in myth or history should that founding moment be situated?

Among ancient writers and artists, these questions spurred a miscellany of interconnecting answers.[1] According to some, Rome's origins were bound up with the myth of Aeneas—his departure from the sacked city of Troy, his arrival at Latium, and his son Ascanius' subsequent founding of Alba Longa. For others, Rome's true foundation came later: with the defiance of Rhea Silvia, the twin exploits of her sons Romulus and Remus, and ultimately, with Romulus' foundational act of fratricide on the Palatine.[2] Others still emphasized subsequent moments—the overthrow of Romulus' kingly successors, the legendary origins of the Republic, the acquisition of Italy and worldwide territories. Of course, these stories were not mutually exclusive, with each "origin" pointing recessively to another. Different myths could likewise be tendered to suit different ideologies of political *re*-foundation: in the late Republic, and under each successive *princeps* in turn, different leaders could spin-doctor their own "official" takes.

What is interesting about these myths is precisely their number and diversity. Rome could be attributed with a whole host of different founding moments, all of them coexistent within the same cultural imaginary. There were multiple myths to be told, each buried in its own social, cultural, and political stratigraphy. Despite all the attempts to talk of a single date or event set in stone—Rome was founded on 21 April 752 BC, according to the monumental *Fasti Capitolini*[3]—the stories told about Roman origins also resisted linearity and narrative closure.

This multiplicity worked on both a collective and an individual level. Whichever myth we focus on, there was never anything quite approximating "gospel truth." Even if one attempted to chronicle a single, processional chain of events (in the manner of Livy's monumental *Ab Urbe Condita*), someone was always at hand to challenge each "fact." An extreme, Second Sophistic example appears in Dio Chrysostom's eleventh oration, composed in Greek and delivered late in the first century AD.[4] Whatever you *think* you know from Homer, the speaker explains, the literary account is riddled with lies and half-truths—and nowhere more so than when it comes to Rome's supposed relationship with Troy. Are we really to believe, the text asks, that Aeneas left a burning city to found a new kingdom? Is it not much more likely that the power-hungry prince sent an army to Italy—that it was through Priam's permission (and indeed, Hector's aid) that Aeneas "founded the greatest city of all" (καὶ πόλιν ᾤκισε τὴν μεγίστην πασῶν, 11.139)? "If anybody does not accept this account under the influence of the old view, let him know that he is unable to get free of error and distinguish truth from falsehood" (ὅστις δὲ μὴ πείθεται τούτοις ὑπὸ τῆς παλαιᾶς δόξης, ἐπιστάσθω ἀδύνατος ὢν ἀπαλλαγῆναι ἀπάτης καὶ διαγνῶναι τὸ ψεῦδος, 11.144).

Rather than follow Dio in (sophistically) attempting to disentangle fact from fiction, the present chapter owns up to the plurality of Roman foundation myths. By exploring, in miniature, some of the ways in which different traditions were played with, my aim is to interrogate the intrinsic discursiveness of Roman foundation fables writ large. All manner of literary case studies could be introduced here. But I have chosen to focus on a single set of material objects, produced in the late first century BC or early first century AD: the *Tabulae Iliacae*, or "Iliac tablets." Although all the tablets are inscribed in Greek, engaging (for the most part) with Greek epic subjects, their stories had an immediate latter-day Roman relevance: the *Tabulae* allude knowingly to an "official" set of Augustan foundation myths, I suggest, while calling into question some of the political ideologies at work.

In turning to the Iliac tablets, my aim is to advance two overriding arguments. First, I demonstrate how, for all their purported Greek literary themes, the tablets (or, more precisely, a substantial number of surviving fragments) seem to have placed Roman foundation stories at their literal and metaphorical center. As we shall see, almost everything about these objects led viewers to understand them in Greek terms. When it comes to composition, however, numerous tablets seem to have pivoted around the story of Aeneas' departure from Troy: for all their canonical Greek literary themes, they framed their epic panoramas around an unrepresented narrative of Roman civic origins. Still more intriguing is the iconography of the central scene. Although the motif of Aeneas fleeing the city had a long artistic pedigree, the presentation here seems to have chimed with that of an important statue group erected by Augustus in his eponymous forum at Rome. At the literal and metaphorical heart of these tablets is a story about (a story about) Rome's foundation—and one that resonated with Augustus' own "official" narrative of imperial beginnings.

This leads to a second and closely related point. For foundational to the tablets' games, I argue, is a narratological self-consciousness about how audiences construct stories, and about how they construct stories about Roman foundations in particular. While setting in stone a specific set of myths, the tablets also spur, prod, and goad: they invite audiences to reflect on the mechanics of making meaning—to reexamine not just what we see and read but also how we do so. As I hope to show, such self-referential games have a particular resonance for the methodological considerations aired so eloquently in the introduction to this book: the tablets do not just monumentalize a single story about civic origins but rather play upon a discourse of myth, and one with particular political charge.

The *Tabulae Iliacae*

Let me begin by saying something about the Iliac tablets more generally. Although the objects were relatively famous in the nineteenth century—cataloged as *griechische Bilderchroniken* ("Greek chronicles in pictures") by Otto Jahn and Adolf Michaelis in 1873—the tablets did not fare well in the twentieth century, and are less known among today's archaeologists and philologists than they should be.[5] Despite a new catalog by Anna Sadurska in 1964, and an even more thorough presentation by Nina Valenzuela Montenegro in 2004, most scholars have paid the tablets relatively little attention.[6] Those who have

Table 6.1. Depicted subjects of the *Tabulae Iliacae*, based on the identification of their surviving sections

	1A	2NY	3C	4N	5O	6B	7Ti	8E	9D	10K
Iliad (Books)	•	•	•	•	•	•			•	
	1, 13–24	19–24	1–5	18	18	1–9			22–24	
Ilioupersis	•	•	•			•	•	•	•	
Aethiopis	•						•		•	
Little Iliad	•						•			
							(ins.)			
Odyssey (Books)					•					
					(ins.)					
Theban cycle									?	•
cycle									(ins.)	
Heraclean cycle										
Historical subjects										

Note: "(ins.)" refers to extant inscriptions that pertain to nonextant sections.

discussed the tablets, especially in the English-speaking world, moreover, have tended to dismiss them in wholly negative terms. "The serious lover of Greek art would have been appalled by such a combination of the obvious, the trivial and the false," wrote Nicholas Horsfall in 1994; likewise, "the serious lover of art cannot have derived much pleasure from pictures so tiny that the sculptor could add little if anything of his own interpretations and emotion."[7] Other Anglophone scholars have generally followed suit: according to Wallace McLeod, the tablets served as "tawdry gewgaws intended to provide the illusion of sophistication for those who had none."[8] I have responded to these arguments at much greater length elsewhere: to my mind, the tablets operate within a much more highbrow literary and artistic milieu than most twentieth-century scholars have assumed.[9]

Although almost all the tablets are fragmentary, we can nonetheless be confident about some essential facts. I restrict myself here to five initial comments, referring to more detailed discussions in the endnotes.[10] First and foremost, there are twenty-two reliefs usually classed under the *Tabulae Iliacae* banner.[11] Following the scheme established by Anna Sadurska, I refer to the tablets using a system of numbers and letters (1A, 2NY, 3C, and so on). As

H	12F	13Ta	14G	15Ber	16Sa	17M	18L	19J	20Par	21Fro	22Get
	•	•	•	•					•	•	
24	22 (+?)	14–18	?3						17–20	22–24	
								•			
•				•							
0				? 3–16							
								•			
					•	•					•

Table 6.1 indicates, the twenty-two tablets depict a variety of subjects. Still, a number of formal features bind the collection together: not just their miniature size but also their Greek inscriptions, compositions, and orthography. It is also worth noting the sheer number of extant reliefs: we have to reckon on possibly thousands of related objects once circulating around Rome.

Second, all the tablets derive from costly marbles, mostly from *palombino* and *giallo antico*.[12] While the different stones vary in color, most consist of relatively pale, off-white shades. At least some of the tablets were once painted: clear traces of gold are to be found on at least two of them, and it seems likely that other examples were decorated in similar fashion (a fact that might go toward explaining their so-called sfumato style, since details were probably painted rather than solely carved).[13]

Third, the issue of date: stylistically, all the tablets can be situated in the late first century BC or early first century AD; additional criteria confirm this chronology.[14] Interestingly, one example was made substantially later: tablet 19J is a mid-second-century imitation that probably combines a number of earlier prototypes. If nothing else, this later imitation seems to confirm the longevity of the phenomenon.[15]

Fourth, it is worth adding something about manufacture and workshops. Unlike others, I am not convinced that all the tablets are necessarily attributable to a single atelier. Nor, by contrast, do I think that we can confidently assign different tablets to distinctive workshops or hands: categorization here must remain speculative. That said, it is worth noting that six tablets do associate themselves with someone or something named "Theodorean," frequently boasting of their "Theodorean craftsmanship" (Θεοδώρηος ἡ τέχνη). Whatever we make of the artistic attribution (why the archaizing adjectival form?), these six attributed objects confirm a shared rationale. There are clear and palpable connections between the tablets, even if it is difficult to reconstruct such connections in terms of production.[16]

Finally, comes arguably the most vexed question: that of provenance and function.[17] The lack of detailed archaeological evidence means that we have to rely on internal rather than external evidence. Working from the tablets themselves, my own view is that the objects functioned as recherché display objects within the Roman *cena*, or dinner party.[18] As learned party pieces, the *Tabulae* were intended to be passed around a room, prompting erudite discussion: they were bite-size opportunities for a host—no less than his guests—to show off literary learning and dazzle assembled audiences. In that sense, one might compare the trappings of contemporary Roman dining *triclinia*—not only silver cups emblazoned with Homeric scenes but also Pompeian wall paintings and mosaics after highbrow literary themes, or indeed the grand sculptural installations at Sperlonga (designed to be enjoyed from the adjacent *triclinium*).[19] The little information that we have about provenance confirms this general picture: where find spots are known, they point exclusively to aristocratic villa contexts around the city of Rome. Although many of the reported find spots cannot be verified, three provenances are fairly secure, and all point to private domestic settings (tablets 1A, 7Ti, and 17M).[20]

So much for the scholarly background. But what do the tablets actually look like? The most famous example (tablet 1A)—and the object on which this chapter concentrates—was discovered in the late seventeenth century and can today be found in Rome's Musei Capitolini (hence its most common name, the "Capitoline Iliac tablet," or *Tabula Iliaca Capitolina*: Figs. 6.1 and 6.2).[21] The surviving fragment contains to its left a depiction of Troy's fall, or *Ilioupersis*, with two additional friezes below, relating to the *Little Iliad* and *Aethiopis*. The scene is framed to the right by a monumental pilaster, inscribed with a summary of *Iliad* 7–24 (in 108 lines, each about a millimeter in height). To the right of the pilaster are twelve lateral friezes (eleven of them inscribed with labels), which

6.1. Obverse of tablet 1A (Capitoline tablet / *Tabula Iliaca Capitolina*: Rome, Musei Capitolini, Sala delle Colombe, inv. 316). Reproduced with permission of the Direzione, Musei Capitolini, Rome.

correspond to the twelve books of *Iliad* 13–24, with the relevant book letters inscribed to the upper left of each frieze (from *nu* to *omega*).[22] The tablet's left-hand section is missing. But we can nonetheless be confident about the original overarching composition (Fig. 6.3): there was once a corresponding pilaster to the left of the *Ilioupersis*, inscribed with a summary of the earlier Iliadic books; to the left of that pilaster was another set of pictorial friezes, this time relating to *Iliad* 1–12. As a result, the first book of the *Iliad* was stretched over the tablet's upper central register (as can clearly be seen on the extant fragment).

The Capitoline tablet evidently visualized a grand panorama of epic. Still more poignantly, it also named its poetic subjects in a series of inscriptions

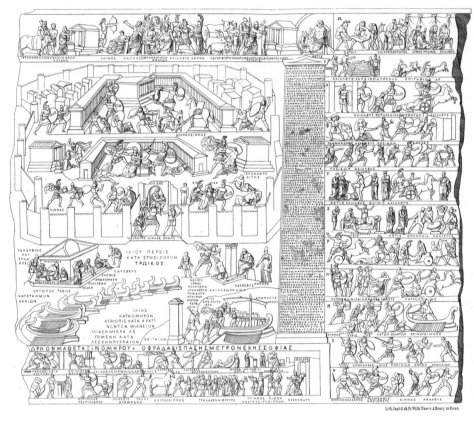

6.2. Drawing of the obverse of tablet 1A (Capitoline tablet) by Feodor Ivanovich.
After Jahn 1873: Tafel I.

underneath its central Trojan scene ("*Iliad* by Homer . . . *Aethiopis* by Arctinus
of Miletus, *Little Iliad* as told by Lesches of Pyrrha": Ἰλίου πέρσις κατὰ
Στησίχορον. Τρωικός. Ἰλιὰς κατὰ Ὅμηρον. Αἰθιοπὶς κατὰ Ἀρκτῖνον τὸν Μιλήσιον.
Ἰλιὰς ἡ μικρὰ λεγομένη κατὰ Λέσχην Πυρραῖον). Predictably, scholarly research
has concentrated on those poetic attributions, debating the object's reliability
for the reconstruction of the lost poetic texts named.[23] Much less attention has
been paid to the tablet's size: the surviving fragment measures just 25 by 30
centimeters (marginally larger than a sheet of A4 paper), despite its careful
decoration with more than two hundred figures. Because the mass of the surviving fragment is just 1.515 kilograms, the whole tablet cannot originally have
weighed more than two kilograms: it could easily be passed from one person to
another, approximating the weight of a small notebook computer today.[24]

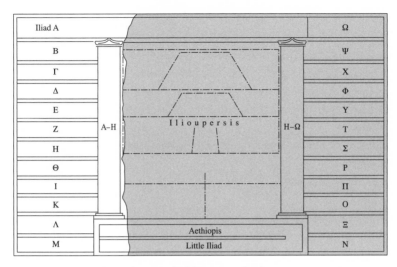

Iliad A				Ω
B				Ψ
Γ				Χ
Δ				Φ
E				Υ
Z	A–H	Ilioupersis	H–Ω	T
H				Σ
Θ				P
I				Π
K				O
Λ		Aethiopis		Ξ
M		Little Iliad		N

6.3. Reconstruction of the obverse of tablet 1A. Author's own.

We cannot be so sure about the compositions of the other tablets. A handful of examples were evidently much smaller, sometimes depicting just one Homeric book (for example, tablets 11H, 12F, ?13Ta). Still, as Table 6.1 shows, thirteen of the tablets are known to have depicted Iliadic themes, and at least eight (and most likely more), arranged their Trojan scenes and inscriptions around a central depiction of Troy's fall (in addition to the Capitoline tablet, compare, for example, tablets 3C [Fig. 6.8], 2NY [Figs. 6.13 and 6.14], 6B, 7Ti, 8E, 9D, and 20Par). As for other subjects, epic themes dominate, with three tablets concerned with the *Odyssey* and two others concerned, respectively, with a Theban cycle and the deeds of Hercules. Finally, three tablets engaged with historical themes, especially (it seems) with the exploits of Alexander the Great.

Rome's "Trojan" Foundation

Foundation myths loom large on the *Tabulae Iliacae*. Although, in what follows, I focus on the tablets with "Trojan" themes, it is worth noting that two of the historical (and most intriguing) tablets probe related ideas about Roman origins and cultural heritage. Not for nothing do fragments 18L and 22Getty seem to have chronicled the grand span of Graeco-Roman history in a truly miniature space, charting the entirety of the past in terms of the present—and counting dates backward from AD 16/17.[25] The subjects of these tablets are not foundation myths as such. Nonetheless, it is significant that these two reliefs interweave past and present, no less than the Greek and Roman, in ways that are at least conceptually related to those found on other tablets. One might also note, in passing, that the marble medium of the *Tabulae*—a most unlikely material for such delicate miniature craftsmanship—bestowed the tablets with an official weight of its own: despite their size and subjects, the medium might make us think of much grander and distinctly Roman monuments, such as the *Fasti Capitolini*.[26]

The Capitoline tablet (1A) engages with Roman foundation myths in a more specific sense. Needless to say, this is not a "Roman" topographic landscape; everything about this tablet suggests a Greek literary, cultural, and intellectual milieu. All the inscriptions are in Greek, and this tablet (like five others) associates itself with a Greek "Theodorean" artist. Greek too are the epic histories depicted, with their characters individually labeled and the plots summarized (again in Greek) on the adjoining stele. An additional inscription, this time emblazoned in the upper frame of the double-frieze band below the *Ilioupersis*, talks of Greek literary precedent alone, and in the language of Greek ekphrastic epigram: "understand [the *technê* of Theod]orus so that, knowing the order of Homer, you may have the measure of all wisdom" (τέχνην τὴν Θεοδ]ώρηον μάθε τάξιν Ὁμήρου / ὄφρα δαεὶς πάσης μέτρον ἔχῃς σοφίας).[27]

For all the Greek talk, audiences seem to have been invited to view the object in contemporary Roman terms. Yes, the subject matter is "Trojan" (hence the word ΤΡΩΙΚΟΣ, inscribed in large letters beneath the ringed city of Troy and interrupting the listed poetic sources mentioned above).[28] At the same time, the tablet hints proleptically forward to events with a key Roman significance. At the bottom right-hand edge of the *Ilioupersis* scene (to the left of the surviving pilaster), we see Aeneas boarding a ship. A first inscription (on Aeneas' left) tells of "Aeneas with his family setting off to the West" (Αἰνήας σὺν τοῖς ἰδίοις ἀπαί[ρ]ων εἰς τὴν Ἑσπερίαν); in case we had missed the point, a second inscription, this time sandwiched between the sails and the inscribed right-hand pilaster, labels the episode once more ("departure of Aeneas": ἀπόπλους Αἰνήου).[29]

Given what we know about the dates of these tablets, such referencing of the future exploits of Aeneas, and in particular his departure "to the West," seems to have had a programmatic contemporary significance. The story of Aeneas' flight and epic journey to Italy had long been a theme of Greek myth and a popular artistic subject.[30] But by the first century BC, the story had become subject to all manner of extensive re-elaborations: for Roman audiences, the destruction of Troy became synonymous with the future founding of Rome. Crucial here was the political intervention of Augustus. As is well known, Augustus founded his own system of political power on a particular story about Rome's "original" foundation. Augustus even traced his own ancestry back to that of Aeneas (and, by extension, to Aeneas' mother, Venus): just as Aeneas and his descendants arrived in Italy and laid the ground for Rome's future rise to power, Augustus' future vision for Rome claimed direct descent from the Trojan ancestral past. Legend has it that the emperor's own great-nephew (and grandson by marriage) visited Troy in AD 18, penning an epigram on the city; "renowned Ilium is rising again" (*Ilios en surgit rursum inclita*), Germanicus is alleged to have written, so that the whole world is now "under the sway of Aeneas' great descendants" (*magnis . . . sub Aeneadis*).[31]

The most famous and elaborate version of this foundation myth came, of course, in the *Aeneid* of Virgil, published posthumously after the author's death in 19 BC. Virgil retold the story of Troy's destruction, focalizing the narrative through the supposed eyewitness account of Aeneas himself (as recounted to the Carthaginians in the poem's second book). Unsurprisingly, perhaps, the *Aeneid* goes unmentioned in the various inscriptions on the Capitoline tablet: there is no room for Latin texts among the various Greek titles cited and (quite literally) synopsized. Whatever the origins of the tablet's production—and not least our conjecture about the precise date—Virgil must have loomed large in the object's reception. The precise relationship between Virgil's epic and the depictions on the Capitoline tablet has been much debated.[32] At least by the end of the first century BC, however, it is hard to imagine elite Roman viewers making sense of these scenes *without* thinking of established Virgilian precedent.[33] As I have argued elsewhere, the very panoply of scenes on the Capitoline tablet, along with their explicit talk of "order" or "arrangement" (*taxis*), might remind viewers of Aeneas' own ekphrastic response before the figurative scenes on the Temple of Juno at Carthage (*Aen.* 1.446–93): like Aeneas, viewers of the tablets are faced with parallel "scenes of Iliac battles laid out in order" (*Iliacas ex ordine pugnas*, *Aen.* 1.456).[34]

But there is one particular way in which the Capitoline tablet frames its Trojan scenes in contemporary, Augustan terms: namely, through the image at its original center (cf. Fig. 6.3). Aeneas recurs three times in the Capitoline tablet's *Ilioupersis* scene, establishing a horizontal-cum-vertical chain of events: in addition to the departure scene in the lower right-hand corner, we see Aeneas rescuing the sacred images from Troy within the city and again at the city gates (Fig. 6.4). Each time, Aeneas is depicted in the same garb, with his name inscribed below; with each occurrence, moreover, we find a slightly different image of Rome's founding hero—as pious devotee, model of familial piety, and as wandering hero setting out on an adventure-filled odyssey.[35] At least in the case of Aeneas' appearance at the center of the *Tabula Capitolina*, though, the inscription is in one sense superfluous (Fig. 6.5). This group of Aeneas, Ascanius, and Anchises—the figures slightly enlarged for increased dramatic effect—would certainly have been familiar to viewers of our tablet. The most famous prototype was to be found in the Forum of Augustus in Rome, constructed between 17 and 5 BC (Fig. 6.6). In the center of the

6.4. Detail of the central *Ilioupersis* scene on the obverse of tablet 1A, highlighting the repetition of Aeneas. Author's own, after Fig. 6.2.

complex's northern exedra, facing a statue of Romulus directly opposite (Rome's other most famous founder, so that the two myths are combined programmatically in one and the same place), stood Augustan Rome's founding hero in a closely related pose, with Anchises and Ascanius again in tow; the group was surrounded on either side by Aeneas' latter-day descendants—the first Trojan kings in Latium, the Julian heirs, and, last but not least, Julius Caesar (Augustus' "father" and the implicit honorand of the Mars Ultor temple that so dominated the complex).[36]

How knowing or self-referential is the relationship between the tablet's motif and the Augustan statue group? Needless to say, there are notable differences between that statue (about four meters high) and this miniature emblem; likewise, the presence of Hermes to the right of Aeneas strikes an additional divine note that is conspicuously absent in the Forum example.[37] Because they go unspoken, iconographic allusions are always dependent upon the mind-set of any given viewer. In this particular scenario, though, there seems little room for doubt: we know of dozens upon dozens of Roman visual allusions to the Forum group, set up in almost every corner of the Roman

6.5. Detail of the central group of Aeneas, Ascanius, Anchises, and Hermes, at the original center of the obverse of tablet 1A. Author's own, after Fig. 6.2.

6.6. Reconstruction of the Aeneas, Ascanius, and Anchises statue group, framed in
the center of the northern exedra in the Forum of Augustus, installed at the end of
the first century BC. Drawing by Maria Luisa Vitali; photograph courtesy of the
Archiv, Institut für Klassische Archäologie und Museum für Abgüsse Klassischer
Bildwerke, Ludwig-Maximilians-Universität, Munich.

Empire—from terracottas and funerary reliefs to irreverent burlesques such
as the mural from the Masseria di Cuomo in Pompeii (which quite literally
"apes" the central character, setting it alongside a parody of the Forum's Romulus group: Fig. 6.7).[38] In the case of the Capitoline tablet, this emblematic
motif might have been seen as nodding not only to the iconography of the
Forum statue but also to its architectural frame: just as the Forum group had
a Latin inscription below, the ruled space for the inscribed names of Ascanius, Aeneas, and Hermes establishes an effective sort of "statue" base; similarly, the architectural aedicule of the Forum group (centered between a pair
of Corinthian columns) is transformed here into a symmetrical city gate. The
prominent placing of this central group on the Capitoline tablet—uncluttered
by surrounding figures—is also paralleled on other examples: we find the

6.7. Painted burlesque of Aeneas, Ascanius, and Anchises, from the Masseria di Cuomo in Pompeii (Museo Archeologico Nazionale di Napoli inv. 9089). Photograph courtesy of the Archiv, Institut für Klassische Archäologie und Museum für Abgüsse Klassischer Bildwerke, Ludwig-Maximilians-Universität, Munich.

same schema on tablet 2NY (Fig. 6.13), for instance; and given the other appearances of Aeneas on tablets 3C (Fig. 6.8), 7Ti, and 8E, it is likely that these compositions (and probably numerous others) similarly placed the motif of Aeneas' flight at their center.[39]

My question, though, is this: What led our artist to frame the tablet's entire composition around this central schema, with all its loaded contemporary Roman cultural and political connotations? Most have answered this question

6.8. Obverse of tablet 3C (Paris, Cabinet des Médailles [Bibliothèque Nationale de France, Département des Monnaies, Médailles et Antiques], inv. 3318). © La Bibliothèque Nationale de France: Monnaies, Médailles et Antiques.

in terms of some "official" Augustan line: the usual argument is that the tablet exploits the panorama of Greek epic to justify a particular foundation myth. "The central panel," writes Richard Brilliant, "transforms the end of an episode into a beginning in medias res, for which a past has been given circumstantially, and circumferentially, while the future has been left to the imagination of the viewer."[40] Others go still further in their politicizing interpretation, arguing that Aeneas' central appearance on the tablet gave it a legitimating "Augustan" stamp. According to de Longpérier in the nineteenth century, this quasi-Virgilian take on events testifies to the tablet's supposed cultic role.[41] Anna Sadurska, on the other hand, supposed that the "discrete allusion to the dynas-

tic ideas of Augustus" was oriented around a slightly different purpose—
that the tablets functioned as "gifts to the emperor or to some important
person in his court."[42] In terms of other contemporary artworks, numerous
parallels can be found for such "official" Augustan recourse to the Aeneas
legend: one might compare the relief on the west side of the Ara Pacis, for
example, where Aeneas' sacrifice (accompanied by Aeneas' son, Ascanius) fore-
shadows the sacrificial procession of Aeneas' latter-day, "august" descendant
on the south frieze (Fig. 6.9).[43]

There can be no doubting that Aeneas' prominence could change responses
to the Capitoline tablet: the iconographic nod to the Forum statue group served
to anchor reactions, reframing the Greek epic vista in Roman politicized terms.
But I would only partly agree with the claim about officiality—the argument
that the tablet enshrines a *single* myth of foundations, one that necessarily
aligns with Augustan versions of events. After all, it is significant that the tablet
does not give a full account of Rome's foundation: as Richard Brilliant notes, it
alludes to a grand story while leaving the narrative poignantly *un*visualized.

6.9. Scene of Aeneas sacrificing, from the south end of the western side of the Ara
Pacis. Photograph courtesy of the Archiv, Institut für Klassische Archäologie und
Museum für Abgüsse Klassischer Bildwerke, Ludwig-Maximilians-Universität,
Munich.

Even in terms of the scenes that are depicted, the tablet leaves it to viewers to piece together an overarching story.

Instead of following a single preestablished account, I would argue that the Capitoline tablet facilitates a series of different stories, from a variety of perspectives. The tablet provides a sort of narrative map, we might say, but leaves viewers free to navigate their own narrative journeys. Indeed, the tablet's miniature size magnifies that sense of authorial control: literally and metaphorically, the tablets place their stories in their audience's hands.

As I have argued elsewhere, the Capitoline tablet (like others) plays knowingly with a variety of storytelling strategies.[44] Upon inspecting the central *Ilioupersis* scene, for example, we find that the picture can be approached geographically and chronologically at once: while depicting Troy as a single geographical entity (with walled city above and harbor and outer-lying monuments below), the scene also arranges events in temporal sequence, ordered from top to bottom (first the Trojan horse, then the sack of Troy, and finally the subsequent aftermath). The same plurality applies to the tablet as a whole (Fig. 6.3). For one thing, the various Iliadic episodes have been arranged at once vertically and horizontally, so that events proceed from left to right within each book-determined frieze, while the friezes themselves are arranged first from top to bottom (on the tablet's left-hand side), and then from bottom to top (on the right). At the same time, the poignant elongation of the upper frieze (pertaining to *Iliad* book 1), so that it stretches across the tablet's central panel, means that, in spatial terms, the first book of the *Iliad* is made to lead directly to its last. As a result, audiences are invited to make sense of the *Iliadic* panels in both clockwise and anticlockwise order—not just to read in a ring all the way through from books *alpha* through to *omega* but also to move straight from beginning to end, and only then to fill in the gaps and complete the circle (for example, first *alpha*, then *omega*, and subsequently *psi* to *beta*).

From this perspective, the compositional centrality of Aeneas might influence a viewer's interpretation in a variety of ways. For one thing, it raises new questions about core and periphery. Aeneas, of course, is a fairly marginal figure in the *Iliad*; by the same token, we find his name inscribed only twice among the surviving *Iliadic* friezes (in the friezes pertaining to books 13 and 15) and nowhere in the extant Greek stele text. Despite that peripheral Homeric role, Aeneas nonetheless occupies the tablet's central spot: on the one hand, the pivotal role given to Aeneas projects, in one sense, the *Iliad* to the margins; at the same time, it raises the problem of reconciling Aeneas' epic history in the wake of Troy's destruction with his somewhat lackluster profile in the Greek literary canon. No less revealing is the uninscribed stele set to the left of Aeneas' ship, toward the lower right-hand center of the *Ilioupersis* panel. This monument recalls—through its shape and appearance— the two stelae inscribed with the Greek résumé of the *Iliad* (one of which borders this scene to the right), as well as the inscribed "tomb of Achilles" (σῆμα Ἀχιλλέως) above. But not only is this stele much smaller than its right-hand counterpart; it is also poignantly uninscribed. The tablet, one might say, draws visual attention to the *un*written story of Aeneas' subsequent epic adventures.

But it is what all this might mean for thinking about Roman foundation myths that I want to draw out here. We have said that the Capitoline tablet might prompt viewers to recall Augustan discourses about Rome's foundation. Ultimately, though, it leaves viewers free to situate that story within a variety of different frameworks. The fascinating elegiac epigram inscribed in large letters in the lower central frame of the tablet flags this theme explicitly, drawing attention to the very mechanics of *taxis* ("order," "organization," "arrangement"—the concept that Latin authors translated as *ordo*):[45] "understand [the *technê* of Theod]orus, so that, knowing the order of Homer, you may have the measure of all wisdom" (τέχνην τὴν Θεοδ]ώρηον μάθε τάξιν Ὁμήρου / ὄφρα δαεὶς πάσης μέτρον ἔχῃς σοφίας). While appearing to privilege the "order of Homer" (τάξιν Ὁμήρου), "Theodorean *technê*" proves a wholly ambivalent "measure of wisdom." Apart from anything else—the ambiguity of the adjective, the combined literary-artistic connotations of *technê*, the size games inherent in this word *metron*, and so on—the inscription hints at something even greater in scope than Homeric poetry. Better, perhaps, the very act of coming to terms with the object opens yet more questions about just what the audiences are holding in their hands. Is there some sort of unspoken order to be found here? To what extent might the *Aeneid* be the true measure of *technê* and *sophia*? In Propertius' prophetic words about the *Aeneid*'s own composition in the 20s BC, might this tiny tablet testify to something even "bigger than the *Iliad*" (*nescio quid maius nascitur Iliade*, 2.34.6)?

The Origins of the Center

The Iliac tablets were not the only early Imperial objects visually to monumentalize Roman foundation myths in relation to the grander literary paradigms of Greek epic. We know from Vitruvius that wall paintings depicting "the battles of Troy or the wanderings of Odysseus through landscapes" were particularly popular in the late first century BC (*Troianas pugnas seu Ulixis errationes per topia*, 7.5.2), and archaeological evidence confirms the general picture.[46] One partial explanation for this newfound popularity was perhaps the renewed cultural relevance of Trojan stories to Augustan myths of foundation. Perhaps this was also the reason that a series of paintings on the "Trojan War in many panels" came to be displayed in the Portico of Philip at Rome, attributed by the Elder Pliny to a certain "Theorus" (*bellumque Iliacum pluribus tabulis*, *Historia Naturalis* 35.144). When Petronius came to send up the theme of Troy's fall as a subject for painting (and, in turn, its set-piece literary description), he was surely responding to a fairly hackneyed visual subject (*Sat.* 89).[47]

One of the best material parallels for the *Tabulae Iliacae*—and the pivotal imagery of Aeneas emblazoned on numerous examples—comes from the painted Trojan cycle in the eponymous entrance hall of the Casa del Criptoportico in Pompeii (I.6.2), usually dated to around 30 BC.[48] Just beneath the vaulted ceiling, and interrupted by raised light wells and make-believe architectural fashionings, Trojan myths are here made to unfold in a series of continuous panels (Fig. 6.10). In contrast to the tablets' own miniature self-contained bands, the stories depicted wind a circular course around the room, following the literal circuits of the perambulating viewer (Fig. 6.11): if we start at the south end of the west wing, we proceed first clockwise through Apollo's plague (on the west wall, originally preceded, it seems, by earlier episodes drawn from the stories of the lost *Cypria*), then Hector's challenging of the Achaeans in *Iliad* 7 (surviving on the north wall of the north wing), and on to the death of Patroclus and the recovery of his body (on the east and south walls of the east wing). At this point, the scenes turn back in on themselves across the opposite wall of the east wing, proceeding back to the same point from which they originally begun. Audiences now move through Achilles' return to battle (*Iliad* 20 and 21: west wall of the east wing), then Patroclus' funerary games (*Iliad* 23: south wall of the north wing), before finally arriving at the scene of, among other subjects, Penthesilea's arrival at Troy (as told in the lost *Aethiopis*: east wall of the west wing).

The complexity of the arrangement is striking. From any given point of the room, viewers could see multiple epic episodes on the walls around them, in a way that thereby broke the strict linear arrangement of each panel's individual sequence. But most interesting is what happens on the south wall of

6.10. Reconstruction of the north wing of the Casa del Criptoportico: the Trojan cycle paintings occupied the upper gray friezes, underneath the vaulted ceiling. After V. Spinazzola (ed.), *Pompei alla luce degli scavi nuovi di Via dell'Abbondanza* (Rome: Libreria della Stato, 1953), 459, fig. 523.

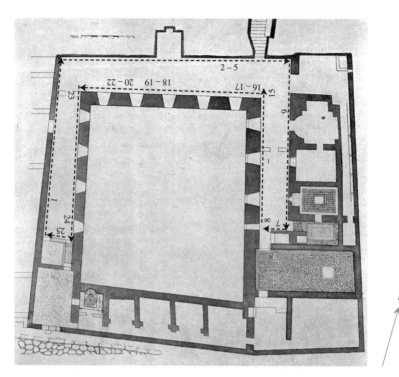

West wing, west wall

1. Apollo and the plague in the Greek camp, relating to *Iliad* 1. (The layout suggests several earlier scenes, probably drawn from events narrated in the *Kypria*, arranged to the left of this one.)

North wing, north wall

2. Exchange of armor between Diomedes and Glaucus, relating to *Iliad* 6.
3. Diomedes with Athena, and Diomedes' combat with (?) Mars or Aeneas, relating to *Iliad* 5.
4. Departure of Hector from Andromache and Astyanax, relating to *Iliad* 6.
5. Counsel of Greek leaders after Hector's challenge, relating to *Iliad* 7.

East wing, east wall

6. Combat of Hector and the Greeks over the body of Patroclus, relating to *Iliad* 17.

East wing, south wall

7. Removal of the body of Patroclus, relating to *Iliad* 17.

East wing, west wall

8. Thetis seated in the workshop of Hephaestus, relating to *Iliad* 18 (with a female figure holding the shield of Achilles, labeled as Euanthe).
9. (?) Achilles beside the body of Patroclus.
10. Three unlabeled and unidentified standing male heroic figures.
11. Return of Briseis to Achilles and a group of seated Achaeans, relating to *Iliad* 19.

12. (?) Athena and other gods intervening in the battle between Trojans and Greeks/council of the gods, relating to *Iliad* 20.
13. Achilles' return to battle and combat between Achilles and Hector (alongside other scenes), relating to *Iliad* 20.
14. Combat between Achilles and Aeneas (who is saved by Poseidon), relating to *Iliad* 20.
15. Achilles raging against the Trojans and the capture of Trojan prisoners, relating to *Iliad* 21.

East wing, south wall

16. Death of Lycaon next to the Scamander river, relating to *Iliad* 21.
17. (?) Pursuit of the Trojans.
18. Lost panel (but inscriptions naming Achilles and Xanthos).
19. Mourning of Andromache, relating to *Iliad* 22.
20. Women mourning Hector's death, possibly relating to *Iliad* 24.
21. Achilles offering a libation before Patroclus' pyre, relating to *Iliad* 23.
22. Funerary games of Patroclus, relating to *Iliad* 23.

West wing, east wall

23. Penthesilea's arrival at Troy (received by Priam), drawn from the *Aethiopis*.
24. (?) Thetis at the tomb of Achilles or Helen on the walls of Troy.

West wing, south wall

25. Aeneas and Anchises fleeing Troy, guided by Hermes.

6.11. Ground plan of the eponymous cryptoporticus of the Casa del Criptoportico, showing the arrangement of Trojan cycle scenes. After V. Spinazzola (ed.), *Pompei alla luce degli scavi nuovi di Via dell'Abbondanza* (Rome: Libreria della Stato, 1953), 455, fig. 517.

6.12. Image of Hermes with Aeneas and Anchises, from the south wall of the west wing of the cryptoporticus in the Casa del Criptoportico. After F. Aurigemma, "Appendice: Tre nuovi cicli di figurazioni ispirate all'Iliade in case della Via dell'Abbondanza in Pompei," in *Pompei alla luce degli scavi nuovi di Via dell'Abbondanza (anni 1920–23)*, ed. V. Spinazzola, 867–1008 (Rome: Libreria dello Stato, 1953), 955, fig. 971. Photograph courtesy of the Archiv, Institut für Klassische Archäologie und Museum für Abgüsse Klassischer Bildwerke, Ludwig-Maximilians-Universität, Munich.

the cryptoporticus' west wing. Situated between the beginning and end of our literal Greek "epic cycle," we find here a Roman aetiological climax: another image of Aeneas' departure from Troy (Fig. 6.12). Although the scene is too fragmentary to allow for a full iconographic reconstruction (and this time, the schema certainly seems to have predated the Forum of Augustus exemplar), there can be no doubting the subject.[49] But it is the panel's position that is significant: not for nothing are Aeneas, Anchises, and Ascanius, shown at the moment of their own departure from Troy, made to occupy the literal liminal space of the room's entrance and exit, greeting viewers at the point where they, too, move into or out of the cryptoporticus. This mythical scene of civic abandonment points the way to viewers' own everyday departure from the room and house, while providing a new focalizing perspective with which to start their stories of this space anew. At the same time, the schema raises questions about whether to go round the cryptoporticus—and hence spin an epic cycle—clockwise or anticlockwise: Just how does the epic story of Rome fit into the lines of Greek epic?[50]

The tablets, I think, take this same foundational concern with order and arrangement and play with it in yet more self-referential ways. To strengthen the point, I want to turn the tablets over. The Capitoline tablet, on which we have so far focused in this chapter, is decorated on one side only: its verso is uninscribed. But of the twenty-two tablets, eleven examples were inscribed on both recto and verso. Of these eleven tablets, moreover, seven feature a particular sort of textual inscription, arranged in so-called magic-square formation.[51]

A fragment in New York (tablet 2NY) offers a particularly enlightening example.[52] We have already mentioned the tablet's obverse because it very clearly preserves the same central schema of Aeneas, Anchises, and Ascanius at its center (Fig. 6.13). The *Ilioupersis* scene is almost identical to that of the Capitoline tablet, even though the lower third of the relief is missing. As with the Capitoline tablet, we can be confident about the tablet's overall composition: each Iliadic book has, this time, been depicted in single "boxed" panels (Fig. 6.14), and both the first and final two books of the poem are sandwiched together in the upper register. Like the Capitoline fragment, moreover, the tablet's obverse was inscribed with an elegiac couplet (albeit now in its upper, rather than lower, frame): although only part of the last four words of the pentameter remains, the text was clearly similar to that found on the Capitoline example; indeed, every word of the New York pentameter finds a parallel in the Capitoline text (". . . [t]echnê, you may have the measure of wisdom": [τ]έχνην μέτρον ἔχῃς σο[φίας).[53]

On this New York tablet, however, an additional set of shallow inscriptions is to be found on the object's reverse side. If we turn the tablet over, we see a most intriguing epigraphic device, set out in a diagrammatic grid of letters (Fig. 6.15). A fragmentary hexameter above explains the principle: "seize the middle letter/stroke [γράμμα] and go whichever way you choose" (γράμμα μέσον καθ[ελὼν παρολίσθα]νε οὗ ποτε βούλει).[54] The missing lower and right-hand sections of the grid can easily be reconstructed (Fig. 6.16), since we find the exact same gridded square of letters on the back of tablet 3C, as well as an almost identical second example on the verso of 20Par (albeit this time, with a slight but revealing orthographic variation). Working outward from the

6.13. Obverse of tablet 2NY (New York Tablet). Metropolitan Museum of Art,
Fletcher Fund, 1924 (24.97.11). Photograph © The Metropolitan Museum of Art.

iota at the square's center, audiences can proceed "whichever way they choose,"
even altering their reading mode along the way (whether vertically, horizontally, or, indeed, diagonally). So long as they continue outward from the middle to any of the four corners, the text holds fast: Ἰλιὰς Ὁμήρου Θεοδώρηος ἡ{ι}
τέχνη ("the *Iliad* is Homer's, but the *technê* is Theodorean").

    This is a truly fascinating inscription and one that knowingly plays with
the boundaries between the linearity of text and the spatiality of pictures: each
of the seven verso magic-square inscriptions develops the intermedial flips of
word and image emblazoned on the tablets' recto sides.[55] In terms of foundation discourses, however, I want to concentrate on just two aspects of the

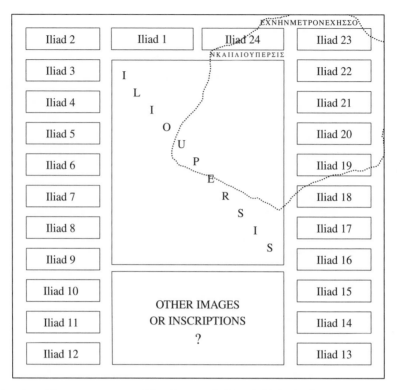

6.14. Possible reconstruction of the obverse of tablet 2NY. Author's own.

verso inscriptions: first, to ask how such magic-square inscriptions affect our reading of the visual imagery depicted on the tablets' obverse sides; and second, to think about their importance for approaching the theme of center and periphery.

Whatever else we make of the magic-square inscription, the format knowingly celebrates the authorial control of the reader-viewer. Indeed, the hexameter inscribed above explicitly instructs as much ("glide/continue wherever you choose!"). The ramifications of this gesture are as important for the tablets' rectos as they are for their versos. Both sides of the New York tablet are inscribed with letters, or *grammata*: on the New York tablet, as on numerous others (for example, 1A, 3C, 6B, 11H, 20Par), each of the twenty-four books of the *Iliad* is delineated in alphabetic letters, often laid out, as it were, from *alpha* to *omega*. In formal terms, the gridded boxes containing the letters on the verso form a sort of counterpoint to the four-square metopes of the

6.15. Reverse of tablet 2NY. Metropolitan Museum of Art, Fletcher Fund, 1924 (24.97.11). Photograph © The Metropolitan Museum of Art.

recto (see, for example, Figs. 6.14–6.16). Linguistically, moreover, the very talk of *grammata* develops that semantic connection: Greek writers (and Hellenistic epigrammatists, in particular) made much of the pun whereby *gramma* could refer to a "stroke" not only of the pen but also of the brush; as *grammata*, the inscribed marks of both recto and verso were signs for reading and seeing.[56]

This leads to a second point and to foundation myths specifically. Just as the verso's talk of *grammata* has a double significance for both sides of the tablet, so its instruction to privilege the center has a pivotal importance for approaching the foundation myth at the core of the recto. In this inscription,

6.16. Reconstruction of the "magic square" on the reverse of tablets 2NY and 3C, incorporating the surviving portions of tablet 2NY (top left) and 3C (top right). Author's own, after Bua 1971: 10, fig. 2.

as in the other six examples, making verbal sense of the verso diagram depends on our working outward from the letter in the middle: the text in the picture works only if we heed the centrifugal force of the initial *iota*. On the verso, of course, this leads to a titular summary that revolves around Homer: *iota* spells out the opening letter of *Iliad*. The situation with the recto is different. Yes, we might begin with the middle *gramma*—the pictorial group of Aeneas, Anchises, and Ascanius at the center. To do so, however, is to make sense of these visual scenes in non-Iliadic terms: privileging the center means revolving around a set of stories that are much more loosely affiliated with the Greek literary canon depicted.

How, then, to square the visual-verbal mode of viewing/reading the tablet's verso with that of responding to its recto? Through the addition of the inscribed magic-square verso, our New York tablet emphasizes the games of periphery and center already latent in the *Tabula Capitolina*. When it comes to the specific stories that we might tell of the obverse scenes, though, the diagrammatic format of the verso inscription proves somewhat destabilizing. However we proceed to make sense of these *grammata*, the reverse inscription reminds us that this can only be one version among many: there are always other interpretative directions to be navigated. In this sense, the dialogue between the two sides of the tablets might be said to throw into relief a certain discursiveness about the very stories that are figured: the tablets allude to a particular, politically charged narrative about Roman (or, more specifically, *Augustan* Roman) origins, but they also delight in a plurality of narrative and interpretive journeys.

Going Whichever Way You Choose?

So where does this leave the *Tabulae Iliacae* in relation to Roman discourses of foundation? The tablets, I have argued, probe the means by which we find meaning in what we see and read. But they also raise questions about the stories that we tell. While hinting at a set of narratives about Aeneas and the origins of Augustan Rome, they incite viewers to piece together their own version of events. If my hypothesis about the social contexts in which the tablets were used is correct, the plurality of potential stories was precisely the point: in every sense, these were intended as discursive objects, serving as *amuse-bouches* for the intimate discussions of the *cena*.

Understood like this, the tiny tablets have a much larger significance for approaching early Imperial foundation myths. While citing a grand (and highly politically charged) story of Roman origins amid their Greek epic landscapes, the tablets do not visualize the whole narrative: they leave it to audiences to construct a narrative framework, situating it in the field of the larger Greek literary canon. It is that sense of open-endedness that strikes me as important: even within an apparently singular myth about civic origins—and one exploited to explain the origins of the Augustan Principate—there was room for innovation. In "going wherever they choose," audiences were invited to look afresh, to visualize variant versions, and to imagine rival points of view.

I want to end this chapter with a final foundational flip. So far, we have concentrated on the idea of interpretative freedom. One way of understanding the tablets, I have suggested, revolves around their potentially destabilizing effect: by encouraging alternatives, they throw into relief the constructedness of any given story. According to this interpretation, the tablets might be thought to have a wholly ambivalent relationship with the stories upon which Augustus founded his own system of political power. If the tablets at once seem to champion a particular story of civic origins, alluding to its contemporary political stakes, they also blow figurative raspberries at such authoritarian authority: choose your *own* adventure![57]

But the precise reverse interpretation is also open to us. For all the semblance of interpretative free play, after all, just how free were audiences to devise their own individual response? Once again, the seven tablets inscribed with magic squares on their verso demonstrate the point with particular self-reflexivity. If we think back to the verso of the New York tablet (Figs. 6.15 and 6.16), the rules of the diagrammatic letter game have, in one sense, been rigged. In making logical sense of the inscribed game, viewers are never quite free to go "wherever they choose": they must not only begin with the central letter but also move outward, never turning back in on themselves. The imperative enshrined in the inscribed hexameter of tablets 2NY and 3C underscores the point: the diagram might disobey the usual conventions of written text, but the inscription also paradoxically *instructs* us to do so. The fact that, whichever way we turn, we always end up with the same verso text might cause us to rethink the heralded hermeneutic freedom: However creative our response, do we not always end up with the same central story?

When dealing with objects as self-referential as the *Tabulae Iliacae*, it should come as no surprise that both interpretations are open to us. In one sense, there are a plurality of myths to be told. In another, interpretive play is never without limits: our stories are necessarily bounded within a singular foundational frame. So are we free to extemporize? Or are we trapped by tradition? As ever, the tablets posit questions. But they leave the answers open: "Go whichever way you choose!"

NOTES

This chapter derives from the paper originally delivered at the Cambridge workshop "Foundation Myths in Dialogue"; it was conceived in connection with a much larger project on the *Tabulae Iliacae*, funded by the Alexander von Humboldt-Stiftung between 2008 and 2010, now published as Squire 2011a. My sincere thanks to the conference participants for their insightful discussions and to Myles Lavan and Naoíse Mac Sweeney for commenting on an earlier draft of the chapter. Needless to say, any errors are my own.

1. The key discussion of the coexistence of different Roman foundation myths (at least by the third century BC) is Cornell 1975, contra, e.g., Strasburger 1968 (on the historical priority of the Aeneas legend). There is a vast bibliography, but Cornell 2000 provides a good preliminary survey, and Poucet 1985 offers a handy single-volume guide. For a helpful epilogue on the history of scholarship concerning Roman origins, see also Fraschetti 2005: 113–19, along with Grandazzi 1991: esp. 17–87. More generally, on the various historical fabrications of Roman myth, readers are referred to the superlative analysis of Wiseman 2004: 16–21 (discussing Trojan stories). For one very readable attempt at writing the history, on the basis of archaeological and textual sources, see Cornell 1995. For the archaeology—and a highly controversial argument about the "real" Romulus—see, most recently, Carandini 2011 (with references to Carandini's earlier foundational work). Visual mediations of Roman foundation myths—structured around public and private poles—have most recently been explored by Dardenay 2010.

2. For a concise and well-referenced discussion of the sources for the Aeneas and Romulus/Remus stories, see Bremmer and Horsfall 1987: 12–24 and 25–48, respectively. As the authors put it (25): "Besides Aeneas, there were always Romulus and Remus." In Augustus' eponymous Forum, dedicated in 2 BC, the two figures would be arranged opposite each other, in the northern and southern exedrae, respectively: see above, pp. 162–64.

3. For discussion, see, e.g., Feeney 2007: esp. 172–82.

4. Hunter 2009 and Kim 2010: 85–139 both provide excellent analyses.

5. Jahn 1873. On the earlier history of scholarship, see Sadurska 1964: 21–22; Valenzuela Montenegro 2004: 11–15; Puppo 2009: 839–40; Squire 2011a: 28–31.

6. Sadurska 1964; Valenzuela Montenegro 2004; cf. Horsfall's useful overview in *IGUR* 4.93–98, nos. 1612–33. For the inscriptions, see *IG* 14: 328–47, nos. 1284–93.

7. Horsfall 1994: 79. The classic articulation of this thesis is Horsfall 1979.

8. McLeod 1985: 164. For other related evaluations, see Squire 2011a: 91–92.

9. See Squire 2010, 2011a: esp. 87–126. Comparable assessments are to be found in, e.g., Valenzuela Montenegro 2002, 2004: esp. 413–19; Puppo 2009; Petrain forthcoming.

10. For a much more detailed discussion of the following issues (and others), see Squire 2011a: 27–86.

11. The most thorough catalog is Valenzuela Montenegro 2004. For the argument of a supposed twenty-third tablet (tablet 23Ky), see Gasparri 2009 (with Squire 2011a: 411–14).

12. On the materials, see Sadurska 1964: 13; Amedick 1999: 198; Valenzuela Montenegro 2004: 297–98.

13. See Lippold 1932: 1896; Sadurska 1964: 8; Valenzuela Montenegro 2004: 297–98 (along with 307 on the sfumato style); Squire 2011a: 64–65. Traces of gold are most visible toward the upper frame of tablet 3C (Fig. 6.8) and on tablet 16Sa, which also displays clear remnants of red paint.

14. On the chronology of the tablets, see Valenzuela Montenegro 2004: 305–9, who argues for a date in the first quarter of the first century AD. But I am not convinced that Sadurska 1964: 16–17 is necessarily wrong to posit a slightly earlier date, toward the end of the first century BC, at least for some of the tablets: cf. Salimbene 2002: 26–27; Squire 2011a: 58–61.

15. Cf. Valenzuela Montenegro 2004: 331–33.

16. For the argument in favor of a single workshop, see Valenzuela Montenegro 2004: 415. For the hypothesis of four different workshops, see Sadurska 1964: 10–15 (followed by Salimbene 2002: 17–29). For my own views, see Squire 2011a: 54–58, along with 283–302. The different hands responsible even for objects that are signed as "Theodorean" are clearest to see in the context of tablets 1A and 3C. Cf. Valenzuela Montenegro 2004: 298–304 (responding to Sadurska 1964: 10–15), although arguing in favor of different artists within a single workshop: "Dass die Tafeln mit der Signatur alle von einer Hand stammen, wie Sadurska sagt, ist m. E. unplausibel. . . . Deshalb ist anzunehmen, dass in der Werkstatt des Theodoros verschiedene, mehr oder minder befähigte Künstler arbeiteten" (300, 302).

17. For discussion of provenance specifically, see Sadurska 1964: 12–13; Salimbene 2002: 27–29; Valenzuela Montenegro 2004: 405; Petrain 2006: 139–47; Squire 2011a: 65–67.

18. See Squire 2011a: 65–85.

19. Cf., e.g., Simon 2008: 235–36 on (among other objects) the Lolland silver cups signed by "Cheirisophos." I would also compare the so-called Megarian Homeric cups from the second century BC with their deliberately riddlesome citations and designs (cf. Giuliani 2003: 263–80).

20. Cf. Squire 2011a: 65–67.

21. For a much more detailed discussion of the tablet and its iconographic derivation, see Mancuso 1909; Maras 1999: 17–68; Valenzuela Montenegro 2004: 22–149. The inscriptions are published in *IG* 14.1284.

22. The letters are contained in the upper left-hand corner of each frieze, although only those pertaining to books *nu*, *omicron*, *pi*, *rho*, *sigma*, and *tau* appear visible today.

23. In particular, scholars have debated the extent to which the tablet can be used to reconstruct the literary content of Stesichorus' *Ilioupersis*. The question goes back to some of the earliest research on the tablets (e.g., Welcker 1829: 233–40; above all, Paulcke 1897), although opinions still remain divided: Nicholas Horsfall has been most vociferous in arguing that the tablets were crafted independently of Stesichorus' poem (Horsfall 1979: 35–43, restated in 2008: 587–91), but others have taken issue both with the conclusions and methodology (e.g., Kazansky 1997: esp. 55–10; Wachter 2001: 316–17; Scafoglio 2005). This has been a rather sterile debate and has underplayed the clear verbal allusion to Stesichorus in the inscribed elegiac epigram below the *Ilioupersis* scene: see Squire 2011a: 106–8.

24. On the semantics of size on the tablets, see Squire 2011a: esp. 247–302, 349–55. The original size of tablet 1A must have been about 25 by 40 centimeters.

25. For an introduction to these two tablets, see Valenzuela Montenegro 2004: 276–96.

26. On marble and monumentality, see, e.g., Corbier 2006: 9–50, esp. 12–23; Thomas 2007: esp. 1–14.

27. On the programmatic significance of the inscription and its allusion to Greek ecphrastic themes, see Squire 2010: 72–77; Squire 2011a: 87–126. Cf. Petrain 2012: 615–19; Petrain forthcoming: ch. 2.

28. For the semantics of this "Trojan" inscription, see Petrain 2010: 51–53; Squire 2011a: 253.

29. For the scenes and inscriptions, see Valenzuela Montenegro 2004: 143–45.

30. See, esp., Galinsky 1969.

31. The poem is collected in Riese (ed.) 1869–70: 2.159, no. 708. Note, too, the corresponding Greek epigram in *Anth. Pal.* 9.387 (the Greek translation inverting the Roman claim to inversion—making Greek once more Rome's own translation of the Greek myth). Cf. Dench 2005: esp. 248–53; Schneider 2007: 69–70; Schneider 2012: 111–12.

32. Many scholars have compared the details of Virgil's description of the sack of Troy with the pictorial version represented here (cf. Valenzuela Montenegro 2004: 387–91, supposing "keinen Anhaltspunkt für einen konkreten inhaltlichen Einfluss der Aeneis auf die Darstellung der Tabula," 391). For further discussion, see Squire 2011a: 155–58.

33. On Virgil's immediate reception in Rome, see (inter alios) Gigante 1984; Barnes 2001; Horsfall 2001; Ziolkowski and Putnam 2008: esp. 5–162. For Virgil's adaptations of the Aeneas myth, see the excellent recent overview of Casali 2010.

34. Cf. Squire 2014b, along with, e.g., Barchiesi 1994: 117.

35. For introductory comments on the underlying Augustan ideology of "pious Aeneas," see, e.g., Galinsky 1969: 3–61; Severy 2003: 99–112.

36. For the motif's iconography on the Capitoline tablet, see, esp., Maras (ed.) 1999: 62–63; Valenzuela Montenegro 2004: 130–32, 306–7. On the statue group in the Forum of Augustus, the most important discussion is Spannagel 1999: 90–131. Cf. Zanker 1968: esp. 16–19; Zanker 1988: 192–215, esp. 201–3; Galinsky 1996: 204–6; Ungaro (ed.) 2007: 159–69; Geiger 2008; Dardenay 2010: 83–107, esp. 83–96; Rutledge 2012: 250–57.

37. Cf. Spannagel 1999: 109.

38. For other instances of the schema in Greek and Roman art, see *LIMC* 1.1: 386–90, s.v. "Aineias," nos. 59–154 (with commentary at 394–95); Fuchs 1973 (with full discussion of iconographic precedents, and analyzing their relation to Virgil at 624–31). Cf. Aichholzer 1983: 2–29, with nos. 1–73; de Vos 1991; Dardenay 2010: 43–51. For the Pompeian pastiche, see, e.g., Zanker 2002: 79–82; Clarke 2007: 143–47. See also Smith 2013: 204–6, no. D4.

39. Cf. Squire 2011a: 177–78.

40. Brilliant 1984: 58. Cf. Valenzuela Montenegro 2004: 418: "Einige Tafeln besitzen eine politische Konnotation: Besonders die Tabula Capitolina ordnet den gesamten Trojazyklus um die zentrale Gestalt des Aineas an, den trojanischen Ahnen des julischen Geschlechts."

41. For de Longpérier, the tablet consequently demonstrated the heroic genealogy of the Julian clan: see de Longpérier 1845: 439–40.

42. Sadurska 1964: 19: "on s'imagine facilement ce genre de monuments comme cadeaux offerts à l'empereur ou à quelque notabilité de la cour."

43. For a brief discussion and references to further bibliography, see Kleiner 2005: 221–25; cf. Galinsky 1996: 319–20 on the "Belvedere Altar."

44. Cf. Squire 2011a: 165–76.

45. For *taxis* as a critical term in contemporary rhetorical theory, see the references collected in Lausberg 1960: 2.878 s.v. τάξις; cf. Meijering 1987: 138–48; Hunter 2009: 52–56 (on Dio Chrys. 11.24–25); Nünlist 2009: 24–25, 89 n. 53; Squire 2014b.

46. For three helpful surveys, see Brilliant 1984: 60–65; Croisille 2005: 154–65; Santoro 2005: 106–9, 113–14. Three extant painted Iliadic cycles from Pompeii are published in Aurigemma 1953.

47. For the Petronian send-up, see Elsner 2007: 177–99, esp. 194–96; Baier 2010.

48. On the paintings from cryptoporticus 17 of the Casa del Criptoportico (inscribed in Greek), see *PPM* 1:201–28, nos. 13–61; cf. Aurigemma 1953: 905–70; Corlàita Scagliarini 1974–76: 20–21; Schefold 1975: 129–34; Brilliant 1984: 60–65; Croisille 2005: 154–65; Santoro 2005: 106–9, 113–14. I discuss some of the circular epic cycle games in Squire 2014a.

49. For discussion, see Aurigemma 1953: 955–56.

50. See Galinsky 1969: 31–32, on how this scene "provides an ennobling mythological parallel to the ordinary, everyday act of leaving the house"; cf. Schefold 1975: 129: "Der Eintretende sah zu seiner Linken die ersten Szenen aus der Ilias und konnte ihrer Fortseztung, immer zu seiner Linken, durch den ganzen Gang folgen, bis er wieder zur Tür zurückkam, und neben dieser, als einziges Bild allein auf einer Wand, das Bild mit Aeneas' Flucht fand."

51. The most important discussion of these reverse magic-square inscriptions is Bua 1971; cf. Valenzuela Montenegro 2004: 347–49. More generally, on the labyrinthine inscriptions and their relations to ancient traditions of pattern poetry, see, e.g., Higgins 1987: 198–200; Ernst 1991: 388–93.

52. For a guide to the tablet and further bibliography, see Valenzuela Montenegro 2004: 185–91. On the reconstruction, see Squire 2011b.

53. For the inscription, see Squire 2011a: 104–5 (with further references). Petrain 2012: 616–17 has tendered the following tentative reconstruction: [τάξιν τὴν Θεοδώρηον μάθε τὴν καθ' Ὅμηρον / ὄφρα δαεὶς τ]έχνην μέτρον ἔχῃς σο[φίας].

54. See Bua 1971: 6–9; Guarducci 1974: 426. The second half of the hexameter is preserved on tablet 3C, although the reconstruction of the missing middle section is contested: Petrain 2010: 53–54 may be correct to prefer the reading of Gallavotti 1989: 49 (γράμμα μέσον καθ[ορῶν παραλάμβα]νε οὗ ποτε βούλει, "Look at the middle *gramma* and continue with whichever/wherever you choose").

55. See Squire 2011a: 197–246.

56. See, esp., Männlein-Robert 2007a: 255–56; Männlein-Robert 2007b: 123–27; Tueller 2008: esp. 141–54. Cf. also Squire 2010: 82–84; Squire 2011a: 235–43. For the *graphein* pun, cf., e.g., Squire 2009: 147–49. In his commentary on the verb *perlegere* at Verg. *Aen.* 6.34, Servius would later comment on the dual meanings explicitly: after all, Servius writes, the Greek verb γράψαι (an aorist infinitive of *graphein*) may be said to mean both "to paint" and "to write" (*cum graece* γράψαι *et pingere dicatur et scribere*: Thilo and Hagen 1923–27: 2:11).

57. In political terms, such subjectivity could prove radical indeed. One might think of Ovid and of the *Metamorphoses'* self-consciously "metamorphosized" reworkings of Virgilian foundation myths, especially in the final books. Needless to say, such a gesture could prove politically subversive: not for nothing did Ovid end up a political outcast on the Black Sea. . . .

REFERENCES

Aichholzer, P. 1983. *Darstellungen römischer Sagen.* Vienna: Verband der Wissenschaftliche Gesellschaften Österreichs.

Amedick, R. 1999. "Der Schild de Achilleus in der hellenistisch-römischen ikonographischen Tradition." *Jahrbuch des Deutschen Archäologischen Instituts* 114: 157–206.

Aurigemma, F. 1953. "Appendice: Tre nuovi cicli di figurazioni ispirate all'Iliade in case della Via dell'Abbondanza in Pompei." In *Pompei alla luce degli scavi nuovi di Via dell'Abbondanza (anni 1920–23),* ed. V. Spinazzola, 867–1008. Rome: Libreria dello Stato.

Baier, T. 2010. "Eumolpe et Encolpe dans une galerie d'art." In *Métamorphoses du regard ancien,* ed. É. Prioux and A. Rouveret, 191–204. Nanterre: Presses Universitaires de Paris-Ouest.

Barchiesi, A. 1994. "Rappresentazioni del dolore e interpretazione nell'Eneide." *Antike und Abendland* 40: 109–24.

Barnes, W. R. 2001. "Virgil: The Literary Impact." In *A Companion to the Study of Virgil,* ed. N. Horsfall, 257–92. Leiden: Brill.

Bremmer, J. N., and N. M. Horsfall. 1987. *Roman Myth and Mythography: Bulletin of the Institute of Classical Studies,* Supplement 52. London: Institute of Classical Studies.

Brilliant, R. 1984. *Visual Narratives: Story-Telling in Etruscan and Roman Art.* Ithaca, NY: Cornell University Press.

Bua, M. T. 1971. "I giuochi alfabetici delle *tavole iliache.*" *Memorie: Atti della Accademia nazionale dei Lincei, Classe di scienze morali, storiche e filologiche* 8 (16): 1–35.

Carandini, A. 2011. *Rome: Day One.* Tr. S. Sartarelli. Princeton, NJ: Princeton University Press.

Casali, S. 2010. "The Development of the Aeneas Legend." In *A Companion to Vergil's Aeneid and Its Tradition,* ed. J. Farrell and M. J. C. Putnam, 37–51. Malden, MA: Wiley-Blackwell.

Clarke, J. R. 2007. *Looking at Laughter: Humor, Power and Transgression in Roman Visual Culture, 100 BC–AD 250.* Berkeley: University of California Press.

Corbier, M. 2006. *Donner à voir, donner à lire: Mémoire et communication dans la Rome ancienne.* Paris: CNRS.

Corlàita Scagliarini, D. 1974–76. "Spazio e decorazione nella pittura pompeiana." *Palladio: Revista di Storia dell'Architectura* 23–25: 3–44.

Cornell, T. J. 1975. "Aeneas and the Twins: The Development of the Roman Foundation Legend." *Proceedings of the Cambridge Philological Society* 21: 1–32.

Cornell, T. J. 1995. *The Beginnings of Rome: Italy and Rome from the Bronze Age to the Punic Wars (c. 1000–264 BC)*. London: Routledge.

Cornell, T. J. 2000. "La leggenda della nascita di Roma." In *Roma: Romolo, Remo e la fondazione della città*, ed. A. Carandini and R. Cappelli, 45–50. Milan: Electa.

Croisille, J.-M. 2005. *La peinture romaine*. Paris: Picard.

Dardenay, A. 2010. *Les myths fondateurs de Rome: Images et politique dans l'Occident romain*. Paris: Picard.

de Longpérier, A. 1845. "Fragment inédit de table iliaque." *Revue de philologie* 1: 438–46.

Dench, E. 2005. *Romulus' Asylum: Roman Identities from the Age of Alexander to the Age of Hadrian*. Oxford: Oxford University Press.

de Vos, M. 1991. "La fuga di Enea in pitture del I sec. d.C." *Kölner Jahrbuch für Vor- und Frühgeschichte* 24: 113–23.

Elsner, J. 2007. *Roman Eyes: Visuality and Subjectivity in Art and Text*. Princeton, NJ: Princeton University Press.

Ernst, U. 1991. "Carmen figuratum." *Geschichte des Figurengedichts von den antiken Ursprüngen bis zum Ausgang des Mittelalters*. Cologne: Böhlau.

Feeney, D. C. 2007. *Caesar's Calendar: Ancient Time and the Beginnings of History*. Berkeley: University of California Press.

Fraschetti, A. 2005. *The Foundation of Rome*. Tr. M. Hill and K. Windle. Edinburgh: Edinburgh University Press.

Fuchs, W. 1973. "Die Bildgeschichte der Flucht des Aeneas." *Aufstieg und Niedergang der römischen Welt* 1 (4): 615–32.

Galinsky, K. 1969. *Aeneas, Sicily, and Rome*. Princeton, NJ: Princeton University Press.

Galinsky, K. 1996. *Augustan Culture: An Interpretive Introduction*. Princeton, NJ: Princeton University Press.

Gallavotti, C. 1989. "Planudea (IX)." *Bollettino dei Classici* 10: 49–69.

Gasparri, C. 2009. "23 Ky: Un nuovo rilievo della serie delle 'tabulae iliacae' dal Foro di Cuma." In *Cuma: Indagini archeologiche e nuove scoperte*, ed. G. Gasparri and G. Greco, 251–57. Pozzuoli: Naus.

Geiger, J. 2008. *The First Hall of Fame: A Study of the Statues in the Forum Augustum*. Leiden: Brill.

Gigante, M. 1984. *Virgilio e la Campania*. Naples: Giannini Editore.

Giuliani, L. 2003. *Bild und Mythos. Geschichte der Bilderzählung in der griechischen Kunst*. Munich: Beck.

Grandazzi, A. 1991. *La fondation de Rome: Réflexion sur l'histoire*. Paris: Les Belles Lettres.

Guarducci, M. 1974. *Epigrafia greca III: Epigrafi di carattere privato*. Rome: Istituto Poligrafico e Zecca dello Stato.

Higgins, D. 1987. *Pattern Poetry: Guide to an Unknown Literature*. Albany: State University of New York Press.

Horsfall, N. 1979. "Stesichorus at Bovillae?" *Journal of Hellenic Studies* 99: 26–48.

Horsfall, N. 1994. "The Origins of the Illustrated Book." In *A History of Book Illustration: Twenty-Nine Points of View*, ed. B. Katz, 60–88. Metuchen, NJ: Scarecrow.

Horsfall, N. 2001. "Virgil's Impact at Rome: The Non-Literary Evidence." In *A Companion to the Study of Virgil*, ed. N. Horsfall, 249–55. 2nd ed. Leiden: Brill.

Horsfall, N. 2008. *Virgil, Aeneid 2: A Commentary*. Leiden: Brill.

Hunter, R. 2009. " 'The Trojan Oration' of Dio Chrysostom and Ancient Homeric Criticism." In *Narratology and Interpretation: The Content of Narrative Form in Ancient Literature*, ed. J. Grethlein and A. Rengakos, 43–61. Berlin: De Gruyter.

Jahn, O. 1873. *Griechische Bilderchroniken: Aus dem Nachlasse des Verfassers herausgegeben und beendigt von A. Michaelis*. Bonn: Adolph Marcus.

Kazansky, N. N. 1997. *Principles of the Reconstruction of a Fragmentary Text*. Saint Petersburg: Russian Academy of Science.

Kim, L. 2010. *Homer Between History and Fiction in Imperial Greek Literature*. Cambridge: Cambridge University Press.

Kleiner, D. E. E. 2005. "Semblance and Storytelling in Augustan Rome." In *The Cambridge Companion to the Age of Augustus*, ed. K. Galinsky, 197–233. Cambridge: Cambridge University Press.

Lausberg, H. 1960. *Handbuch der literarischen Rhetorik*. 2 vols. Stuttgart: Franz Steiner.

Lippold, G. 1932. "Tabula iliaca." *Real-Encyclopädie der klassischen Altertumswissenschaft* 4 (2): 1886–96.

Mancuso, U. 1909. "La 'tabula iliaca' del Museo Capitolino." *Memorie: Atti della Accademia nazionale dei Lincei, Classe di scienze morali, storiche e filologiche* 5 (14): 661–731.

Männlein-Robert, I. 2007a. "Epigrams on Art: Voice and Voicelessness in Hellenistic Epigram." In *Brill's Companion to Hellenistic Epigram Down to Philip*, ed. P. Bing and J. S. Bruss, 251–71. Leiden: Brill.

Männlein-Robert, I. 2007b. *Stimme, Schrift und Bild: Zum Verhältnis der Künste in der hellenistischen Dichtung*. Heidelberg: Winter.

Maras, D. F. (ed.). 1999. *La Tabula Iliaca di Bovillae*. Boville: Proloco di Boville.

McLeod, W. 1985. "The 'Epic Canon' of the Borgia Table: Hellenistic Lore or Roman Fraud?" *Transactions of the American Philological Association* 115: 153–65.

Meijering, R. 1987. *Literary and Rhetorical Theories in Greek Scholia*. Groningen: E. Forsten.

Nünlist, R. 2009. *The Ancient Critic at Work: Terms and Concepts of Literary Criticism in Greek Scholia*. Cambridge: Cambridge University Press.

Paulcke, M. 1897. *De Tabula Iliaca Quaestiones Stesichoreae*. Ph.D. diss. Königsberg.

Petrain, D. 2006. "Epic Manipulations: The *Tabulae Iliacae* in Their Roman Context." Ph.D. diss., Harvard University.

Petrain, D. 2010. "More Inscriptions from the *Tabulae Iliacae*." *Zeitschrift für Papyrologie und Epigraphik* 174: 51–56.

Petrain, D. 2012. "The Archaeology of the Epigrams from the *Tabulae Iliacae*: Adaptation, Allusion, Alteration." *Mnemosyne* 65: 597–635.

Petrain, D. Forthcoming. *Homer in Stone: The Tabulae Iliacae in Their Roman Context*. Cambridge: Cambridge University Press.

Poucet, J. 1985. *Les origines de Rome: Tradition et histoire*. Brussels: Latomus.

Puppo, P. 2009. "Le Tabulae Iliacae: Studio per una riedizione." In *Immagine e immagini della Sicilia e di altre isole del Mediterraneo antico*, vol. 2, ed. C. Ampolo, 829–49. Pisa: Edizioni della Normale.

Riese, A. (ed.). 1869–70. *Anthologia Latina, sive Poesis Latinae Supplementum*. 2 vols. Leipzig: G. Teubner.

Rutledge, S. 2012. *Ancient Rome as a Museum: Power, Identity, and the Culture of Collecting*. Oxford: Oxford University Press.

Sadurska, A. 1964. *Les tables iliaques*. Warsaw: Państwowe Wydawnictwo Naukowe.

Salimbene, C. 2002. "La Tabula Capitolina." *Bollettino dei Musei Comunali di Roma* 16: 5–33.

Santoro, S. 2005. "I temi iliaci nella pittura pompeiana." In *Troia tra realtà e leggenda*, ed. G. Burzacchini, 97–123. Palma: Monte Università Parma Editore.

Scafoglio, G. 2005. "Virgilio e Stesicoro: Una ricerca sulla *Tabula Iliaca Capitolina*." *Rheinisches Museum* 148: 113–25.

Schefold, K. 1975. *Wort und Bild: Studien zur Gegenwart der Antike*. Mainz: Philipp von Zabern.

Schneider, R. M. 2007. "Friend and Foe: The Orient in Rome." In *The Age of the Parthians*, ed. V. S. Curtis and S. Stewart, 2:50–86. London: I. B. Tauris.

Schneider, R. M. 2012. "The Making of Oriental Rome: Shaping the Trojan Legend." In *Universal Empire: A Comparative Approach to Imperial Culture and Representation in Eurasian History*, ed. P. F. Bang and D. Kolodziejczyk, 76–129. Cambridge: Cambridge University Press.

Severy, B. 2003. *Augustus and the Family at the Birth of the Roman Empire*. New York: Routledge.

Simon, E. 2008. "Die Rezeption in Rom." In *Homer. Der Mythos von Troia in Dichtung und Kunst. Eine Ausstellung des Antikenmuseums Basel, des Art Centre Basel und der Reiss-Engelhorn-Museen Mannheim*, ed. J. Latacz et al., 232–44. Munich: Hirmer.

Smith, R. R. R. 2013. *Aprodisias VI: The Marble Reliefs from the Julio-Claudian Sebasteion*. Darmstadt: Philipp von Zabern.

Spannagel, M. 1999. *Exemplaria Principis: Untersuchungen zu Entstehung und Ausstattung des Augustusforums*. Heidelberg: Verlag Archäologie und Geschichte.

Squire, M. J. 2009. *Image and Text in Graeco-Roman Antiquity*. Cambridge: Cambridge University Press.

Squire, M. J. 2010. "Texts on the Tables: The *Tabulae Iliacae* in Their Hellenistic Literary Context." *Journal of Hellenic Studies* 130: 67–96.

Squire, M. J. 2011a. *The Iliad in a Nutshell: Visualizing Epic on the Tabulae Iliacae*. Oxford: Oxford University Press.

Squire, M. J. 2011b. "Three New *Tabulae Iliacae* Reconstructions." *Zeitschrift für Papyrologie und Epigraphik* 178: 63–78.

Squire, M. J. 2014a. "Running Rings Round Troy: The Epic Cycle in Hellenistic and Roman Visual Culture." In *A Companion to the Epic Cycle*, ed. M. Fantuzzi and C. Tsaglis. Cambridge: Cambridge University Press.

Squire, M. J. 2014b. "The *Ordo* of Rhetoric and the Rhetoric of *Ordo*." In *Art and Rhetoric in Roman Culture*, ed. J. Elsner and M. Meyer, 353–417. Cambridge: Cambridge University Press.

Strasburger, H. 1968. *Zur Sage von der Gründung Roms*. Heidelberg: Winter.

Thilo, G., and H. Hagen (eds.). 1923–27. *Servii grammatici qui feruntur in Vergilii carmina commentarii*. 2nd ed. 3 vols. Leipzig: Teubner.

Thomas, E. V. 2007. *Monumentality and the Roman Empire: Architecture in the Antonine Age*. Oxford: Oxford University Press.

Tueller, M. A. 2008. *Look Who's Talking: Innovations in Voice and Identity in Hellenistic Poetry*. Leuven: Peeters.

Ungaro, L. (ed.). 2007. *The Museum of the Imperial Forums in Trajan's Market*. Milan: Electa.

Valenzuela Montenegro, N. 2002. "Die Tabulae Iliacae als Kommentar in Bild und Text: Zur frühkaiserzeitlichen Rezeption des trojanischen Sagenkreises." In *Der Kommentar in Antike und Mittelalter: Neue Beiträge zu seiner Erforschung*, ed. W. Geerlings and C. Schulze, 2:67–100. Leiden: Brill.

Valenzuela Montenegro, N. 2004. *Die Tabulae Iliacae: Mythos und Geschichte im Spiegel einer Gruppe frühkaiserzeitlicher Miniaturreliefs*. Berlin: Dissertation.de.

Wachter, R. 2001. *Non-Attic Greek Vase Inscriptions*. Oxford: Oxford University Press.

Welcker, F. G. 1829. "Sur la table iliaque." *Annali dell'Instituto di Corrispondenza Archeologica* 1: 227–43.

Wiseman, P. 2004. *The Myths of Rome*. Exeter: University of Exeter Press.

Zanker, P. 1968. *Forum Augustum: Das Bildprogramm*. Tübingen: E. Wasmuth.

Zanker, P. 1988. *The Power of Images in the Age of Augustus*. Tr. A. Shapiro. Ann Arbor: University of Michigan Press.

Zanker, P. 2002. *Un'arte per l'impero: Funzione e intenzione delle immagine nel mondo romano*. Milan: Electa.

Ziolkowski, J. M., and M. C. J. Putnam. 2008. *The Virgilian Tradition: The First Fifteen Hundred Years*. New Haven, CT: Yale University Press.

CHAPTER 7

Beyond Greece and Rome: Foundation Myths on Tyrian Coinage in the Third Century AD

ALFRED HIRT

During the Roman Principate, foundation myths—stories and images of historical or mythical foundation—were part of civic self-presentation in the Greek East of the Roman Empire. Mythical (hi)stories were told and referred to in local literary texts and orations, or they were presented in evocative images in local architectural sculpture or monuments set up in public and private spaces.[1] Greek foundation myths played an important role in inter-civic rivalries, and civic representatives referenced the mythical prehistory of their polities when making their case before emperor and senate in Rome.[2] Narratives of historical and mythical founders and foundations were propagated by a variety of communities in Anatolia, Syria-Palestine, and on Cyprus; some could field legitimate claims to a Greek origin, and others merely appropriated and adapted episodes and heroes from a shared Greek history, often from Homeric epics. Polities in the Roman Near East sometimes even refrained from making reference to a distant mythical past by opting to go with either their (re-)foundation by Alexander the Great or by Seleucid dynasts, or by choosing a civic era marking other significant beginnings from which the years were counted.[3] Irrespective of the means (literature, art, calendar) by which a polity anchored itself in the past, story lines and images steeped in the shared language of Greek foundation narratives seemed mandatory. Reference had to be made to actual or fictional founders of Greek or Macedonian extraction. For some communities, however, claiming to be of Greek origin was impossible: Phoenician cities, foremost Sidon and Tyre, were engrained in the collective memory of the educated Roman world as the embodiment of the "other." Greek and Latin literary texts played a pivotal role in cementing the image of the Phoenicians often (but not exclusively) as antagonists of Greek and Roman heroes.[4] And in the Hellenistic period, most Phoenician cities were not refounded as Greek settlements, but instead kept their Semitic names. In short, these cities could not field a convincing claim to have Greek origins.[5]

Since the days of Alexander's conquest, however, Phoenician cities had modeled their civic life after Greek poleis. Local dynasts disappeared and were quickly replaced with regular polis institutions by the mid-third century BC. Greek became the main written language on buildings and monuments in the public sphere, relegating the Phoenician script to cultic and funerary contexts. On the surface, Tyre, Sidon, and other Phoenician cities were to become almost indistinguishable from other poleis in the Greek East.[6]

The surviving epigraphic and archaeological evidence at Roman Tyre, for example, strongly professes the self-perception of this civic community as part of the Greek world in the Roman Empire: monuments inscribed in Greek attest the full array of polis institutions (assembly, council, magistrates). Honorific monuments inscribed in Greek and Latin record scores of Roman dignitaries and officers, benefactors, orators, and athletes; there are votive dedications to Greek and Roman gods and Egyptian deities. Even funerary inscriptions reveal the civic values and religious and funerary customs that Tyre shared with other communities throughout the eastern Mediterranean. On its bronze coinage (cf. Period 1 below) and on inscriptions abroad, the city proudly boasted its Greek honorific titles: *hiera, asylos, autonomos, metropolis*.[7] The urban plan, with colonnaded streets, arches, temples, shrines, an aqueduct, and a hippodrome in the ubiquitous architectural style of the Principate, exemplifies Tyre's ambition to conform with the visual styles and system of symbols of the Roman world.[8]

The self-image as a Greek town professed by Tyre clashes with Greek and Roman perceptions as non-Greek alterity. It is this dichotomy that sets the parameters defining the range of mythical foundation narratives that Tyre can pursue. This provides us with the unique opportunity to examine how

these communities constructed their mythical origins, given the require-
ment to demonstrate kinship with the Greek world despite a forceful literary
tradition clearly stating the contrary.

The abundant evidence for Tyrian bronze coinage allows us to explore
the imagery relating to mythical foundation narratives from the late second to the mid-third century AD. Coupled with literary and archaeological
sources, the Tyrian coin emissions provide an interesting insight into how the
community defined its mythical past in light of the given constraints and, as
we shall see, under changing political circumstances. The use of coinage to
convey a civic self-image also raises the important questions of who the
audience(s) were in this important harbor town, for whom the visual messages
were intended, and what was hoped to be achieved.

Before we set out to answer these questions, we will provide a survey of
reverses on Tyrian bronze coinage during the Principate down to the mid-
third century (after this, Tyrian emissions cease). Then we will turn to the
use of mythical foundation imagery under changing political circumstances.
Finally, we will explore the social milieus and geographical provenance of
the audience of coin users, consider the diverging reception of these foundation narratives, and ponder the reasons for picking these particular visual
messages.

Overview of Tyrian Bronze Coin Types[9]

The development of Tyrian bronze coinage can be charted over four main
periods, each displaying varying ranges of imagery.

Period 1: First and Second Centuries

During the first century AD, three and later four denominations display either the laureate head of Heracles or the turreted and veiled bust of Tyche on
the obverse. The reverses consist of three or four types: a monogram for Tyre
(*TYP*) surmounted on a Herculean club; a galley; a palm tree; and a female
figurine standing on a galley. All reverse types are inscribed with TYP or
TY(P) IERA AΣY (Τύρου ἱερᾶς [καὶ] ἀσύλου); the title μητροπόλεως is added
from AD 86/87 onward. The reverses show the date in the Tyrian era; the
coins' origin is indicated with *lṣr*, Phoen. "of Tyre." An eight-column temple

with the captions Κοινού Φοινίκες and Ἄκτ/ι is added to the reverse types (second century AD).[10]

Period 2: Septimius Severus to Elagabalus

With the grant of colonial status (AD 198), the coinage now shows the emperor or members of the imperial family on the obverse. On the reverse, Latin legends give the civic title *Sep(timia) Tyrus Metrop(olis) Col(onia).*[11] The range of reverse types is expanded significantly: a female figurine (Tyche?/Astarte?) wearing a turreted crown, standing on the bow of a galley together with a trophy and Nike, is depicted repeatedly. Other reverses show this scene within a hexastyle temple, indicating that it may render the cult image of a deity central to Tyre.[12] Apart from his bust, Hercules is also shown standing with a club resting in his left arm near a trophy, or performing a libation on an altar with two stelae/rocks in the background.[13] Also shown are Dionysus and Egyptian deities.[14] Other coins show prize crowns with the Greek legends "Heraclian" (games) and "Actia Heraclia";[15] or the temple of the *koinon*(?), often with the Latin legend *Coenu Phoenices.*[16] The only foundation imagery of this period depicts a figure, *capite velato*, with an ox and a cow, representing the ritual of plowing the *sulcus primigenius*, the sacred furrow; in the background, a legionary standard renders *leg(io) III Gal(lica)*. Other types show a bull (the emblem of the legion) or an eagle before a legionary standard with *leg(io) III Gal(lica).*[17]

Period 3: Elagabalus

For a short period during the reign of Elagabalus (AD 218–22), the caption *Sep(timia) Turus Metrop(olis) Coloni(a)* on reverse types is replaced with the ethnic TVRIORVM. The colonial foundation and legionary types are not in use; nor are *koinon* types.[18] Other reverse types are continued,[19] and new motifs are introduced.[20] Regarding foundation imagery, reverses render Dido as founder of Carthage; the city is shown as a gate under construction, and the veiled woman standing in the foreground is clearly identified by the Greek caption ΔΕΙΔΩΝ.[21] Dido may furthermore be depicted on a different reverse type without an identifying caption: a woman with *aphlaston* in her left arm and giving directions with a short staff is standing on a galley, accompanied by two men to the left and right of her, one dumping a bag overboard.[22] Further motifs seem to show a naked hero with chlamys hurling a stone with his right arm toward a snake. The scene is reminiscent of a story from the Kadmos cycle: before founding Thebes, Kadmos sends companions to a water source, where the serpent of Ares kills them; the enraged Kadmos slays the serpent with a stone.[23] In another scene, a hero, tentatively identified as Kadmos (?), is shown rushing aboard a ship while looking back.[24] One type depicts two stones/stelae on both sides of an olive tree with the caption AMBROCIC PAETRE, the "divine" or "immortal" rocks.[25] Intriguing is the motif of a naked hero standing on a line and holding a staff and the reins to four stags; on later coins, he is identified by the caption *pgmljn* (see Theme 4 below).[26]

Period 4: Severus Alexander to Gallienus

After Severus Alexander is made emperor in AD 222, Tyre puts the full title, *Sep(timia) Tvro(s) Metrop(olis) Col(onia) P(ho)enic(es)*, back on its reverses.[27] Roman legionary emblems are shown again; the Roman founder image, however, is not reused.[28] Cult, festival, and temple imagery, as well as deities,[29] and, most important, foundation imagery—Dido, Kadmos, and the "ambrosial stones"—continue to be shown.[30] New motifs expand the range of reverse types, referring not only to the local cult imagery (for example, a portable shrine) but to mythical heroes—for example, "Kadmos and Harmonia (?)" and deities.[31] Significantly, Europa is shown on Tyrian reverses under Trebonianus Gallus (AD 251–53) and Valerian (AD 253–60); identified by the caption Εὐ|ρώ|πη, she is portrayed standing upright beside a bull emerging from the water, the ambrosial rocks / two stelae with an olive tree behind her. A similar type shows Europa standing to the right of an olive tree between two stelae, to the lower left a bull, above an inscription reading [Ε]ὐρώ|<π>η, ἱ<έ>ρια ἀ|μβρο|cιῶν πετ|ρ|ῶν, "priestess of the ambrosial stones."[32] A reverse coined under Gallienus (AD 253–68) depicts the naked Kadmos standing with *phiale* in his right hand and staff in his left, beside a lying heifer; in the background, a turreted city gate is shown. The caption ΘΗΒΕ identifies the scene: the Delphic oracle advises the Tyrian hero to give up his search for his sister Europa and instead follow a heifer; where the heifer sits down, he was to found a city, Thebes.[33] Another type (Gallienus, AD 253–68) depicts Kadmos handing a papyrus roll (the *phoinikeia grammata?*) to three Hellenes. The figures are identified by the sobriquets ΚΑΔΜΟϲ and ΕΛΛΗΝΕϲ.[34]

Civic Status and Messages Through Coin Imagery

This survey of the main reverse types coined by the Tyrian mint during the Principate allows us to describe the emergence and concurrent use of four themes, two regarding the foundation(s) of Tyre: its foundation as a Roman titular colony (Theme 1); and the ambrosial rocks and Hercules as part of a local foundation myth (Theme 4). Two further narratives highlight the role of Tyre in the foundation of Carthage and Boeotian Thebes (Themes 2 and 3). The introduction of these four foundation themes does not happen at random but coincides with two significant alterations to the overall appearance of Tyrian coinage: the change to colonial types under Septimius Severus; and the short-lived TVRIORUM emissions under Elagabalus. These alterations, it shall be argued, reflect important changes to the status of the city of Tyre. This corroborates the notion that, at least for these four foundation themes, we may postulate a message of a political nature.

Theme 1: A Roman Foundation

The elevation to colonial rank in AD 198, following Tyre's early support for Septimius Severus against Pescennius Niger in the spring of AD 194, had a significant impact on the civic self-image of the city presented in its coinage.[35] Tyrian coin emissions of the first and second century AD professed the idea of Tyre as an autonomous Greek polis (Period 1). Conversely, there was no reference to the Roman Empire: unlike most civic coinages, Tyrian obverses did not show the emperor.[36] With the grant of colonial status, the self-image of Tyre experienced an almost paradigmatic shift (Period 2): it now presented itself as a Roman colony. From Septimius Severus onward, obverses now depicted the emperor's head and his Latin titles. The reverses gave the full colonial title of the city in Latin. Besides cult imagery and "Greek" and Egyptian deities,[37] reverse types now showed colonial themes: one scene on coins under Septimius Severus, and repeated sporadically until Elagabalus, showed a Roman founder outlining the limits of the colony's territory with an ox and a plow (Fig. 7.1). From

7.1. Caracalla (AD 211–17). Rev. SEP. TVRVS MET. // LEG. / III / GAL. Münzen & Medaillen GmbH, Auction 32, lot 330, 26.05.2010.

the start, Tyre visualized its elevation to colonial status on its coins with an evocative yet fictional Roman founder image—a generic scene characteristic of coins minted at Roman colonies throughout the Roman Near East (for example, Ptolemais, Berytus, Caesarea, Sebaste, Aelia Capitolina) and elsewhere. In other words, Tyre presented a mythicized illustration of its colonial refoundation. For most communities, the grant of colonial status was merely a titular matter. Tyre, however, may have seen an actual settlement of alien Roman citizenry in the town: the depiction of standards and emblems of *legio III Gallica* not only as a backdrop to the founder scene but as a central image of other reverse types is understood to reflect the influx of legionary veterans to the city.[38]

Theme 2: Dido, Kadmos, and the Metropolis

The abrupt replacement of colonial titles with TVRIORVM under Elagabalus (Period 3) constitutes an anomaly in the comparatively well-documented series of Tyrian coin emissions, suggesting more than just a cosmetic modification of reverses.[39] Since the late Hellenistic period, the Tyrian mint had consistently and accurately reflected the honorary titles bestowed on the city of Tyre, which were similarly presented in public and private inscriptions by the Tyrian polity and its members. The sudden and temporary removal of the honorary titles *Colonia Septimia* and *Metropolis* suggests a demotion of Tyre, for whatever reason, by the emperor Elagabalus. This hypothesis is further corroborated by contemporary

coin emissions of neighboring Sidon. While Tyre emitted its TVRIORVM reverses, Sidon rekindled its bronze coinage after a long hiatus (since Hadrian). The
Sidonian reverses now rendered the civic title *A(urelia) P(ia) Sid(on) Col(onia)
Metro(polis)* and displayed founder scenes with a standard in the background,
inscribed with *l(egio) III Gal(lica)* or an image of three military standards.[40] Sidon
used exactly the epithets and colonial imagery on its coins, which disappeared
from Tyrian reverses. As a working hypothesis, it is thus suggested that Tyre was
demoted, and Sidon, in turn, awarded the titles *colonia* and *metropolis* instead.[41]

The written sources remain mute on the reasons for the loss of status. The
degradation of a community, however, was not unprecedented: Septimius
Severus had reduced Antiochia to a κώμη and added its territory to Laodicea ad Mare. Laodicea received the titles of *metropolis* and *colonia*, which
Antiochia had held—a harsh punishment for the latter's support of Pescennius Niger in the civil war of AD 193/94.[42] Based on this analogy, it is plausible
that the loss of prestigious titles and, therefore, the humiliation of the Tyrian
community significantly influenced the choice of reverse types on TVRI-
ORVM coinage. Inconspicuous reverses depicting Tyrian cult imagery, such
as the female deity, or Hercules, were continued, of course. Yet the introduction of a new genre of images may be read in terms of a visual reaction to, and
perhaps even a protest of, Tyre's loss of status. Reverse types on TVRIORVM
coins suddenly evoked Tyre's mythical past by making potent references to
two well-known scions of Tyre: Dido, founder of Carthage; and, probably,
Kadmos. The first depiction of Dido as mythical founder of Carthage on
TVRIORVM reverses coincides with the loss of civic titles, first and foremost
the title of *metropolis* (Fig. 7.2). The motif of Dido sacrificing at an altar while
the new city is constructed in the background emphasized Tyre's role as

7.2. Iulia Maesa (AD 218–24?). Rev. TVRIORVM; Rouvier 2406; Münzen &
Medaillen GmbH, Auction 11, lot 181, 07.11.2002.

mother city of Carthage—and thus expressed visually what perhaps could not be voiced.

The term *metropolis* has a dual meaning: first, it identified Tyre as the foremost town of the *eparchia* of Phoinike (and Koile-Syria);[43] second, it signified the founder city of overseas settlements. The latter, as we shall see, was likely more important to the Tyrian community. In an inscription at Didyma for a former governor of Syria (c. AD 100–103/4), the city reveals its full title as ὁ δῆμος Τυρίων τῆς ἱερᾶς καὶ ἀσύλου καὶ αὐτονόμου μητροπόλεως Φοινείκης καὶ τῶν κατὰ Κοίλην Συρίαν καὶ ἄλλων πόλεων καὶ ναθαρχίδος.[44] A Latin version is inscribed on a statue base honoring Septimius Geta at Lepcis Magna (late second century AD), adding the newly acquired status of *colonia*: *Septimia Tyros colonia metropolis Phoenices et aliarum civitatium*.[45] The full civic title given in the inscriptions of Didyma or Lepcis Magna not only elevate Tyre to *metropolis* of Phoenicia (and Koile-Syria) but, more important, ἄλλων πόλεων or *aliarum civitatium*, of "other cities," clearly alluding to the connotation as mother city of overseas foundations. These "other towns" reinforced Tyre's claim by setting up monuments honoring their mother city: during the second century AD, Lepcis Magna and one or two other polities commissioned statues in Tyre with Lepcis Magna dedicating its statue to *Tyron et suam metropolin*.[46] Thus, for Tyre, being "the" *metropolis* was of utmost significance. Pointedly, Tyre was involved in a long-standing dispute with its neighbor Sidon over exactly this title. An inscribed monument of the late third century BC names Sidon the "house of the descendants of Agenor" and metropolis of "Cadmeian Thebes."[47] Since 170 BC, Tyre had minted bronzes claiming, in Phoenician, to be mother of the Sidonians. Sidonian bronze coins of the same period give the Phoenician caption "(coin?) of the Sidonians, the mother of [the settlements] Kambe(?), Hippo, Kition, (and) Tyre."[48] Strabo relates an ongoing dispute on whether Tyre or Sidon can rightfully declare to be a *metropolis*.[49] The varying claims are mirrored in other literary sources: Sallust describes Lepcis, Hippo, and Hadrumetum as foundations *ab Sidoniis*, Pliny the Elder Lepcis, Utica, Gades, and Carthage as Tyrian colonies. Moreover, Pliny calls Sidon *thebarumque boeotiarum parens*, and Achilles Tatius deemed Sidon to be μήτηρ Φοινίκων ἡ πόλις and its people the father of the Thebans.[50] The title of *metropolis* was finally granted to Tyre by the emperor Domitian.[51] According to the *Suda*, a Paulus, an orator sent from Tyre to the emperor Hadrian, was able to secure the title of *metropolis* for his city; another town, probably Sidon, had likely contested the title.[52] Herodian reports that on the eve of the civil war of AD 193/94, Tyre lay in dispute with Berytus, possibly over claims to be the rightful *metropolis*.[53]

Given the extended history of the rivalry among "Phoenician" cities for the title of *metropolis,* Tyre likely was not pleased over its temporary loss to Sidon under Elagabalus. One Sidonian reverse type showed a male figure rushing onto a prow looking back; the figure probably represented Kadmos in a posture eerily similar to images fielded simultaneously on TVRIORVM coins (Figs. 7.3 and 7.4).[54] Evidently, the Phoenician Kadmos, founder of Boeotian Thebes, was claimed by both cities to be its son.[55] Tyre and Sidon employed mythical founders of overseas settlements, such as Dido or Kadmos, to bolster their respective claims of being the true mother city. Even after the restoration of Tyre to its full civic titles under Severus Alexander, Tyrian coinage almost incessantly repeated

7.3. Sidon. Elagabalus (AD 218–22). Rev. AVR. PIA [SID.] COL. MET.; Classical Numismatic Group, Inc., Auction 85, lot 677, 15.09. 2010.

7.4. Iulia Maesa (AD 218–24?). Rev. [TVRIORVM?]. Classical Numismatic Group, Inc., Electronic Auction 193, lot 167, 6.08.2008.

the founding scenes with Dido and, in the mid-third century AD, added the foundation of Thebes by Kadmos to its reverse types.

Theme 3: Kadmos, Europa, and Greek Kinship

The repeated reference to Dido and Kadmos from Elagabalus onward must not necessarily be read only in the context of the *metropolis* dispute. Through Vergil's *Aeneid* and the works of various mythographers, Dido and Kadmos provided Tyre with two mythical heroes well known among the educated of the Greek East and the Roman West. Both allowed Tyre to claim at least the entangledness of their "other" or "Phoenician" history with the mythical past of Greece and of Rome. In the case of Kadmos, Tyre could even declare direct ancestry to a host of Greek mythical heroes and heroines said to be descendants of Kadmos and Harmonia.[56] A similar claim could be fielded in the case of Europa, whose image was introduced to Tyrian coin reverses in the mid-third century AD. The surviving Greek narratives on Europa do not identify her as founder of overseas settlements; but after being abducted by Zeus to Crete, she emerges as the mother of Minos, Rhadamanthys, and, later, Sarpedon, all fathered by Zeus; her sons figure as progenitors of a whole stemma of Greek mythical heroes.[57] With the display of Kadmos and Europa, Tyre may have promulgated the message that this Phoenician city was closely linked with the mythical past of Greece, and perhaps even that heroes and heroines from Tyre stood at the origin of Greek mythical genealogies. Instead of establishing descent from a fictional or real *ktistes* of Greek origin, the prominent role of Kadmos and Europa in Greek mythology may have allowed Tyre to put forward a different argument: it was by Tyrian founders and progenitors that the Greeks were related to the Tyrians. This fits in well with the spiel on antecedence not only evidenced in literary sources such as the *Phoinikika* of Herennius Philo: the bronze reverse showing Kadmos introducing the Greeks to the alphabet is the most conspicuous of the coin images asserting cultural preeminence (see below).[58]

Theme 4: Hercules, the Ambrosial Stones, and the Creation of Tyre

The Tyrian reverses depicting Europa with the ambrosial rocks/stelae (Fig. 7.5) linked a prominent narrative centered on Europa with the rather obscure local foundation tale on the ambrosial stones (Period 4). With the addition of Europa to the range of types, Tyre appropriated a Sidonian icon, which had been displayed almost incessantly on Sidonian issues since the late Hellenistic period,[59] for its own past. Regarding the foundation tale of the ambrosial rocks, it was first alluded to on TVRIORVM coins bearing two rounded stones or stelae beside an olive tree and identified by the sobriquet AMBRO-CIC PAETRE (Fig. 7.6; Period 4). The early fifth-century author Nonnus of Panopolis, in his *Dionysiaka*, retold one, if not the main, version of the underlying foundation narrative. In conversation with Dionysus, Hercules relates the story of the creation of Tyre as the result of his own intervention. After the Tyrians emerged from mud, Hercules, by way of prophecy, told them to construct a boat to travel on water, and ordered them to set out to sea. As foretold by Hercules, the Tyrians found two "ambrosial" rocks floating amid the waves, upon which grew an olive tree. The tree stood in flames but was not consumed by the fire. A chalice and an eagle sat in its branches, and a snake coiled around its stem, all unharmed by the flames. As instructed by Hercules, the Tyrians caught the eagle and sacrificed it to Poseidon; they poured out its blood onto the rocks. The rocks immediately merged with the seabed into an island, upon which the Tyrians built their city.[60] For this episode, Nonnus perhaps made use of a local tradition: he may have known Tyre and Berytus (both cities take up significant space in the *Dionysiaka*) and distilled works on the foundation of cities, so-called *pátria*, or other literary sources, for his epic.[61] Elements of

7.5. Valerian (AD 253–60). Rev. [COL. TVRO. ME]TR. // EV/RW/ΠΗ; *BMC* 468; Münzen & Medaillen GmbH, Auction 20, lot 916, 10.10.2006.

7.6. Elagabalus (AD 218–22). Rev. TVRIORVM // AMB/ROCIC // ΠΑΕ/ΤΡΕ; Rouvier 2391; Heidelberger Münzhandlung Herbert Grün e.K., Auction 53, lot 246, 20.05. 2010.

the story told by Nonnus emerge in other contexts: Achilles Tatius describes the isle of Tyre as floating, that is, not rooted on the bottom of the sea, and has Sostratos, one of his main characters, explain that in an enclosed sacred area, the branches of an olive tree are set alight by a fire in the ground.[62] We thus might be looking at a local foundation narrative, existing in different versions, perhaps combining Near Eastern elements with the Greek concept of a foundation myth.[63]

This said, the reverse types depicting the stelae or stones beside the olive tree allow for divergent readings inspired by other Tyrian foundation tales: Herennius Philo relates the story of the cultural hero Ousoos, who, during his flight from a forest fire near Tyre—a city founded by his brother and rival Samemroumos—jumped onto a log and swam out to sea, thereby inventing seafaring. On his return to the shore, he set up two stelae to fire and wind, on which he poured out animal blood. The Tyrians were to worship the stelae and conduct yearly festivals. Ousoos thus provided the city formed by his brother with its central sanctuary; in Philo's tale, the two stelae are closely linked with the creation of the city.[64] Also, the reverse types link Hercules with the two stelae, perhaps referring to Herodotus' visit to Tyre (Fig. 7.7). He describes two stelae—one of gold, the other of emerald—inside the sanctuary of Hercules; on recording the age of the sanctuary, Herodotus conjoins the creation of it with the city's foundation by qualifying the sanctuary to be "as old as Tyre."[65] Both Herodotus' description of the sanctuary at Tyre and the Ousoos story link the two stelae/stones to the settlement or foundation of Tyre.[66] This notion is reflected in a Greek decree in 154/53 BC from Delos, in

7.7. Iulia Domna (AD 193–217). Rev. [SE]P. TVRVS METRO. COLONI.; Classical Numismatic Group, Inc., Mail Bid Sale 76, lot 1128, 12.09.200.

which the Tyrians describe their god Hercules as ἀρχηγός τῆς πατρίδος, "founder of the hometown/fatherland."[67]

From Elagabalus onward, varying foundation images centered on the ambrosial stones appear regularly on Tyrian coins, clearly identified by the caption AMBROCIC PAETRE; these may have evoked different versions of the foundation myth on purpose, multiplying the possibilities of how they might be read and thus integrating a diverse audience of users. The unifying message of these reverses did not emphasize Tyre's mythical past in relation to Greece and Rome. Their obscurity points in the opposite direction: Tyre's difference from, rather than kinship with, Greece was markedly accentuated. Its own foundation myth was proudly put center stage, setting it on a par with Greek foundation narratives.

This emphasis on difference, of not being Greek, is furthermore conveyed by reverses coined under Gordian III (238–44): the well-known "Dido and Carthage" type with the inscription ΔΕΙΔΩΝ also shows the Phoenician caption 'lt ṣr, "Goddess of Tyre."[68] Another reverse type, the opaque "hero with four stags," is identified by the Phoenician vignette pgmljn, rendering the Greek name Pygmalion in Phoenician letters.[69] The use of Phoenician in the mid-third century AD is striking: it had disappeared as a written language from the public sphere by the early first century (except during Period I).[70] Phoenician may still have been in use as a script in private or religious contexts, but the literary sources referring to Phoenician as a spoken idiom are hardly conclusive.[71] It is entirely possible that by the third century AD, Aramaic was spoken instead.[72] In consequence, the point of Phoenician captions lay not in their textual content but in the pictorial value of the letters; the forms of Phoenician letters were recognizably different from Greek, Latin, and Aramaic, and familiar to Tyrians and other inhabitants of the Phoenician coast; monuments and dilapidated buildings inscribed with Phoenician were likely still visible, if not in Tyre itself, then certainly throughout the Tyrian countryside.[73]

The use of the Phoenician script and of the ambrosial stones on its coinage celebrated the uniqueness and distinctiveness of Tyre and its past. While other foundation imagery either highlighted the Roman colonial foundation of Tyre or alluded to its role as *metropolis* or as progenitor of mythical Greek kinsfolk, these foundation narratives possibly reflect a look inward, perhaps even a withdrawal from the dominant discourse centered on Greek origins. Through these reverse types, Tyre may have stated that it was not Greek and highlighted its "Phoenicity."

Audience(s) and Authority

The survey of Tyrian coin emissions reveals that there were a number of reverse types, which can be read as visualizations of foundation myths related to Tyre. These types have been interpreted here to be deliberate and timely additions to a wide range of Tyrian coin motifs, mirroring the reaction of the civic body to changes in status and the rivalries over position and prestige with neighboring communities. This is contingent upon the tentative notion that a mint executed coin designs decided on by Tyrian authorities intent on employing bronze coinage as a vehicle to convey particular messages. But to whom? And to what effect?

These questions have been put to the imagery on civic coin emissions in the Greek East in general. The answers are disheartening; it remains unclear whom these images were aimed at, what impact they had on the audience of coin users, and, in the vast majority of cases, what the intrinsic message of the coin imagery and the intent of the issuing body was.[74] In this respect, the Tyrian foundation types are exceptional: the temporal correlation between their issue and significant political events argued here, along with the effort to improve the apprehension of these types by adding captions in Greek or Latin, strongly implies an intent to get across specific messages of a political nature. Consequently, this merits a reconsideration of audience(s) and authority.

The constraints to the possible audience of coin users are set by the circulation pattern of civic bronze coinage, usually limited to the territory of the issuing city. This likely applied to Tyrian bronze coinage as well, although some specimens were found as far away as Berytus, Si' in the Hauran, or Gerasa in Jordan.[75] The potential audience thus consisted mainly of citizens and residents of and visitors to Tyre and its territory.

To conclude economic transactions in the territory of Tyre, silver and bronze coins needed to be exchanged for the local currency, its users being exposed automatically to the imagery. Within the city, civic coinage was put into circulation through payments to public servants, moneychangers, and bankers licensed by the city, or distributions or gifts at public festivals.[76] Could the images conveyed on Tyrian coins be understood? Apart from a few literary quotations, the reception or impact of coin motifs cannot be tested. Although Lucian of Samosata, for example, was aware that Sidon minted coins depicting Europa and the bull, it is far from evident that others read the image in the same way.[77] The complexity and obscurity of the visual language employed in Tyrian coin imagery prima facie points to the civic aristocracy as the audience most able to decode this specific genre of Greek narrative art. Their *paideia*, their literate and cultural edification, likely equipped them to comprehend the images and understand their implications. During the Principate, elementary education for at least some of the local aristocracy at Tyre was sophisticated enough to enable "academic" and imperial careers as philosophers in Athens and Rome or, respectively, as equestrian officials in the imperial administration.[78] More important, the civic aristocracy participated in the dominant cultural discourse and was well accustomed to the visual system of symbols of the Greek East:[79] statuettes, sculptures, paintings, and mosaics, all adorning the private houses of the ruling elite, expressed their *paideia* and effectively pronounced their cultural sophistication over the commoner.[80] Other literate members of Tyrian citizenry might have difficulties comprehending most reverse types, but in the case of Tyrian foundation imagery, they were cued by captions. Surely, the sobriquets were intended to clarify the basic meaning to a literate audience.[81]

We need to be careful not to overemphasize the role of a literate education in the reception of the coin motifs. Even without having endured *enkyklios paideia*, the foundation images could well be appreciated by urban Tyrians, provided that the reverses captured iconic scenes in sculpture, paintings, or mosaics in the public and religious spaces and cult settings of Tyre. Circumstantial evidence from Sidon provides a convenient illustration: Achilles Tatius describes a painting in a Sidonian temple exhibiting a swimming bull carrying Europa with her billowing veil; Europa's posture is well known from Sidonian coins.[82] One reverse depicts "Europa on bull" in the tympanum of a distyle temple front, indicating that the Europa scene was copied from an existing religious building.[83] By the same token, an attentive urban audience, including the illiterate and non-Greeks, possibly understood the foundation narratives on Tyrian reverses if they reflected narrative art of the public sphere. Perhaps readings of the reverses were shared orally among the urban citizenry of Tyre. Mythic figures such as Kadmos and Europa, and even Dido, and the ambrosial stones may have formed part of a communal memory—a memory that was regularly reaffirmed at cult rituals, festivals, games, and processions in the public sphere. It is open to question, however, whether all Tyrians shared the same interpretation of the coin imagery and whether their reading diverged from the core message of the reverses.[84] A divide between town and country may have played a role as well: the majority of the rural community rarely visited Tyre.[85] Less embedded in the Greek visual culture of the urban center, the foundation imagery may have meant nothing to the rural populace.

The audience of these coin motifs was not limited to citizens and residents of Tyre: honorific monuments inscribed in Latin and Greek set up for senatorial officials and equestrian officers indicate the occasional attendance or even permanent presence of representatives of Roman power at Tyre.[86] Dedications in Latin also document soldiers and civilians with Roman names in Tyre; the civic epithet ναυαρχίς may emphasize the role of Tyre's harbor as port of call for the *classis Syriaca*.[87] Moreover, the city received veterans of *legio III Gallica* after the grant of colonial status (cf. Period 2). As a *metropolis*, Tyre likely was a regular place of assemblies for delegations from the eparchy or *koinon* of Phoenicia (and Koile-Syria)—and perhaps on occasion, from all four Syrian eparchies.[88] Honorific monuments attest to ties as far as Lepcis Magna, implying perhaps groups or individuals from former *apoikiai* visiting the "mother city"(?).[89] Agonistic and religious festivals, cultic rituals, races at the hippodrome, and economic opportunities in maritime trade and local purple and glass production, as well as other central functions fulfilled by the city, likely pulled many people from the coastal hinterland and Roman Syria to Tyre.[90]

Given the wide range of social milieus and geographic origins, it is difficult to isolate a group that was targeted by one certain foundation image.[91] The use of the traditional Roman founder image, for example, signaled to members of other civic elites that Tyre had risen in status; for the representatives of imperial power and travelers from the West, it assured them of Tyre's *romanitas*; the legionary veterans perhaps saw the founder image combined with their legionary emblem as a confirmation that they were an integral part of this newly forged community. The "Dido and Carthage" type probably played rather well with representatives of the Roman state and army officers, as well as delegates, merchants, and travelers from the western Mediterranean. Popularized in the Roman West by Vergil's *Aeneid*, the core text of Latin literate education, Dido was likely familiar to all those who had learned to read and write Latin.[92] Given the Greek caption ΔΕΙΔΩΝ, however, a literate Greek audience, especially Tyrians familiar with Dido, were addressed as well; the later addition of a Phoenician caption reinforces this hypothesis (cf. Theme 4). Literate outsiders from the Greek East coming to Tyre were perhaps targeted as well: the motifs "Kadmos and Thebes," "Kadmos giving Hellenes the alphabet," and "Europa" are likely to have been understood by literate non-Tyrians; the Greek sobriquets made sure of this. Regarding the more obscure foundation images, particularly the ambrosial stones, or motifs not illuminated by Greek or Latin captions (Dido, Kadmos; cf. Period 2), it is questionable whether they had outsiders in mind at all. Only those well versed in Greek visual language or the initiated Tyrians could read or knew of their intended meaning. The opaque types were perhaps more reflective of an internalized discourse limited to Tyre's ruling elite.

We are generally left in the dark about the decision process and the parties involved in choosing civic coin images. Whether some of the more obscure motifs reflected not a communal agenda but were coined for the self-promotion or legitimization of partisan factions, elite families, and individuals within Tyre, remains an open question. Given that coin emissions were probably an expensive enterprise, much might have depended upon who financed particular coin emissions or offered to provide the base metal. Whether institutions of the polity or, perhaps, provincial authorities had a say in the choice of coin motifs or at least sanctioned them, is beyond our knowledge.[93] That said, the foundation narratives displayed on the coinage surely were chosen in the interests of the whole community. We just do not know by whom.

The flurry of minting activity by Tyre during the first half of the third century implies that it provided more than just income (the city likely received a commission from the exchange of coins).[94] The high frequency of Tyrian issues and costs of minting indicate that emitting coins was a matter of civic prestige. The considerable expansion in the range of types and the use of captions from Septimius Severus onward furthermore suggests that there was perhaps more at play here: with the choice of foundation narratives, the authorities not only reacted to the grant, removal, and restitution of prestigious civic titles (*colonia, metropolis*) but utilized coin reverses as a medium. We have postulated plausible political messages expressed by the foundation imagery and thought about the possible audiences to whom specific foundation types were addressed. But what did the Tyrian authority issuing these coins hope to achieve? Were foundation types just part of a coordinated and multifaceted information strategy aimed at regaining and retaining the civic status of *metropolis*? Or do the divergent foundation messages reflect a conflict of goals and interests? Were particular groups of audiences targeted? Or were the visual messages left ambiguous, to reach many coin users? Was the authority keen on addressing outsiders to garner their support and fortify the rightfulness of their claims? Or were these foundation types issued to reach a Tyrian audience in order to rekindle the civic pride of its citizens in a humiliated community and restore the legitimacy of the ruling elite?

Conclusion

In his epochal book *The Roman Near East*, Fergus Millar suggests that a cultural amnesia about the pre-Hellenistic "history," widely attested in the Roman Near East, did not pertain to the cities of Sidon and Tyre.[95] A part of the Tyrian reverse types on bronze coinage emitted throughout the first half of the third century AD prima facie provides good evidence for Millar's statement; Dido, Kadmos, and Europa—figures closely linked to Tyre (and/or Sidon)—evoke a distant past entwined with the Greek and Roman world by emphasizing Tyre's role in the foundation of Carthage and Boeotian Thebes and as progenitor to a host of Greek heroes and communities. It is, however, not Tyre's pre-Hellenistic past that is retold; it is the past according to Greek and Roman literary sources. The myths connecting Tyrian founder heroes or progenitors such as Kadmos and Europa with Greece allowed Tyre to easily bridge the dichotomy between being a Greek city and the literary perception as a non-Greek alterity. Europa and Kadmos permitted Tyre to claim ancestry and therefore kinship with the Greeks.

Conversely, Tyre sidestepped the subject of Greek kinship by minting coins mythicizing the grant of colonial status and the settlement of legionary veterans; the self-image professed was that of a Roman colony founded in accordance with ancient Roman rites and settled with Roman citizens. This was visualized by showing the traditional founder scene and "legionary standards"; although the bulk of colonial themes were shown before the reign of Elagabalus, legionary standards were still depicted in the mid-third century in remembrance of the colonial foundation. Another theme coined simultaneously was a foundation narrative centered on the role of the "ambrosial rocks/stelae" in the creation and foundation of Tyre. These reverse types might have signaled a departure from the ruling Greek foundation discourse; rather than trying to explain Tyre's kinship with Greece by using mythic figures well known from core texts of Greek and Roman literature, the obscurity of these narrative scenes indicates a foundation story told locally that links the temple of Hercules or Ousoos and its two stelae with the foundation of Tyre. According to these narratives, Tyre was distinctly non-Greek and created by Tyrians on the instigation of its main god, Hercules, or of Phoenician cultural heroes Samemroumos and Ousoos. With the depiction of ambrosial stones on coins, Tyre perhaps emphasized its distinctiveness, which was further underpinned by the use of Phoenician captions on "Dido and Carthage" or "hero with stags" (*pgmljn*) types.

The Tyrian community seems quite comfortable playing simultaneously with a plurality of foundation themes highlighting diverging civic self-perceptions as ancestor to Greek lineages, as a Roman colony, or as a Phoenician city. For the Tyrian authorities, these distinctions appear not mutually exclusive or contradictory. The foundation themes were possibly directed at distinct groups of coin users. The "Dido and Carthage" motif perhaps played well with the veteran settlers and representatives of Roman power present at Tyre, but the Greek caption may also suggest an educated Greek elite as intended audience; the later addition of a Phoenician caption even suggests local Tyrian addressees. This ambivalence with respect to the intended audience of this particular coin type appears almost deliberate. Other types seem more straightforward: Kadmos and Europa could have been coined with literate visitors from Roman Syria and the Greek East in mind, whereas the ambrosial stones probably focused exclusively on an urban Tyrian audience. Scholarly consensus has it that only the educated elite could read the coin images. An illiterate or a non-Greek urban audience, however, perhaps recognized the imagery from the public sphere and could decode the coin types as well. It is remarkable that the different foundation themes on reverse types at one time or another were explained by captions, whereas the majority of Tyrian types are not. Clearly, the authorities were intent on clarifying the narrative foundation scenes in particular (though not exclusively), to ensure that a wider audience could read the pictorial messages.

Perhaps the most significant contribution of this survey of Tyrian civic coinage is the observation that the choice of foundation imagery is closely linked to the grant, loss, and restitution of the civic epithets *colonia* and *metropolis*. Prior to Tyre's degradation, foundation narratives (with the exception of colonial motifs) are not part of the Tyrian self-presentation on coins. The political humiliation of Tyre by Elagabalus and the subsequent challenges fielded by Sidon (and Berytus) for the prestigious honor of *metropolis* prompted the Tyrians to display foundation episodes of its own mythic past as perceived by Greek and Roman authors (Dido, Kadmos). The sudden appearance of such images was not only down to the crisis and challenges to its civic status; the evocation of foundation myths and founder heroes as a technique to argue kinship with Greece was widely practiced by many civic communities in the eastern Mediterranean and defined the mind-set of the Tyrian authorities choosing coin dyes. Narrative scenes of foundation myths were the obvious choice to push a political message. The motifs on Tyrian coins, however, reveal a unique twist in the normal use of foundation themes by Greco-Roman polities. Tyrians skillfully employed the full range of Greco-Roman literary traditions in their favor. However, this did not stop them from making full use of their own myths on the origins of Tyre.

NOTES

1. Graf 2011: 222f.; Strubbe 1984–86; Scheer 1993; Lindner 1994; Sartre 2002; Butcher 2003b: 237–59, 273–77, 313–21.

2. Tac. *Ann.* 3.60–61; Woolf 1994: 132; Rigsby 1996: 580–86; Jones 1999: 106ff.; Price 2005: 123, bibliography.

3. Scheer 1993: ch. E II.5 and F; Butcher 2003b: 122–24; Butcher 2004: 224–28; Marek 2010: 585–89.

4. Briquel-Chatonnet 1992; S. Ribicchini, in Krings 1995: 72–83; Isaac 2004: 324–35; Gruen 2011: 115–40.

5. "Sidon/*Ṣdn*"; "Tyre/*Ṣr.*" Millar 2006a: 34. Exceptions: cf. Cohen 2006: 201–22.

6. E.g., Millar 2006a.

7. Assembly and council: *SEG* 2 330 (Delos); *IG* 14 830, 1.2; *IGLTyr* 29, 40, 411: *I.Didyma* 151. Magistrates: *IG* 14 830, *IGLTyr* 53, 54, 55, 56; Mouterde (1944–46): 62; Le Lasseur 1922; Chéhab 1962.

8. For Roman Tyre, cf. Chéhab 1970, 1983, 1984, 1985, 1986; Salamé-Sarkis 1986; Bikai et al. 1996; De Jong 2010: 598–602.

9. For silver, cf. *RPC* 1:4619–706. *RPC Suppl.* 1, 45f. On Tyrian silver coinage, cf. Weiser and Cotton 2002; Butcher 2004: 81–92.

10. "Hercules/Monogram-Club": *RPC* 1:4707–19, 2:2058–66. "Tyche/Galley": *RPC* 1:4720–32, 2:2067–76. "Tyche/Palm Tree": *RPC* 1:4733–9A, 2:2077–83. "Tyche/Woman on Galley": *RPC* 2:2085–87. "Head of Hercules/Monogram": cf. *RPC* 2:2057. "Hercules/ Koinon?-Temple": *BMC Phoenicia* (= *BMC*) 361–66; Rouvier 1903: 2246; *RPC* online temp. 5662; cf. Ziegler 1999: 138f.

11. *BMC* 269ff.; Rouvier 1904 (= Rouvier): 65ff.; cf. *IRT* 437 (Lepcis Magna).

12. "Female deity with trophy and Nike": *BMC* 369, 372f., 385, 388–92; Rouvier 2298, 2301; 2310–12; 2329; 2332; 2348f., 2357–59. "Female deity with trophy and Nike in hexastyle temple": *BMC* 393; Rouvier 2363, "Nike with victory wreath": *BMC* 375. Cult imagery and coins: Howgego 2005: 3; Heuchert 2005: 48.

13. "Hercules with trophy": Rouvier 2299. "H. with altar, two stelae": *BMC* 370?; Rouvier 2313f., 2333, 2342. H.'s bust: Rouvier 2334. H.'s club: Rouvier 2368.

14. Dionysos: *BMC* 406; Rouvier 2366. Harpocrates: *BMC* 374; Rouvier 2317, 2327, 2370. *Isis lactans*: Rouvier 2326. "Athena/Roma": Rouvier 2369. "Emperor? in quadriga": Rouvier 2344.

15. *BMC* 379; Rouvier 2323f.

16. *BMC* 376? , 381f.; Rouvier 2318, 2335–37, 2343, 2384.

17. "Founder": *BMC* 367–68, 394–95; Rouvier 2300, 2392. "Bull and standard": *BMC* 371, 377–78, 383; Rouvier 2304, 2320, 2339; cf. Ritterling 1925: 1518. "Eagle and standard": *BMC* 380; Rouvier 2303, 2310, 2330. For *sulcus primigenius*, cf. Burnett et al. 1992: 45. On "Marsyas of the Forum" (Rouvier 2371; *BMC* 325) as indication of colonial status, cf. Butcher 2004: 223.

18. Servais-Soyez 1983: 99f.

19. Continued types: "Female deity with trophy and Nike": *BMC* 396–403, 416. "Female deity with trophy and Nike in hexastyle temple": *BMC* 404–5; Rouvier 2360–63, 2398. "Hercules with altar, two stelae": Rouvier 2365, 2399. "H.'s head": Rouvier 2407. "Dionysus": *BMC* 406; Rouvier 2367. "Prize crowns": Ἡράκλια Ὀλύμπ(ια) Καισάρ(εια), cf. *BMC* 414–15, 418; Rouvier 2394, 2404; Ἡράκλια Κομμόδεια, cf. Rouvier 2488. "Emperor? in quadriga": *BMC* 412; Rouvier 2387.

20. "Artemis": Rouvier 2412. "Nike with palm branch": *BMC* 407, 417; Rouvier 2385f., 2401, 2409. "Snake coiled around stone": *BMC* 413; Rouvier 2390, 2402. "Two hands": Rouvier 2389. "Ovoid stone" with legend: Rouvier 2410.

21. Dido: *BMC* 409; Rouvier 2375. On Theiosso/Elissa/Deido, cf. Timaios *FGrH* 566 F82; Iust. *Ep.* 18.4f; Verg. *Aen.* 1.335–71 and *Aen.* 1.421–29 with Simon 1997: 561.

22. *BMC* 410; Rouvier 2377–79, with Imhoof-Blumer 1910: 38f.

23. Rouvier 2372. Hellanikos *FGrH* 4 F96.

24. Imhoof-Blumer 1910: esp. 36–39. Kadmos?: *BMC* 411; Rouvier 2372f., 2380–82.

25. Rouvier 2391, 2403, 2411, 2422; cf. Will 1950–51; Naster 1986; Bijovsky 2005; Aliquot 2009: 169.

26. *BMC* 408; Rouvier 2388, cf. Bijovsky 2000; Gitler and Bijovsky 2002.

27. For the use of TVRIORVM on reverse types under Severus Alexander, cf. Rouvier 2416f. For full title SEP TVRO METROP COL PENIC, cf. Rouvier 2421.

28. "Marsyas": Rouvier 2417f. "Eagle and standard": *BMC* 492; Rouvier 2473, 2512f. "Bull and standard": *BMC* 443; Rouvier 2474.

29. "Female deity with trophy and Nike": *BMC* 419, 423, 431, 436, 449–51, 474f.; Rouvier 2413–18, 2423, 2439f., 2453, 2456, 2460f., 2479f., 2489–91, 2520, 2563. "Female deity with trophy and Nike in hexastyle temple": *BMC* 424, 445, 452f., 476f.; Rouvier 2424, 2441, 2492f., 2521f. "Nike": *BMC* 460–63, 481–84, 495; Rouvier 2511, 2545. "Hercules with trophy": *BMC* 459, 485. H. with altar and two stelae: *BMC* 427; Rouvier 2313f., 2426–27, 2444, 2464, 2494–96, 2523–24. "Prize crowns": *BMC* 444, 493, 498; Rouvier 2438, 2451f., 2455, 2560f. "Koinon-Temple": *BMC* 420–22?; Rouvier 2421, 2509f. "Snake coiled around stone": Rouvier 2435, 2476, 2516, 2555f. "Man with snake coiled around stone": Rouvier 2551f. "Hero with four stags": *BMC* 428; Rouvier 2434, 2514, 2548.

30. "Dido and Carthage": *BMC* 440f., 447, 470; Rouvier 2430, 2454, 2458, 2483, 2501, 2533f., 2566. "Ambrosial stones": *BMC* 429f., 442, 473; Rouvier 2436f., 2477, 2487, 2518f., 2557f. "Kadmos and serpent": *BMC* 425f., 486, 496; Rouvier 2428f., 2530f., 2564. "Kadmos? on/without prow": *BMC* 446, 469, 489; Rouvier 2432, 2449, 2459, 2484, 2505f., 2539f.

31. Hermes-Thoth: *BMC* 448, 494; Rouvier 2445, 2466, 2497, 2563. "Kadmos and Harmonia(?)": *BMC* 434. "Two Nikes": *BMC* 492. "Female deity with palm tree and Nike venerated by four cities with turreted crowns": *BMC* 433, 438. "Portable shrine": *BMC* 435, 437, 471f., 478–80; Rouvier 2554. "Hercules and Apollo": *BMC* 439. "Reclining Okeanos" with Greek sobriquet (ΩΚΕΑΝΟC): *BMC* 464, 497; Rouvier 2517, 2553. "River/Lake god": *BMC* 465f., 491. Diomedes with palladium: *BMC* 467; Rouvier 2433, 2542f. Female figure at altar before temple with club of Hercules: *BMC* 490; Rouvier 2448.

32. Europa and Zeus, cf. Hdt. 4.147; Hellanikos *FGrH* 4 F51. On coins: *BMC* 468; Rouvier 2471, 2507. Cf. Mouterde 1942–43: 77–79; Aliquot 2009: 169.

33. Kadmos and Thebes: *BMC* 487; Rouvier 2457, 2469, 2500. Literary sources, cf. Hdt. 2.49,3; Ps.-Apollod. 3.4.1. Eur. *Phoen.* 638–39, 660–75, 1062–63. Cf. Geisau 1979; Bonnet 1992; Kühr 2006; Heinze 2008.

34. *BMC* 488; Rouvier 2446, 2468.

35. Herod. 3.3.3–5. Ulpianus *De censibus lib.* 1 (*Dig.* 27.1.6.2ff.); Ziegler 1999: 142f.; Millar 2006b: 195.

36. On "pseudo-autonomous" coins and the status of Tyre in relation to Rome, see Burnett et al. 1992: 41f., with *CIL* 10:1601 (Puteoli); Ulpian *Dig.* 50.15.1.pr. (. . . *foederis quod cum Romanis percussit . . .*). *autonomos* in civic title cf., *IG* 14 830, 1.2 (Puteoli);

I.Didyma 151, l.9f., cf. Jones 1937: 260f. n. 45; Millar 2006b: 195. On civic era, cf. Rigsby 1996: 482f.

37. Egyptian sanctuaries at Tyre: *SEG* 38: 1571; *IGLTyr* 5; *Sammelbuch griechischer Urkunden aus Aegypten* 3: 6214 with Parlasca 2004: 2f.; Iamb., *vit. Pyth.* 13f.; *Epiph. Anc.* 104; see Aliquot 2004, 2009: 175f.

38. *BMC* 316; Sayada 2009: 391; *BMC Palestine*, 326. Veterans, cf. Birley 1988: 64; Dąbrowa 2004: 400: Sayada 2009: 232.

39. Contra Millar 2006b: 196 n. 127.

40. *BMC* pp. 181f., 266–73, 288, 301–5; Rouvier 1902: pp. 257f. and 1508, 1511–13, 1523, 1525, 1552, 1563, 1583, 1593–95.

41. Ziegler 1978: 512f.; Sawaya 2009: 255. Perhaps Tripolis was granted *neôkóros* instead of Tyre?, cf. Burrell 2004: 252.

42. Malal. 294.3; *HA Sept. Sev.* 9.4; Herodian 3.6.9; with Ziegler 1978: 495; Millar 2006b: 191f. *BMC Galatia, Cappadocia, Syria* 258f., nos. 81ff. Antiochia, cf. Butcher 2004: 41f. Berytus, cf. Millar 1993: 124; Millar 2006b: 193; Sawaya 2009: 230.

43. This is suggested by the civic titles of Tyre (cf. *I.Didyma* 151; *AE* 1927: 95; *IRT* 437). The choronyms *Phoineíkê/Phoenice* and *Koilê Suría / Coele Syria* are linked to the term *metropolis*, indicating preeminence in status within a region (ἐπαρχία?). The province of Syria contained three or four eparchies (*IGLTyr* 54 [AD 43/44]; *I.Gerasa* 53 [AD 119/20]; coins, Laodikeia ad Mare [third century AD], cf. Meyer 1987/88: 71; Butcher 2003b: 371, 461; Butcher 2004: 234, fig. 65). The four eparchies/"provinciae" are a formation on a sub-provincial level, cf. Ziegler 1999, 139f.; Sartre 2001a: 179f.; Sartre 2005: 58f.; Butcher 2003b: 370f.; Marek 2010: 449–52; Vitale 2012. Contra: Eck 2007a: 200. The names of these eparchies occur in honorific inscriptions for former Syrian governors, cf. ἀντιστρατεγος . . . ἐπαρχείας Συρίας Φοινείκης Κομμαγηνῆς (*I.Didyma* 151; *I.Ephesos* 3:614; *I.Pergamon* 2:437; 3:21). For an analogy, cf. *AE* 1961: 320: ἡγεμόνα Κιλικίας Λυκαονίας Ἰσαυρίας (in c. AD 144–47; cf. Habicht 1959/60: 109ff.; Birley 2005: 253, no. 26) with *I.Anazarbos* 4, 6, 12 (AD 207): μητροπόλις τῶν τριῶν ἐπαρχειῶν Κιλικίας Ἰσαυρίας Λυκαονίας, and *OGI* 578 = *IGR* 3:880+1526, cf. Laminger-Pascher 1974: 32; Ziegler 1999: 148. Consequently, the chain of choronyms in Syrian gubernatorial titles of the early second century AD identify the three eparchies, i.e., Syria/Seleukis, Phoenicia (and Koile-Syria), and Commagene. A fourth eparchy, Koile-Syria, was created under Hadrian (cf. Sartre 2001a: 170f.).

44. *I.Didyma* 151 with Eck 1997; *PIR*[2] 1:507; Dąbrowa 1998: 79f.; cf. *I.Ephesos* 3:614, 7:3033–34; *AE* 1929: 98 (Milet). *I.Pergamon* 2:437 = *IGR* 4:374. *IG* 14:830 with Freis 1994: 207–9 (Puteoli, AD 174).

45. *IRT* 437, cf. also *AE* 1927: 95 (Eumeneia, Hadrianic) with Buckler et al. 1926: 74–78, no. 201; Ritterling 1927.

46. *IGLTyr* 48–51.

47. Bickerman 1939: 92.

48. Strabo 16.2.23; *BMC* cxxxiii f.; *BMC Sel. Kings* p. 39, nos. 54f.; Rouvier 1842f. A Hellenistic inscription at Tyre (post-200 BC) refers to ἀποικίας, the overseas foundations,

by Tyre (?), cf. *IGLTyr* 387; Daubner 2009. For *lßdnm* | *'m kmb* | *'p' kt* | *ßr*, cf. *BMC* cvii
and nos. 87–91; Meyer 1965: 112 n. 223; Huss 1990; Krahmalkov 2000: 68; Lipiński 2004:
384 n. 238.

49. *IRT* 437 (Lepcis Magna); *IGLTyr* 8 = *AE* 2006: 1581; *IGLTyr* 28 = *AE* 1988: 1051;
IGLTyr 32 = Chéhab 1962: 19f. *IGLTyr* 378 = *AE* 2006: 1606.

50. Sall. *Jug.* 19.1, 78.1; Pliny *NH* 5.76. Cf. also Silius Italicus 3.256–58; Ach. Tat. 1.1.1.

51. *RPC* 2:294f.

52. *Suda*, s.v. Παῦλος (ed. Adler 4:69), with Millar 1993: 289.

53. Herodian 3.3.3–5. The matter festered until the mid-fifth century AD; cf. *CJ*
11.22.1; *ACO, Concilium universale Chalcedonense anno 451,* 2.1.3 14. 1 line 11; see, esp.,
Millar 2006b: 198.

54. Imhoof-Blumer 1910: 37.

55. Edwards 1979: 46 n. 49; Kühr 2006: 93 n. 67.

56. E.g., Gantz 1993: 467–73, 818, table 15; Heinze 2008.

57. Gantz 1993: 816, table 13; Harder 2009.

58. Kadmos as cultural hero: Hdt. 5.58–61; Ephoros *FGrH* 70 F105. Baumgarten
1981: 140–79; Attridge and Oden 1981: 40–47.

59. *BMC* 229–35, 293, 295, 311–12; Rouvier 1902: 1481f., 1481, 1487, 1503–5; 1574; 1590;
1615f.

60. Nonnus *Dion.* 40, 428–537. Commentary: Simon 1999: 150–60; Naster 1986: 361–
63; Bonnet 1988: 31f.; Bonnet and Lipiński 1992. Dionysus and Tyre: cf. Ach. Tat. *Leuc. et
Cleit.* 2.2.1, cf. Simon 1999: 134–61; Aliquot 2009: 168f.

61. Bowersock 1990: 45–49; Chuvin 1991: 224–53; Chuvin 1994: 168–71; Simon 1999:
134f.

62. Ach. Tat. 2.14.5. For a Tyrian relief showing a burning tree, snake, and eagle, cf.
Will 1950–51; Seyrig 1963; Naster 1986; Bijovsky 2005; Aliquot 2009: 169.

63. On "eagle, snake, and tree," cf. versions of Etana and Gilgamesh epics. Cf. Foster 2005: 533–54 (Etana); Will 1995: 247.

64. Eusebius *PE* 1.10.10 with Attridge and Oden 1981: 43 and 82 n. 56; Baumgarten
1981: 164f.; Bonnet 1988: 27–30.

65. Temple of H., cf. Hdt. 2.44; Arrian *Anabasis* 2.24.5: Polyb. 31.12.11f. On emerald
stela, cf. Theophr., *Lap.* 25; Pliny *HN* 37.74–5; Josephus *AJ* 145f.; *c.Ap.* 1.118f. with Bonnet
1988: 34f.; Lipiński 1995: 233f. Chariton 7.2.7–9, 8.5.2; Ach. Tat. 2.15, 7.14.2, 8.18.1; Heliod.
Aeth 4.16.3–17.1 with Lightfoot 2003: 295. Inviolability declared in c. 141/0 BC, cf. Justin
39.1.7, Dio 42.49, with Rigsby 1996: 481–85. See also Seyrig 1951: 225–28; Lipiński 1995:
231f. nn. 74, 79. On Hercules aka Melkart, e.g., Arr. 2.16.1; Lucian *Dea Syria* 3; Philo of
Byblos (Eusebius *PE* 1.10.27.3, 1.20.28). Cf. also *IGLSyr* 8:4001 (25/24 BC) with Bonnet
1988: 47–77.

66. On Ousoos, cf. Baumgarten 1981: 142, 159–61; Attridge and Oden 1981: 82.

67. *ID* 1519 with Bonnet 1988: 372; Bonnet and Niehr 2010: 98.

68. For Bijovsky's reading *'lt,r* 2000: 321 n. 9, see Howgego 2005: pl. 1.4 no. 41 (photo),
correcting Robinson 1999: 43.

69. The scene cannot be linked to the known myths on Pygmalion. Cf. Just. 18.4–6; Clem. Alex. *protr.* 57.3; Ov. *Met.* 10.243–97; Bijovsky 2000; Gitler and Bijovsky 2002. On *pgmljn*, cf. *pgmlwn*: *KAI* 73; Krahmalkov 2000: 394.

70. The "last" publicly displayed inscription is a Greek/Phoenician bilingual at Aradus (25/24 BC: cf. *IGLSyr* 7:4001; Briquel-Chatonnet 1991: 5f.).

71. Luc. *Alex.* 13; Eus. *PE* 1.9.20, 21. Cf. also Origen, *c.Cels.* 1.6; Meleagros of Gadara *Anth. Pal.* 7.419. *Poenus sermo,* cf. Ulpian, *Dig.* 32.11, pr. 45.1.1.6 with Millar 1993: 293f., Briquel-Chatonnet 1991: 13f., Anm. 63; Jongeling and Kerr 2005: 4f.; Butcher 2003b: 285. "Phoenician" onomastics, cf. Briquel-Chatonnet 1991: 16–18; Zadok 1999: 289; Zadok 2000: 635; Sartre 2005: 293.

72. Butcher 2003b: 285. On Theodoret, *Quaestiones in Iudices* 19 (*PG* 80, cols. 507–9), cf. Millar 2006d: 385.

73. E.g., Umm al-'Awāmīd: Dunand and Duru 1962. Further Tyrian monuments, cf. Gubel 2002: 117–48.

74. Heuchert 2005: 40; Butcher 2005: 143–45.

75. On circulation in Roman Syria, cf. Butcher 2003a: 36–41; Butcher 2003b: 218f.; Butcher 2004: 144f.; Butcher 2005: 144. Finds of Tyrian coins, cf. Butcher 2003a: 66, 70–76.

76. Burnett et al. 1992: 16; Butcher 2004: 144f.

77. Luc. *Dea Syr.* 4.

78. E.g., Paulus of Tyre, orator under Hadrian (*Suda* s.v. Παῦλος; *P.Oxy.* 1242 lines 10f.; *IGLTyr* 47), Hadrianus, sophist (second century AD), *ab epistulis Graecis* under Commodus (AD 180–91) (*PIR²* H 4); Domitius Ulpianus, jurist, *a libellis*(?), *praefectus annonae,* and praetorian prefect under the Severans, member of the *consilium* to Severus Alexander between AD 205 and 223 (*PIR²* D 169).

79. Bowersock 1990; Woolf 1994: 125–30; Swain 1996: 409–22; Butcher 2003b: 273f.; Howgego 2005; Sartre 2005: 274–91.

80. For Roman Syria, cf. Butcher 2003b: 289–327 bibliography.

81. Heuchert 2005: 40. On literate education and Greek literature, cf. Morgan 1998: 90–151.

82. Achilles Tatius *Leucippe et Cleitophon* 1.1.2.

83. Rouvier 1902: 1550; with Price and Trell 1977: 13, 156–58, fig. 277; Lightfoot 2003: 298.

84. For misinterpretation, cf. Socr. *Hist. Eccl.* 3, 17; Julian, *Misopogon* 355 (ed. Kent); Howgego 1995: 74 bibliography.

85. Tyrian territory: Meimaris et al. 1992: 60–65; Aliquot 2007: 56f.; Aliquot 2008: 17f., 21f., 24f., 28.

86. C. Vibius Marsus(?), governor of Syria in AD 42–44 (*IGLTyr* 26); A. [—] Sempronianus, *tribunus laticlavius* in *legio IV Ferrata* and quaestor to Trajan in Rome (*IGLTyr* 27); Tib. Iulius Alexander, procurator of Syria under Nero (*IGLTyr* 29); T. Flavius Sallustius Paelignianus (*CIL* 3:12094 = *IGRR* 3:1101; early third century AD; P. Valerius Protogenianus, equestrian officer of Syrian auxiliary units (Latin; *IGLTyr* 30; mid- to late second century AD); unknown procurator or governor under Vespasian (Latin; *IGLTyr*

37), cf. Haensch 1997: 254f., 259–61. On the use of Latin in the Roman Near East, cf. Millar 2006e; Eck 2007b: 157–200.

87. *IGLTyr* 38 (*optiones*), 39 (*speculator*), 383 (*signifer coh. Italica mil.*), 384 (*optio de liburna Dulfino*); in Greek, cf. *IGRR* 3:1104 (veteran). Latin inscriptions by civilians(?): *IGLTyr* 45, 46, 348–65. Tyre and *nauarchis*: *I.Didyma* 151; *IGLTyr* 51. Gebhardt 2002: 164–96; Sartre 2001b: 622 n. 60.

88. Tyrian reverses (mid-third century AD) show four female figures with mural crowns (personifications of ἐπαρχίαι?) sacrificing to "Tyche," cf. *BMC* 432, 438; Rouvier 2440, 2461. Laodicea ad Mare, *metropol(is) IIII prov(inciarum)* in the early third century AD, minted a similar motif; cf. Butcher 2004: 234. The addition of Tyre to choronyms of one gubernatorial title (*I.Ephesos* 7:3033–34 lines 15f., ἀντιστράτεγος . . . ἀπαρχείας Συρίας Φοινείκης Κομμαγηνῆς Τύρου) perhaps reflects Tyre's status as *metropolis* of the three eparchies(?); for a different view, cf. Sartre 2001a: 172.

89. *IGLTyr* 48–52; cf. *IRT* 437.

90. Sartre 2001b: 682 n. 183. Games at Tyre, 2 *Macc.* 4.18–20. *BMC* 414–15, 418; Moretti 1953, nos. 87, *l.* 22. 90, *l.* 29. Millar 1993: 289; 1992: 449, 451f. for a different view Rey-Coquais 1993: 1344. *IGRR* 3:1012 = Moretti 1953: no. 85 = *IGLSyr* 4:1265 with Bonnet 1988: 57. Athletes at Tyre: *IGLTyr* 58–61.

91. Cf. Howgego 1995: 71.

92. On Hellenistic D(e)ido: Timaios *FGrH* 566 F82, cf. Period 4. On Latin literate education, see Morgan 1998: 97ff.; Heather 1994: 182–85; Uytterhoeven 2009: 323 n. 9, further bibliography.

93. For civic coinage in Roman Syria, cf. Butcher 2003a: 214–20; Butcher 2004: 241f., 250f. On choice and intention in civic coin production, see Howgego 1995: 70–44; Weiss 2005; Burnett et al. 1992: 1–5..

94. Burnett et al. 1992: 16; Butcher 2004: 145.

95. Millar 1993: 275.

REFERENCES

Aliquot, J. 2004. "Aegyptiaca et Isiaca de la Phénicie et du Liban aux époques héllenistique et romaine." *Syria* 81: 201–28.

Aliquot, J. 2007. "Burqush-Barkousa: Du village à la cite." In *Mélanges en l'honneur de Jean-Paul Rey-Coquais* (Mélanges de l'Université Saint-Joseph 60), ed. P.-L. Gatier and J.-B. Yon, 241–67. Beirut: Institut français du Proche-Orient.

Aliquot, J. 2008. *Inscriptions grecques et latines de la Syrie* 11. *Mont Hermon (Liban et Syrie).* Beirut: Institut français du Proche-Orient.

Aliquot, J. 2009. *La vie religieuse au Liban sous l'empire romain.* Bibliothèque Archéologique et Historique 189. Beirut: Institut Français du Proche-Orient.

Attridge, H. W. and R. A. Oden. 1981. *Philo of Byblos: "Phoenician History." Introduction, Critical Text, Translation, Notes.* Washington: Catholic Biblical Association.

Augé, C. 1985. "Les monnaies de fouille de Si' et la circulation monétaire antique dans le Hauran." In *Hauran I*, ed. J.-M. Dentzer, 203–27. Paris: Institut Français d'Archéologie Orientale.

Augé, C., and P. Linant de Bellefonds. 1986. "Dionysos (in peripheria orientali)." *LIMC* 3: 514–31.

Baumgarten, A. I. 1981. *The Phoenician History of Philo of Byblos: A Commentary*. Leiden: Brill.

Bellinger, A. R. 1938. *Coins from Jerash, 1928–1934*. Numismatic Notes and Monographs. New York: American Numismatic Society.

Benz, F. L. 1972. *Personal Names in the Phoenician and Punic Inscriptions: A Catalog, Grammatical Study and Glossary of Elements*. Studia Pohl 8. Rome: Biblical Institute.

Betz, H. D. (ed.). 1986. *The Greek Magical Papyri in Translation: Including the Demotic Spells*. Chicago: University of Chicago Press.

Bijovsky G. 2000. "More About Pygmalion from Tyre." *Quaderni Ticinesi: Numismatica e Antichità Classiche* 29: 319–32.

Bijovsky, G. 2005. "The Ambrosial Rocks and the Sacred Precinct of Melqart in Tyre." In *XIII Congreso Internacional de Numismatica*, Madrid 2003, 1:829–34. Madrid: Ministeria de Cultura.

Bikai, P. M., W. J. Fulco, and J. Marchand. 1996. *Tyre: The Shrine of Apollo*. Amman: American Center of Oriental Research.

Bickerman, E. 1939. "Sur une inscription grecque de Sidon." In *Mélanges Syriens offerts a Monsieur René Dussaud*, 91–99. Paris: P. Geuthner.

Birley, A. R. 1988. *Septimius Severus: The African Emperor*. London: Routledge.

Birley, A. R. 2005. *The Roman Government of Britain*. Oxford: Oxford University Press.

Bonnet, C. 1988. *Melqart: Cultes et mythes de l'Héraclès tyrien en Méditerranée*. Studia Phoenicia 8. Leuven: Peeters.

Bonnet, C. 1992. "Kadmos." In *Dictionnaire de la civilisation phénicienne et punique*, ed. E. Lipiński, 241. Leiden: Brepols.

Bonnet, C. 2007. "Melqart." In *Iconography of Deities and Demons in the Ancient Near East*, ed. C. Uehlinger et al. (http://www.religions-wissenschaft.unizh.ch/idd/pre publications/e_idd_melqart.pdf).

Bonnet, C., and E. Lipiński. 1992. "Ambrosiai Petrai." In *Dictionnaire de la civilisation phénicienne et punique*, ed. E. Lipiński, 26. Leiden: Brepols.

Bonnet, C., and H. Niehr. 2010. *Religionen in der Umwelt des Alten Testaments II: Phönizier, Punier, Aramäer*. Studienbücher Theologie 4.2. Stuttgart: Kohlhammer.

Bowersock, G. 1985. "Hadrian and Metropolis." In *Bonner Historia-Augusta-Kolloquium 1982–1983*. Beiträge zur Historia-Augusta-Forschung 17, ed. J. Straub, 75–88. Bonn: Habelt.

Bowersock, G. 1990. *Hellenism in Late Antiquity*. Ann Arbor: University of Michigan Press.

Briquel-Chatonnet, F. 1991. "Les derniers témoignages sur la langue phénicienne en Orient." *Rivista di Studi Fenici* 19 (1): 3–21.

Briquel-Chatonnet, F. 1992. "L'image des Phéniciens dans les Romans grecs." In *Le monde du roman grec: Actes du colloque international tenu à l'École normale supérieure*, December 17–19, 1987, ed. M.-F. Baslez, Ph. Hoffmann, and M. Trédé, 189–97. Paris: Presses de l'École normale supérieure.

Buckler, W. H., W. M. Calder, and C. W. M. Cox. 1926. "Asia Minor 1924. III. Monuments from Central Phrygia." *Journal of Roman Studies* 16: 53–94.

Burrell, B. 2004. *Neokoroi: Greek Cities and Roman Emperors.* Cincinnati Classical Studies, n.s., vol. 9. Leiden: Brill.

Burnett, A. 2002. "Syrian Coinage and Romanisation from Pompey to Domitian." In *Les monnayages syriens: Quel apport pour l'histoire du Proche-Orient hellénistique et romain? Actes de la table ronde de Damas*, November 10–12, 1999, ed. Chr. Augé and F. Duyrat, 115–22. Beirut: Institut Français d'Archéologie du Proche-Orient.

Burnett, A., M. Amandry, and P. P. Ripollès. 1992. *Roman Provincial Coinage*, vol. 1: *From the Death of Caesar to the Death of Vitellius (44 BC–AD 69)*, part 1: *Introduction and Catalogue.* London: British Museum Press.

Butcher, K. 2003a. *Small Change in Ancient Beirut: The Coin Finds from BEY 006 and 045: Persian, Hellenistic, Roman, and Byzantine Periods* (Berytus XLV–XLVI, 2001–2). Beirut: American University of Beirut.

Butcher, K. 2003b. *Roman Syria and the Near East.* London: Getty.

Butcher, K. 2004. *Coinage in Roman Syria: Northern Syria, 64 BC–AD 253.* London: Royal Numismatic Society.

Butcher, K. 2005. "Information, Legitimation or Self-Legitimation? Popular and Elite Designs on the Coin Types of Syria." In *Coinage and Identity in the Roman Provinces*, ed. C. Howgego et al., 143–56, pl. 12.1. Oxford: Oxford University Press.

Chéhab, M. 1962. "Tyr à l'époque romaine: Aspects de la cité à la lumière des textes et des fouilles." *Mélanges de l'Université Saint-Joseph* 38: 11–40.

Chéhab, M. 1970. *Tyr: Histoire, topographie, fouilles.* Beirut: Société d'Impression et d'Edition Libanaise.

Chéhab, M. 1983. "Fouilles de Tyr: La nécropole, 1. L'arc de triomphe." *Bulletin du Musée de Beyrouth* 33: 7–132.

Chéhab, M. 1984. "Fouilles de Tyr: La nécropole, 2. Description des fouilles." *Bulletin du Musée de Beyrouth* 34: 1–482.

Chéhab, M. 1985. "Fouilles de Tyr: La nécropole, 3. Description des fouilles." *Bulletin du Musée de Beyrouth* 35: 483–805.

Chéhab, M. 1986. "Fouilles de Tyr: La nécropole, 4. Description des fouilles." *Bulletin du Musée de Beyrouth* 36: 1–268.

Chuvin, P. 1991. *Mythologie et géographie dionysiaques: Recherches sur l'oeuvre de Nonnos de Panopolis.* Adosa: Clermont-Ferrand.

Chuvin, P. 1994. "Local Traditions and Classical Mythology in the Dionysiaca." In *Studies in the Dionysiaca of Nonnus*, ed. N. Hopkinson, 167–76. Cambridge: Cambridge Philological Society.

Cohen, G. 2006. *The Hellenistic Settlements in Syria, the Red Sea Basin, and North Africa.* Berkeley: University of California Press.

Dąbrowa, E. 1998. *The Governors of Roman Syria from Augustus to Septimius Severus.* Antiquitas 1, vol. 45. Bonn: Habelt.

Dąbrowa, E. 2000. "Legio III Gallica." In *Les légions de Rome sous le Haut-Empire: Actes du Congrès de Lyon*, September 17–19, 1998, ed. Y. Le Bohec, 309–15. Lyon: Université Jean Moulin-Lyon.

Dąbrowa, E. 2003. "Les colonies honoraires ou les colonies de vétérans? Observations sur l'iconographie de quelques types de revers de monnaies colonials." In *Hommages à Carl Deroux*, vol. 3, *Histoire et épigraphie, Droit*, ed. P. Defosse, 127–34. Brussels: Latomus.

Dąbrowa, E. 2004. "Le vexillum sur les monnaies coloniales (IIe–IIIe s. après J.-C.)." *Latomus* 63 (2): 395–405.

Daubner, F. 2009. "Eine ἀποικία in einer hellenistischen Inschrift aus Tyros." *Zeitschrift für Papyrologie und Epigraphik* 168: 177–82.

Deininger, J. 1965. *Die Provinziallandtage der römischen Kaiserzeit von Augustus bis zum Ende des dritten Jahrhunderts n. Chr.* Munich: C. H. Beck.

De Jong, L. 2010. "Performing Death in Tyre: The Life and Afterlife of a Cemetery in the Province of Syria." *American Journal of Archaeology* 114: 597–630.

Delcor, M. 1986. "Astarte." *LIMC* 3 (11): 1077–85.

Dunand, M. 1965. "Tombe peinte dans la campagne de Tyr." *Bulletin du Musée de Beyrouth* 18: 5–49.

Dunand, M. and R. Duru. 1962. *Oumm El-'Amed: Une Ville de l'époque hellénistique aux échelles de Tyr.* Paris: A. Maisonneuve.

Eck, W. 1997. "Zu kleinasiatischen Inschriften (Ephesos; Museum Bursa)." *Zeitschrift für Papyrologie und Epigraphik* 117: 107–16.

Eck, W. 2007a. "Die politisch-administrative Struktur der kleinasiatischen Provinzen während der Hohen Kaiserzeit." In *Tra Oriente e Occidente. Indigeni, Greci e Romani in Asia minore: Atti del convegno internazionale Cividale del Friuli*, September 28–30, 2006, ed. G. Urso, 189–207. Pisa: ETS.

Eck, W. 2007b. *Rom und Judaea: Fünf Vorträge zur römischen Herrschaft in Palaestina.* Tübingen: Mohr Siebeck.

Edwards, R. B. 1979. *Kadmos the Phoenician: A Study in Greek Legends and the Mycenaean Age.* Amsterdam: Adolf M. Hakkert.

Eissfeldt, O. 1948. "Tyros." In *Paulys Real-Encyclopädie der classischen Altertumswissenschaft* 7, A 2, 1876–1907.

Elsner, J. 1997. "The Origins of the Icon: Pilgrimage, Religion and Visual Culture in the Roman East as 'Resistance' to the Centre." In *The Early Roman Empire in the East*, ed. S. E. Alcock. Oxford: Oxbow.

Elsner, J. 2001. "Describing Self in the Language of Other: Pseudo(?) Lucian at the Temple of Hierapolis." In *Being Greek Under Rome: Cultural Identity, the Second Sophistic and Development of Empire*, ed. S. Goldhill, 123–53. Cambridge: Cambridge University Press.

Erskine, A. 2003. *Troy Between Greece and Rome: Local Tradition and Imperial Power.* Oxford: Oxford University Press.

Foster, B. R. 2005. *Before the Muses: An Anthology of Akkadian Literature.* Bethesda, MD: CDL.

Freis, H. 1994. *Historische Inschriften zur römischen Kaiserzeit. Von Augustus bis Konstantin.* Darmstadt: Wissenschaftliche Buchgesellschaft.

Freyberger, K. S. 1996. "Zur Funktion der Hamana im Kontext lokaler Heiligtümer in Syrien und Palästina." *Damaszener Mitteilungen* 9: 143–61.

Freyberger, K. S. 2007. "Der Tempel von Medjel Andjar: Kulte in der südlichen Beka' in hellenistisch-römischer Zeit." *Mélanges de l'Université Saint-Joseph* 60: 77–110.

Gantz, T. 1993. *Early Greek Myth: A Guide to Literary and Artistic Sources.* Baltimore: Johns Hopkins University Press.

Gebhardt, A. 2002. *Imperiale Politik und provinziale Entwicklung: Untersuchungen zum Verhältnis von Kaiser, Heer und Städten im Syrien der vorseverischen Zeit.* Klio. Beiträge zur alten Geschichte NF 1. Berlin: Akademie.

Geisau, H. von. 1979. "Kadmos." In *Der kleine Pauly*, ed. K. Ziegler und W. Sontheimer, 41–42. Leiden: Brill.

Geissen, A. 2005. "The Nome Coins of Roman Egypt." In *Coinage and Identity in the Roman Provinces*, ed. Chr. Howgego et al., 167–70. Oxford: Oxford University Press.

Gitler, H., and G. Bijovsky. 2002. "The Coins of Pygmalion from Tyre: A Chronological Sequence from Elagabalus to Gallienus." *Quaderni Ticinesi: Numismatica e Antichità classiche* 31: 317–24.

Graf, F. 2011. "Myth and Hellenic Identities." In *A Companion to Greek Mythology*, ed. K. Dowden and N. Livingstone, 211–26. Malden, MA: Wiley-Blackwell.

Gruen, E. S. 2011. *Rethinking the Other in Antiquity.* Princeton, NJ: Princeton University Press.

Gubel, E. 2002. *Art phénicien: La sculpture de tradition phénicienne.* Paris: Réunion des musées nationaux.

Gzella, H. 2006. "Das Aramäische in den Römischen Ostprovinzen: Sprachsituationen in Arabien, Syrien und Mesopotamien zur Kaiserzeit." *Bibliotheca Orientalis* 63: 16–39.

Habicht, C. 1959–60. "Zwei neue Inschriften aus Pergamon." *Istanbuler Mitteilungen* 9–10: 109–27.

Haensch, R. 1997. *Capita Provinciarum: Statthaltersitze und Provinzialverwaltung in der römischen Kaiserzeit.* Mainz: Philipp von Zabern.

Hajjar, J. 1965. "Un hypogée romain a Deb'aal dans la région de Tyr." *Bulletin du Musée de Beyrouth* 18: 61–104.

Hall, S. 1999. "Kulturelle Identität und Globalisierung." In *Widerspenstige Kulturen: Cultural Studies als Herausforderung*, ed. K. H. Höring and R. Winter, 393–441. Frankfurt am Main: Suhrkamp.

Harder, R. E. 2009. "Europe. [2] Geliebte des Zeus auf Kreta." In *Der neue Pauly*, ed. H. Cancik and H. Schneider. Brill Online. (http://www.brillonline.nl/subscriber/entry?entry=dnp_e406180).

Heather, P. 1994. "Literacy and Power in the Migration Period." In *Literacy and Power in the Ancient World*, ed. A. K. Bowman and G. Woolf, 177–97. Cambridge: Cambridge University Press.

Heinze, Th. 2008. "Kadmos. [1] Sohn des Agenor und der Telephassa." In *Der neue Pauly*, ed. H. Cancik and H. Schneider. Brill Online. (http://www.brillonline.nl/subscriber/entry?entry=dnp_e604970).

Heuchert, V. 2005. "The Chronological Development of Roman Provincial Coin Iconography." In *Coinage and Identity in the Roman Provinces*, ed. C. Howgego et al., 29–56, pl. 3.1–5. Oxford: Oxford University Press.

Hirt, A. M. 2009. "Bild und Kontext: Eine Annäherung an die tyrische Bronzeprägung des 3. Jhs. n.Chr." *Hefte des archäologischen Seminars der Universität Bern* 21: 77–94.

Howgego, C. 2005. "Coinage and Identity in the Roman Provinces." In *Coinage and Identity in the Roman Provinces*, ed. C. Howgego et al., 19–28, pl. 1.1–4. Oxford: Oxford University Press.

Huss, W. 1990. "Die punischen Namen der nordafrikanischen Städte Hippon Diarrhytos und Hippo Regius." *Semitica* 38: 171–74.

Imhoof-Blumer, F. 1910. "Beiträge zur Erklärung griechischer Münztypen. I. Seefahrende Heroen." *Nomisma: Untersuchungen auf dem Gebiete der antiken Münzkunde* 5: 26–39, pl. 1–3.

Imhoof-Blumer, F. 1911. "Beiträge zur Erklärung griechischer Münztypen." *Nomisma: Untersuchungen auf dem Gebiete der antiken Münzkunde* 6: 7f.

Isaac, B. 2004. *The Invention of Racism in Classical Antiquity*. Princeton, NJ: Princeton University Press.

Jones, A. H. M. 1937. *The Cities of the Eastern Roman Provinces*. Oxford: Clarendon Press.

Jones, C. P. 1999. *Kinship Diplomacy in the Ancient World*. Cambridge, MA: Harvard University Press.

Jongeling, K. 2008. *Handbook of Neo-Punic Inscriptions*. Tübingen: Mohr Siebeck.

Jongeling, K., and R. M. Kerr. 2005. *Late Punic Epigraphy: An Introduction to the Study of Neo-Punic and Latino-Punic Inscriptions*. Tübingen: Mohr Siebeck .

Kindler, A. 1982–83. "The Status of Cities in the Syro-Palestinian Area as Reflected by Their Coins." *Israel Numismatic Journal* 6–7: 79–87.

Klose, D. O. A. 2005. "Festivals and Games in the Cities of the East During the Roman Empire." In *Coinage and Identity in the Roman Provinces*, ed. C. Howgego et al., 125–33, pl. 10.1–3. Oxford: Oxford University Press.

Krahmalkov, Ch. 2000. *Phoenician-Punic Dictionary*. Orientalia Lovanensia Analecta 90. Leuven: Peeters.

Krings, V. (ed.). 1995. *La civilisation phénicienne et punique: Manuel de recherche* Handbuch der Orientalistik 20. Leiden: Brill.

Kühr, A. 2006. *Als Kadmos nach Boiotien kam: Polis und Ethnos im Spiegel thebanischer Gründungsmythen.* Hermes Einzelschriften 98. Stuttgart: Franz Steiner.

Laminger-Pascher, G. 1974. "Kleine Nachträge zu kilikischen Inschriften." *Zeitschrift für Papyrologie und Epigraphik* 15: 31–68.

Leibner, U. 2009. *Settlement and History in Hellenistic, Roman, and Byzantine Galilee: An Archaeological Survey of the Eastern Galilee.* Texts and Studies in Ancient Judaism 127. Tübingen: Mohr Siebeck.

Le Lasseur, D. 1922. "Mission archéologique à Tyr." *Syria* 3: 1–26, 116–33.

Lightfoot, J. L. 2003. *Lucian: On the Syrian Goddess.* Oxford: Oxford University Press.

Lindner, R. 1994. *Mythos und Identität: Studien zur Selbstdarstellung kleinasiatischer Städte in der römischen Kaiserzeit.* Stuttgart: Franz Steiner.

Lipiński, E. 1992. "Bétyle." In *Dictionnaire de la civilisation phénicienne et punique*, ed. E. Lipiński, 70–71. Leiden: Brepols.

Lipiński, E. 1995. *Dieux et déesses de l'univers phénicien et punique.* OLA 64; Studia Phoenicia 14. Leuven: Peeters.

Lipiński, E. 2004. *Itineraria Phoenicia.* Studia Phoenicia 18. Leuven: Peeters.

Marek, Chr. 2010. *Die Geschichte Kleinasiens in der Antike.* Munich: C. H. Beck.

Marot, T. 1998. *Las monedas del Macellum de Gerasa (Yaray, Jordania): Aproximación a la circulación monetaria en la provincia de Arabia.* Madrid: Museo Casa de al Moneda.

Meimaris, Y. E., K. Kritikakou, and P. Bougia. 1992. *Chronological Systems in Roman-Byzantine Palestine and Arabia.* Athens: Kentron Hellenikes kai Romaikes Archaiotetos Ethnikon Hidryma Ereunon.

Meshorer, Y. 1975. *Nabatean Coins.* Qedem 3. Jerusalem: Hebrew University of Jerusalem.

Meyer, E. 1965. *Geschichte des Altertums.* 4th ed. Stuttgart: J. G. Cotta'sche Buchhandlung Nachfolger.

Meyer, E. 1987–88. "Die Bronzeprägung von Laodikeia in Syrien 194/217." *Jahrbuch für Numismatik und Geldgeschichte* 37 (8): 56–92.

Millar, F. 1992. *The Emperor in the Roman World (31 BC–AD 337).* 2nd ed. Ithaca, NY: Cornell University Press.

Millar, F. 1993. *The Roman Near East, 31 BC–AD 337.* Cambridge, MA: Harvard University Press.

Millar, F. 1998. "Il ruolo delle lingue semitiche nel vicino oriente tardo-romano (V–VI secolo)." *Mediterraneo Antico* 1: 71–94.

Millar, F. 2006a. "The Phoenician Cities: A Case-Study of Hellenisation." In F. Millar, *The Greek World, the Jews, and the East.* Rome, the Greek World and the East 3, 32–50. Chapel Hill: University of North Carolina Press.

Millar, F. 2006b. "The Roman *Coloniae* of the Near East: A Study of Cultural Relations." In F. Millar, *The Greek World, the Jews, and the East.* Rome, the Greek World, and the East 3, 164–222. Chapel Hill: University of North Carolina Press.

Millar, F. 2006c. "Porphyry: Ethnicity, Language and Alien Wisdom." In F. Millar, *The Greek World, the Jews, and the East*. Rome, the Greek World and the East 3, 331–50. Chapel Hill: University of North Carolina Press.

Millar, F. 2006d. "Ethnic Identity in the Roman Near East, A.D. 325–450: Language, Religion, and Culture." In F. Millar, *The Greek World, the Jews, and the East*. Rome, the Greek World and the East 3, 378–405. Chapel Hill: University of North Carolina Press.

Millar, F. 2006e. "Latin in the Epigraphy of the Roman Near East." In F. Millar, *The Greek World, the Jews, and the East*. Rome, the Greek World and the East 3, 223–42. Chapel Hill: University of North Carolina Press.

Moretti, L. 1953. *Iscrizioni agonistiche greche*. Rome: Angelo Signorelli.

Morgan, T. 1998. *Literate Education in the Hellenistic and Roman Worlds*. Cambridge: Cambridge University Press.

Mouterde, R. 1942–43. "Monuments et inscriptions de Syrie et du Liban." *Mélanges de l'Université Saint-Joseph* 25 (3): 23–79.

Mouterde, R. 1944–46. "Tyr, les agoranomes de l'an 66." *Mélanges de l'Université Saint-Joseph* 26: 60–63.

Naster, P. 1986. "Ambrosiai Petrai dans les textes et sur les monnaies de Tyr." In *Religio Phoenicia*. Studia Phoenicia 4, ed. C. Bonnet et al., 361–70. Namur.

Parlasca, K. 2004. "Ägyptische Skulpturen als Griechische Votive in Heiligtümern des Ostmittelmeerraums und des Nahen Ostens." In *Sepulkral- und Votivdenkmäler östlicher Mittelmeergebiete (7. Jh. v. Chr. - 1. Jh. n. Chr.). Kulturbegegnungen im Spannungsfeld von Akzeptanz und Resistenz*, ed. R. Bol and D. Kreikenbom, 1–5. Mainz: Paderborn.

Price, S. 2005. "Local Mythologies in the Greek East." In *Coinage and Identity in the Roman Provinces*, ed. C. Howgego et al., 115–24, pl. 9.1–5. Oxford: Oxford University Press.

Price, M. J. and B. L Trell. 1977. *Coins and Their Cities: Architecture on the Ancient Coins of Greece, Rome and Palestine*. London: Vecchi.

Rey-Coquais, J.-P. 1973. "Inscriptions grecques d'Apamée." *Annales Archéologiques Arabes Syriennes* 23: 39–84.

Rey-Coquais, J.-P. 1977. *Inscriptions grecques et latines découvertes dans les fouilles de Tyr (1963–1974). I. Inscriptions de la nécropole*. Bulletin du Musée de Beyrouth 29. Paris: A. Maisonneuve.

Rey-Coquais, J.-P. 1978. "Syrie romaine de Pompée à Dioclétien." *Journal of Roman Studies* 68: 44–73.

Rey-Coquais, J.-P. 1981. "Philadelphie de Coelésyrie." *Annual of the Department of Antiquities of Jordan*, 25–31.

Rey-Coquais, J.-P. 1987. "Une double dédicace de Lepcis Magna à Tyr." *L'Africa romana* 4: 597–602.

Rey-Coquais, J.-P. 1993. "Tyr, métropole de Carthage et de beaucoup d'autres villes, aux époques romaine et paléochrétienne." *L'Africa Romana* 10: 1339–53.

Rey-Coquais, J.-P. 2006. *Inscriptions Grecques et Latines de Tyr.* BAAL, special issue 3. Beirut: Bulletin d'Archéologie et d'Architecture Libanaises.

Rigsby, K. J. 1996. *Asylia: Territorial Inviolability in the Hellenistic World.* Berkeley: University of California Press.

Ritterling, E. 1925. "Legio." In *Paulys Real-Encyclopädie der Classischen Altertumswissenschaft* XII, ed. W. Kroll, 1186-830. Stuttgart: J. B. Metzler.

Ritterling, E. 1927. "Military Forces in the Senatorial Provinces." *Journal of Roman Studies* 17: 28–32.

Robinson, M. 1997a. "Phoenician Inscriptions on the Late Roman Bronze Coinage of Tyre. Part 1: A Coin Depicting Pygmalion." *Numismatic Circular* 105: 199–201.

Robinson, M. 1997b. "Phoenician Inscriptions on the Late Roman Bronze Coinage of Tyre. Part 2: Coin with Elissa/Dido Reverse." *Numismatic Circular* 105: 234–36.

Robinson, M. 1999. "Gordian III's Bronze Coinage of Tyre: A Further Specimen with Phoenician Letters." *Numismatic Circular* 107: 43.

Rouvier, J. 1901. "Numismatique des villes de la Phénicie." *Journal International d'Archéologie Numismatique* 4: 35–66.

Rouvier, J. 1902. "Numismatique des villes de la Phénicie." *Journal International d'Archéologie Numismatique* 5: 229–84.

Rouvier, J. 1903. "Numismatique des villes de la Phénicie." *Journal International d'Archéologie Numismatique* 6: 17–46, 269–332.

Rouvier, J. 1904. "Numismatique des villes de la Phénicie." *Journal International d'Archéologie Numismatique* 7: 65–108.

Salamé-Sarkis, H. 1986. "La nécropole de Tyr: A propos de publications récentes." *Berytus* 34: 193–205.

Sartre, M. 2001a. "Les manifestations du culte impérial dans les provinces syriennes et en Arabie." In *Rome et ses provinces: Genèse et diffusion d'une image du pouvoir: Hommages à Jean-Charles Balty*, ed. C. Evers and A. Tsingarida, 167–86. Brussels: Etudes d'Archéologie Classique de l'Université Libre de Bruxelles.

Sartre, M. 2001b. *D'Alexandrie à Zénobie: Histoire du Levant antique, IVe siècle avant J.-C.* Paris: Fayard.

Sartre, M. 2002. "La construction de l'identité des villes de la Syrie hellénistique et imperial." In *Idéologies et valeurs civiques dans le Monde Romain: Hommage à Claude Lepelley*, ed. H. Inglebert, 93–105. Nanterre: Picard.

Sartre, M. 2005. *The Middle East Under Rome.* Cambridge, MA: Harvard University Press.

Sawaya, Z. 2009. *Histoire de Bérytos et Héliopolis d'après leurs monnaies (Ier siècle av. J.- C.–IIIe siècle apr. J.-C.).* Beirut: Institut français du Proche-Orient.

Sayada, Z. 2009. *Historie de Bérytos et d'Héliopolis d'après leurs monnaies Ier siècle av. J.-C.–IIIe siècle apr. J.-C.* Bibliothèque archéologique et historique 185. Beirut: Institute Français du Proche-Orient.

Scheer, T. S. 1993. *Mythische Vorväter: Zur Bedeutung griechischer Heroenmythen im Selbstverständnis kleinasiatischer Städte.* Münchner Arbeiten zur Alten Geschichte 7. Munich: Münchener Universitätsschriften.

Servais-Soyez, B. 1983. "Le monnaies impèriales de Tyr." In *Studia Phoenicia. I. Sauvons Tyr. II. Histoire Phénicienne*, ed. E. Gubel et al., 97–112. Leuven: Peeters.

Seyrig, H. 1951. "Antiquitées syriennes, No. 48. Adradus et Baetocaecé." *Syria* 28: 191–228.

Seyrig, H. 1963. "Antiquitées syriennes, No. 83. Les grands dieux de Tyr à l'époque grecque et romaine." *Syria* 40: 19–26.

Simon, E. 1997. "Dido." *LIMC* 8 (1): 559–62.

Simon, B. (ed.) 1999. *Nonnos de Panopolis, Les Dionysiaques*, vol. XVI: *Chants XLIV–XLVI*. Paris: Less Belles Letters.

Soyez, B. 1972. "Le bétyle dans le culte de l'Astarté phénicienne." *Mélanges de l'Université de Saint-Joseph* 47: 149–69.

Strubbe, J. 1984–86. "Gründer kleinasiatischer Städte: Fiktion und Realität." *Ancient Society* 15–17: 253–304.

Swain, S. 1996. *Hellenism and Empire: Language, Classicism, and Power in the Greek World, AD 50–250*. Oxford: Oxford University Press.

Uytterhoeven, I. 2009. "Know Your Classics! Manifestations of 'Classical Culture' in Late Antique Elite Houses." In *Faces of Hellenism: Studies in the History of the Eastern Mediterranean (4th Century B.C.–5th Century A.D.)*. Studia Hellenistica 48, ed. P. Van Nuffelen, 322–42. Leuven: Peeters.

Vitale, M. 2012. *Eparchie und Koinon in Kleinasien von der ausgehenden Republik bis ins 3. Jh. n. Chr*. Asia Minor Studien 67. Bonn: Rudolph Habelt.

Weiser, W., and H. M. Cotton. 2002. "Neues zum 'Tyrischen Silbergeld' herodianischer und römischer Zeit." *Zeitschrift für Papyrologie und Epigraphik* 139: 235–50.

Weiss, P. 2005. "The Cities and Their Money." In *Coinage and Identity in the Roman Provinces*, ed. C. Howgego et al., 57–68. Oxford: Oxford University Press.

Will, W. 1950–51. "Au sanctuaire d'Héraclès a Tyr: L'olivier enflammé, les stèles et les roches ambrosiennes." In idem, *De l'Euphrate au Rhin: Aspects de l'Hellénisation et de la romanisation du Proche-Orient*. B.A.H. 135, 1995, 243–55. Beirut: Institut Français d'Archéologie du Proche-Orient.

Will, E. 1995. *De l'Euphrate au Rhin: aspects de l'hellénisation et de la romanisation du Proche-Orient*. Beirut: Institut français d'archéologie du Proche-Orient.

Woolf, G. 1994. "Becoming Roman, Staying Greek: Culture, Identity and the Civilizing Process in the Roman East." *Proceedings of the Cambridge Philological Society* 40: 116–43.

Zadok, R. 1999. "The Ethno-Linguistic Character of the Semitic-Speaking Population (Excluding Judeo-Samaritans) of Syria in the Hellenistic, Roman and Byzantine Periods: A Preliminary and Tentative Survey of the Onomastic Evidence." In *Michael: Historical, Epigraphical and Biblical Studies in Honor of Prof. Michael Heltzer*, ed. Y. Avishur and R. Deutsch, 267–301. Tel Aviv: Archaeological Center.

Zadok, R. 2000. "On the Prosopography and Onomastics of Syria-Palestine and Adjacent Regions." *Ugarit-Forschungen* 32: 599–674.

Ziegler, R. 1978. "Antiochia, Laodicea und Sidon in der Politik der Severer." *Chiron* 8: 493–514.

Ziegler, R. 1999. "Das Koinon der drei Eparchien Kilikien, Isaurien und Lykaonien im späten 2. und frühen 3. Jahrhundert n. Chr." *Asia Minor Studien* 34: 137–53.

Epilogue

ROBIN OSBORNE

In the beginning was the lie. That is the founding perception of Greek literature, explicit in its earliest lines—for the Muses who taught Hesiod beautiful
song announced themselves to him as "knowing how to speak many lies like
the truth" (*Theogony* 27). Had Hesiod lived in a world of one truth, rather
than many lies, his world would have needed only one muse, perhaps even
only one god. Instead, Hesiod's is a world of many muses and many lies, with
various alternative stories always available. Even if Hesiod was the first to
commit himself to papyrus, oral epic had already brought its listeners up
against the lying tales of Odysseus and the impossibility of telling the limits
of a liar's lies; *Odyssey* 19.203 even uses the *Theogony*'s phrase of Odysseus' lying
speech to Penelope—"many lies like the truth." Everywhere we look in early
Greek literature, we find lies. In the second book of the *Iliad*, Agamemnon
tests the Greek troops by deliberately lying to them to discover their true
mettle. But if a king is not above lying, neither is a god. Hera's deception of
Zeus in *Iliad* 14 is only the most daring, and most amusing, of the many lies
told by gods in epic.

For all that classical scholars have contributed to such collections as *Lies
and Fiction in the Ancient World*,[1] they have generally been reluctant to acknowledge the fundamental place of the lie in all communications—above
all, in history. It is the willingness of the contributors to this volume to see
that the stories of history are all lies—and therein lies history—that makes
this volume so important and such a breath of fresh air. From Thucydides
onward, historians have advertised themselves—and the function of "history"

as a genre—as distinguishing truth from fiction, wanting to place history firmly on the side of truth. While the actual practice of writing history often involved playing games with truth and falsehood, the explicit rhetoric of historiography is overwhelmingly focused on truth. Lucian's *How to Write History* (39) challenges the reader to accept that "if you are going to write History you must sacrifice to Truth alone." The old question of whether Herodotus is the father of history or the father of lies depends upon this exclusive opposition between history and fiction, truth and lies. A lot is at stake in belief in this opposition—including the successful functioning, both in antiquity and today, of law courts. But that does not stop it being a lie.

Accusations about telling lies hurt. All sorts of circumlocution are adopted to avoid talking of lies. Look at the chapter titles of *Lies and Fiction in the Ancient World*: only two of the eight authors are prepared to use "lies" or "lying" in their titles; the others prefer "falsehood" or "untruth" or "make-believe" or "fictive belief." A generation ago, a British Cabinet Secretary added a phrase to the English language when he coined the euphemism "being economical with the truth." But for all that mendacity takes a variety of forms (and may be adopted for a variety of noble or honorable motives), words, images, and actions designed to deceive are lies.

Origins encourage deceit. That is best explained by Eliot's perception (in "East Coker") that "In my beginning is my end."[2] What we tell about our beginning is indicative of the end(s) we aim to achieve. Did Herodotus tell us in the first two words of his *History* that he was "Herodotus of Halikarnassos," thereby emphasizing the origin of his text in a community poised between the Greek world and the Persian Empire? Or did he tell us, as Aristotle implies (*Rhetoric* 1409a) that he was Herodotus of Thourioi, emphasizing the origin of his text in a settlement sponsored by the Athenians and made possible by their imperial might? How we read Herodotus' *History*—indeed, what the *History* is all about—will be profoundly affected by which of these two foundations we believe the text to have been built upon. For the reader who finds in this text either a warning or an *apologia* for the Athenians, it will always be a lie to identify Herodotus as a Halikarnassian. For the reader who finds in this text a profound account of the encounter between two distinct cultures that possess only partial understanding of each other, it will always be a profound truth that Herodotus was a Halikarnassian. Whatever Herodotus wrote in the manuscript that he first consigned to the copyist, he was not telling the whole truth.

Foundations are not foundations if nothing is founded upon them, and all that is founded must have a foundation. And since much is founded in any foundation, there will always be multiple stories to account for any foundation. Unlike the cities of history, which must decide their end before making concrete their beginning, the history of cities can conjure up, after the event, foundations to match the end. But the history of cities is never simple (what on earth would a simple city be? Well, it would not be on earth, that is for sure)—and no city has a simple end. Within any community, there is contestation about where its priorities, if not also its physical limits, lie, about what the salient qualities of the community are, about which past residents deserve to be remembered and which forgotten. There can be no original truth where there is no final truth—not for nothing do Plato's Forms provide both. How could the *faex Romuli*, or any city other than Plato's Kallipolis, have a single uncontested foundation story?

This book has told two stories. One has been explicit. It has been a story of lies (even if the term "lies" has only once been used, "truth" has been clearly problematized). In every chapter, we have met lies told about the past in order to influence the hearer or reader's view not just of the past but of the present. As scholars have increasingly emphasized over the last generation, Greek and Roman cities were strongly interdependent. They were nodes in a whole range of different networks through which they accessed a variety of material and immaterial resources. Maintaining the links with other cities, and turning those links into means by which advantages could be gained, depended upon presenting an image that impressed the other party. Every city wanted to believe that it was exceptional in the eyes of other cities, and the stories that cities told about their past were ways of showing why, of inscribing the special standing on which their relationship with this city or that city was based. A single story might give grounds for a special relationship with more than one city—as the Theran story of the foundation of Cyrene, as related to and by Herodotus (Herodotus 4.151–2) offered grounds for claiming special relationships with Itanos on Crete and with Samos as well as with Cyrene. But no single story could offer grounds for special relationships with *every* other city. As we have seen throughout this book, truth does and cannot rest in any individual foundation story. The very existence of multiple stories, from Hesiod's many muses onward, demonstrates their falsehood. If there is any truth at all to be gained, it rests not in any single story but rather in entire collections of lies together—in what this book has termed "foundation discourses."

Sometimes there is no doubt that the lies told by the representatives of a city were made up on the spot in particular circumstances, taking advantage of sympathies that the tellers thought they had just detected in the listener.

But more commonly, what we find is a tissue of lies upon lies upon lies. It was, for example, the claim that Xanthos had already made that it was the place where Leto gave birth to Apollo and Artemis that allowed Kytenion to claim a link through having been the birthplace of Apollo's son Asklepios.[3]

This claim by Xanthos to be the birthplace to Apollo and Artemis is apparently already advertised in one of the poems in honor of Arbinas inscribed in the early fourth century,[4] and it was almost certainly grounded in the Homeric epithet for Apollo, λυκηγενής (*Il.* 4.101, 119) which Homeric scholiasts explained as meaning "born in Lykia."[5] It is impossible to excavate fully the sequence of imaginative opportunism here, but whether the Xanthians start with Homer and proceed to the sanctuary of Apollo and Artemis' mother, Leto, or start with the sanctuary of a female deity and proceed, via identification of that deity with Leto and use of Homer to localize in that sanctuary the place where she gave birth, does not affect the basic issue. The Homeric epithet certainly did not dictate the creation of the Letoon sanctuary, nor does the existence of the Letoon require the claim of being the birthplace to Apollo and Artemis.

Kytenion's claim to be the birthplace of Asklepios was even more opportunist. Already in the *Iliad*, Asklepios' sons are recorded as coming from Trikka, the site of one of the most famous sanctuaries of Asklepios,[6] but Trikka was just one of three sites where Asklepios was said to have been born (Lakereia in Thessaly and Epidauros being the others). Cicero exploited the plurality of birthplaces to claim that there were three different Asklepioses (*De Natura Deorum* 3.57), and Pausanias argued for the priority of Epidauros (2.26). Kytenion could pass itself off as effectively the same place as Trikka, since Trikka could be reckoned to have been, like Kytenion, part of Doris (Strabo 9.5.17, 10.4.6). This Dorian identification of Trikka was helped again by the occurrence in Homer of a word of uncertain meaning, "τριχάϊκες" (*Odyssey* 19.177), as an epithet of the Dorians. The great advantage of fabricating lies upon lies is that it is unlikely that there will be a whistle-blower to give the lie.

The story told by Kytenion is a story of origins but not a story of foundation. The power of beginnings is not reduced by there being many different aspects of any community that need establishing and explaining. Stories of foundation should not be divorced from stories about how a city got its first laws, for instance, or how it acquired its walls or its particular cults. Kipling exploited the universal appeal and familiar structure of this kind of narrative in his *Just So Stories*, first published in 1902, but such stories can be traced back at least as far as *The Epic of Gilgamesh.* "Just so" stories explain and, in doing so, draw attention to difference—"natural" differences, in the case of Kipling's tales; cultural differences, in many other cases. Current distinctiveness is the end to which these celebrations of beginning draw attention. But these stories are also intensely conservative. They promise that although something is distinctive because it has a distinctive history, its condition is now stable. The elephant has his trunk and is stuck with it; we need not fear that he will develop some other frightening feature, or that we will acquire a trunk if we associate closely with him. The elephant's trunk and, indeed, Leto's labor in Xanthos are stable facts of life. However readily they are made up, these lies promise to endure to the end—the end that is contained in every beginning.

It is the determination to believe lies to be true that is the other story told in this book, but a story left largely implicit after the Introduction. Lies do not get past their first telling unless those who hear them are prepared to accept them. What matters here is not the truth flagged by Thucydides the idealist but the expediency flagged by the cynical Thucydides. It is once the people of Xanthos found it expedient to accept and write up the story told them by Kytenion, or once the people of Cyrene found it expedient to accept and write up the story told them by the Theran ambassadors, that what these tellers invent becomes part of history. Once the listeners have bought the lie, they have an interest in denying that it is a lie. They now have a stake in this story. From its form as a story, the lie becomes manifested in ritual, civic imagery, and everyday social practices. These shifting protean forms are, no less than the original story, part of the foundation discourse. The initial lie is no longer singular. In the process of transforming it into a social truth, it is splintered into a myriad of other lies.

This will to truth, this determination to turn lies into truth, does not merely affect the ancients. It is prevalent among modern scholars. Scholars are reluctant to acknowledge that what they are reading is lies—as if once they admitted that they were reading lies, they would be revealed in the emperor's new clothes. If all historians study is lies, what distinguishes them from literary scholars? There must be a kernel of truth, even if that kernel is hard to detect.

Scholars who have emphasized that what we study in ancient history—above all, in the study of the early history of Greek cities—is lies get branded as skeptics. It is, the implication goes, easy to be skeptical. Skeptics are presented as destroyers of truth, as persons who are ungrateful for what they are offered and hard to please. But to recognize a lie as a lie is no more to be a skeptic than to refuse to recognize a lie as a lie. Those who are skeptical about whether lies are lies are no less destroyers of history than those who are skeptical about the truth of lies. To recognize the lie is to add a chapter to history, not to destroy one. It is to realize that counterclaims do not necessarily cancel each other out but that they coexisted in antiquity and that that very coexistence made the claimants—and the divine and human actors about whom the claims were made—more enigmatic and less limited. Herein lies the essential contribution of this book: its insistence on this coexistence of claims and on the complicated network of personal and corporate links that the rival claims reveal.

Acts of lying are arguably much more revealing than acts of telling the truth (whatever that may be). People might tell the truth for no better reason than that it *is* the truth. Those who tell lies tell them for a reason—without a reason, no lie can take shape, for it is the reason that suggests its content. Those who tell the truth write themselves out of history. Those who tell lies write themselves into history. If the answer to the question of why someone tells the truth may be utterly uninteresting, the reasons that someone lies are often—and have been throughout this book—fascinating (even if they are and have been also sometimes predictable and depressing).

Scholars who would write definitive history must insist that there is a true story. The value of this book lies not least in the recognition by its contributors that just as there is no true story of foundations, so there can be no definitive history of foundations, or even of foundation stories—or rather, that when it comes to foundation stories, the lie was the truth. And the other lie was also the truth.

NOTES

I am grateful to Naoíse Mac Sweeney for the invitation to contribute this epilogue. I thank all the contributors for extending the range of my thinking on the topic, and I thank Naoíse and Caroline Vout for their helpful comments on an earlier draft.

1. Gill and Wiseman 1993.

2. It requires a conviction of a very different set of values to affirm, with Mary Queen of Scots, in prison shortly before her execution, "En ma Fin gît mon Commencement."

3. *SEG* 38.1476; Curty 1995: no. 75.

4. *Fouilles de Xanthos* 9, pp. 157–58, line 11; cf. p. 179.

5. Herakleitos, *Homeric Allegories* 7.

6. Cf. Herodas *Mimiambi* 4.1; cf. 2.97; Strabo 9.5.17.

REFERENCES

Curty, O. 1995. *Les parentés légendaires entre cités grecques: Catalogue raisonné des inscriptions contenant le terme syngeneia et analyse critique.* Geneva: Librairie Droz.

Gill, C., and T. P. Wiseman. 1993. *Lies and Fiction in the Ancient World.* Exeter: University of Exeter Press.

Kipling, R. 1902. *Just So Stories for Little Children.* London: Macmillan.

CONTRIBUTORS

Lieve Donnellan completed her Ph.D. at the University of Ghent in 2012. She is a postdoctoral fellow of the Belgian-American Educational Foundation, at the Department of Classics of the University of Chicago in 2013–14. She is interested in colonization, ethnicity, and networks and has excavated widely across sites in the Black Sea, North Africa, Sicily, and Portugal. She is currently working on networks and interaction in Euboea and the Mediterranean.

Alfred Hirt is a Lecturer in Roman History at the University of Liverpool. He is the author of *Imperial Mines and Quarries in the Roman World* (2010) and has published on Roman military history. He is currently working on Greek geographic concepts of the Levant.

Naoíse Mac Sweeney is a Lecturer in Ancient History at the University of Leicester. She is the author of *Community Identity and Archaeology* (2011) and *Foundation Myths and Politics in Ancient Ionia* (2013). She is interested in cultural interactions between the Greek world and the Near East and is currently working on archaic authors from Ionia.

Rachel Mairs is a Lecturer in Classics at the University of Reading. She is the author of *The Archaeology of the Hellenistic Far East* (2011), *The Hellenistic Far East: Archaeology, Language and Identity in Greek Central Asia* (forthcoming), and works on Hellenistic Central Asia as well as Roman and Hellenistic Egypt, with a particular interest in multilingualism.

Irad Malkin is a Professor of Greek History at Tel Aviv University and holds the Cummings Chair for Mediterranean History and Cultures. He is cofounder (1986) and coeditor of the *Mediterranean Historical Review*. His major publications include *Religion and Colonization in Ancient Greece* (1987), *Myth and*

Territory in the Spartan Mediterranean (1994), *The Returns of Odysseus: Colonization and Ethnicity* (1998), *Ethnicity and Identity in Ancient Greece* (in Hebrew, 2003), and *A Small Greek World: Networks in the Ancient Mediterranean* (2011).

Daniel Ogden is a Professor of Ancient History at the University of Exeter and a Research Fellow at the University of South Africa. His books include *Polygamy, Prostitutes and Death: The Hellenistic Dynasties* (1999), *Greek and Roman Necromancy* (2001), *Alexander the Great: Myth, Genesis and Sexuality* (2011), and *Drakōn: Dragon Myth and Serpent Cult in the Greek and Roman Worlds* (2013).

Robin Osborne is a Professor of Ancient History at the University of Cambridge. His major publications include *Classical Landscape with Figures: The Ancient Greek City and Its Countryside* (1987), *Archaic and Classical Greek Art* (1998), *Athens and the Athenian Democracy* (2010), and *The History Written on the Classical Greek Body* (2011). He is currently working on Greek inscriptions and the iconography of daily life on Athenian pottery.

Michael Squire is a Lecturer in Classical Greek Art at King's College London and currently a Fellow at the Wissenschaftskolleg zu Berlin. He is the author of *Panorama of the Classical World* (2nd ed., 2008), *Image and Text in Graeco-Roman Antiquity* (2009), *The Art of the Body: Antiquity and Its Legacy* (2011), and *The Iliad in a Nutshell: Visualizing Epic on the Tabulae Iliacae* (2011). He is especially interested in the relationship between ancient literary and visual cultures, as well as in ancient and modern aesthetics.

Susanne Turner is the Curator of the Museum of Classical Archaeology in Cambridge. She is interested in classical Greek art—in particular, the role of the viewer in funerary and ritual contexts. She is currently working on gods and their viewers in the Greek temple, as well as plaster casts and their viewers in the museum.

INDEX

Abraham, 23–24, 26–28
Achaemenid, 12, 106–9, 114–15, 120. *See also* Persians
Aegean, 5, 20, 104
Aeneas, 13, 34, 151–13, 160–70, 172–74, 178–79, 181 nn.1–2, 183 nn.33–42
Agathos Daimon, 13, 127–43
agora, 34, 42, 55–56, 58, 59 n.4, 71–73
Aigeus, 12, 72–74, 77, 79–80, 84–92
Ai Khanoum, 12–13, 103–22
Alexander of Macedon: in Bactria, 106, 109–10, 118–21, 124 n.48, 129; in Egypt, 129–35, 140–41; in general, 12–13, 190; *Romance*, 130–34, 140, 142, 143 nn.2–3, 144 n.10, 145 n.15, 147 n.52; on the *Tabulae Iliacae*, 159. *See also* coinage
Alexandria: in Egypt, 10, 13, 129–43; other Alexandrias, 103–4, 118–20
Anatolia, 83, 190. *See also* Asia Minor
Antiochus, 110, 117–19, 123 n.20
Apollo, 22, 25, 135, 170, 230; Archegetes, 11, 44–48, 51, 52, 54–59, 61 nn.22–3; on coinage, 53–55; in Delos, 47, 61 n.23; at Delphi, 32, 42, 47, 73, 83
Aramaic, 106, 108, 115, 119–20, 204
archegetes, 24, 30. *See also* Apollo Archegetes
Argos, 22–23, 29, 141–42
Asia Minor, 4–6, 20. *See also* Anatolia
Athens, Athenians: campaigning in Sicily, 45–46, 49; control of Chalkis, 49; foundation myths of, 1–3, 10, 15 n.1, 20–21, 36 n.3, 44; as a *metropolis*, 4–5, 49–50; in the Troad, 26. *See also* Theseus
Attica, 2, 4, 73, 85
Augustus, 153, 161–64, 167, 172, 180, 181 n.2, 183 n.36
autochthony, 1–3, 5–6, 20–22, 25, 36 n.3, 88–89, 91–92

Bacchylides, 75, 77–78, 81, 83–86, 94 n.26, 96 n.70
Bactria, 10, 12, 105–6, 122
barbarian, 21, 23–24, 48–51, 85
Bible, 23–24, 26, 32, 33
Black Sea, 20, 185
Bronze Age, 107, 108

Cadmus. *See* Kadmos
Canaan, 23–24, 26, 138
Carians, 5–6, 8–9
Catane, 44–46, 49–50, 52–55, 57–59
Christian, 130, 138–42
citizenship (*or* citizen body), 44, 61 n.50, 73, 75, 85, 94 n.21
civic space, 55–56
coinage: Ai Khanoum (*see* mint); Alexander, 110; Sicilian, 11, 52–55; Tyrian, 14
colonia status, 14, 194–98, 204, 206, 208–10, 211 n.17
colonization: Greek, 11, 31–36, 42–46, 51–52, 59 n.3, 83, 113. *See also* Delphi; Hebrew
colony, 23, 26, 29, 32, 37 n.24, 46, 49, 58, 62 n.48, 104, 113, 121, 195, 209
conquest, 4, 6, 21–24, 26, 28, 31–32, 35, 83, 108, 119–21, 191
Corinth, Corinthian, 22–23, 44, 54
Crete, Cretans, 5–6, 8, 73, 77, 91, 147 n.50, 200
Cyrene, 2, 16 n.2, 22, 24–26, 30, 132, 229, 231

"Dark Age," 20. *See also* Iron Age
Delphi: and the foundation of Greek colonies, 12, 29–32, 37 n.31, 51, 60 n.5, 103–6, 112–13, 116, 122 n.2, 35, 42, 47, 51–52, 57, 71, 73, 106–7, 121, 133
Dido, 14, 193–94, 196–200, 203, 206–10
Dorian, 21–23, 25, 28–29, 31–32, 35, 36 n.3, 44, 46, 48, 50–52, 59, 60 n.16, 230

ACKNOWLEDGMENTS

This volume was first conceived in 2011, in a series of discussions between the editor, authors, and a wider network of scholars. We planned to present a volume addressing plurality in ancient foundation myths—in particular, the dialogue or discourse between alternative versions of myths. The discussions proved so engrossing that our own dialogues and discourses spilled over into the months and years afterward. Many people have been crucially important in sustaining these conversations, not least the contributors to this volume, whose impressive intellectual weight is matched only by their equally impressive patience.

In addition to the authors whose work is published here, many other individuals have contributed to this project at various stages. These include Jeanne Pansard-Besson, Alexander Herda, Joe Skinner, Gillian Ramsay, Catherine Draycott, Dirk Booms, Myles Lavan, Hyun Jin Kim, Graham Shipley, Lin Foxhall, Renaud Gagné, Kostas Vlassopoulos, Franco Basso, Dorothy Thompson, Jeremy Tanner, Llewelyn Morgan, Rosalind Thomas, Peter Agocs, Alex Mullen, Carrie Vout, Carol Atack, Emily Kneebone, Sophie Schoess, Athina Mitropoulos, Chris Noon, Jenny Zhao, Alisa McDermid, Natalie Arrowsmith, Daniel Unruh, Hannah Wiley, Karen Petersen, Maya Feile Tomes, Naomi Carless Unwin, Margarita Devine, and Dacia Viejo-Rose. I am also grateful to Deborah Blake for her patience, advice, and suggestions, as well as to the entire team at the University of Pennsylvania Press for their invaluable contributions.